SOME MINOR ROMAN HISTORIANS

SOME MINOR ROMAN HISTORIANS

BY

W. DEN BOER

LEIDEN
E. J. BRILL
1972

ISBN   90 04 03545 1

PRINTED IN THE NETHERLANDS

CONTENTS

INTRODUCTION

This book is devoted mainly to three little-known authors of the fourth century A.D. Their erroneous treatment of Roman history has been emphasized sufficiently often in the past to make it unnecessary for me to enlarge on the subject, far less to act as apologist.

The aim of this book is to elucidate the degree to which these historians may be considered authoritative for their own time, with special emphasis on one aspect, namely, the extent to which they reflect certain prevailing ideas about the Roman Empire and its history. This question has never yet, to my knowledge, been raised. In the case of the three historians to be discussed here, Aurelius Victor, Eutropius and Festus, the point is not only of interest in itself, but also in view of the fact that their works are far from similar, though they were written within about ten years of each other.

The first chapter is devoted to Florus, the first of the epitomists of Roman history to attain individual stature in our eyes. Numerous problems with which his successors had to deal two hundred years later are already to be found in his writings.

A considerable part of my spare time during the last seven years has been spent on this study. Some of the preliminary results have already been published in *Mnem.* 18 (1965) and *Mnem.* 21 (1968). Apart from the first chapter, however, no detail whatsoever has previously been published in its present form; even the first chapter has been revised in places.

In recent years I was granted several opportunities for discussing a number of problems that arise in this book with colleagues abroad, for whose helpfulness I am most grateful. I lectured on various aspects of the subject-matter in Munich, Erlangen, Würzburg, Rome, Leeds, and London. I recall with gratitude the illuminating discussions with many colleagues and their students in seminars held during my visits to a number of German and British universities. I profited greatly from my discussions with E. Badian, K. von Fritz, F. Klingner, S. Mazzarino, and A. D. Momigliano. To all of these, named and unnamed, I am greatly indebted.

The translation is the result of the combined efforts of Mrs I. Rike and Miss M. Jokel. The author is greatly in their debt for the skill with which they have avoided the numerous pitfalls involved in any work of translation. For any faults that in spite of their vigilance still remain I am of course responsible. The fact that this book can appear in 1972 is due to the kind assistance of Drs. E. Ch. L. van der Vliet and R. S. Brink of the Department of Ancient History at Leiden, who helped see this volume through the press during my absence in Ann Arbor in the academic year 1971-1972.

Thanks are due to the Netherlands Organisation for the Advancement of Pure Research (Z.W.O.) for subsidising the work of translation. I should also like to express my gratitude to E. J. Brill and their Classical Editor, T. A. Edridge, for helping to make this publication possible.

W. den Boer

LIST OF ABBREVIATIONS

AHR   American Historical Review
ALL   Archiv für lateinische Lexikographie und Grammatik
ARW   Archiv für Religionswissenschaft

Bull. Comm.   Bollettino della Commissione Archeologica Communale di Roma
Bull. Inst. Cl. Stud. (London)   Bulletin of the Institute of Classical Studies of the University of London
BSAF   Bulletin de la Société nationale des antiquaires de France

CAH   Cambridge Ancient History
Class. et Med.   Classica et Mediaevalia
CPh   Classical Philology
CQ   The Classical Quarterly
CR   The Classical Review

Ec. Hist. Rev.   Economic History Review

Fleckeis. Jahrb.   Jahrbücher für Classische Philologie herausgegeben von Alfred Fleckeisen

Heidelb. Jahrb.   Heidelberger Jahrbücher
HZ   Historische Zeitschrift

Jahrb. f. A. u. Chr.   Jahrbuch für Antike und Christentum
JHS   Journal of Hellenic Studies
JRS   Journal of Roman Studies

Mnem.   Mnemosyne

P.I.R.   Prosopographia Imperii Romani
Proc. of the Cambr. Philol. Soc.   Proceedings of the Cambridge Philological Society

RAC   Reallexikon für Antike und Christentum
RE   Paulys Realencyclopädie der classischen Altertumswissenschaft

REA	Revue des Études Anciennes
REL	Revue des Études Latines
Rev. Hist.	Revue Historique
Rev. Phil.	Revue de Philologie, de Littérature et d'Histoire anciennes
RFIC	Rivista di Filologia e di Istruzione Classica
RhM	Rheinisches Museum für Philologie
TLL	Thesaurus Linguae Latinae
ZNum.	Zeitschrift für Numismatik

CHAPTER ONE

THE EPITOME OF FLORUS AND THE SECOND CENTURY A.D.

The picture that a nation has of its own history is hardly ever determined by the best sources available. Legend overshadows history, people only remember remarkable events, and thus other, sometimes more important, facts are lost sight of. In the long run, what appeals to popular imagination is reduced to a series of anecdotes, a number of sensational details, which stem from deliberate bias on the part of the historians.

It is fascinating to examine the traditional history of Rome as current in various social strata of the population. Their idea of the past can best be gauged from sources which were not originally intended to be historical. Cicero's speeches, for instance, offer an excellent hunting ground for this purpose. These sources indicate what was handed down as history in senatorial circles; the stultified traditions of one's own clan, spirited and arrogant stories, as unreliable as the rival traditions of one's ancestral enemies. We must also take the *equites* into consideration: they too were divided into mutually hostile factions, they too had their own traditional history. The true story of Marius' life, for instance, is obscured by all kinds of unhistorical anecdotes, which partly owe their existence and tenaciousness to contradictory oral (and possibly written) legends of the *ordo equester* to which he belonged.

The idea of history held by the common people must be distinguished from that of the senate and the *equites*. It was influenced by both, but had an independent existence. We seldom, if ever, get a hint of what the Roman common man knew of the history of his own people. The cannibalism to which the desperate citizens of Saguntum and Numantia were reduced is, according to Petronius (*Satiricon* CXLI), just another blood-curdling story of the past with which everyone was familiar. A similar story is that dubious legend kept alive by the worthy citizens of Leiden. Just about all they know of the Spanish siege is that Burgomaster van der Werff offered his own body as food for the desperate, starving populace. In fact, he never did so, despite the evidence of the painting in that city's museum that represents his supposed heroic sacrifice.

However, not much information of the same nature as that furnished by Petronius is available about the ordinary Roman citizen. Our knowledge of attitudes towards history is derived from general works—school textbooks for everyone, which did not appear until the second century A.D. Among the oldest of these abridged general history books is the *Epitome* of L. Annaeus Florus, a work which must be seen within the context of the traditions of the *senatores* and the *equites*, and the striking details that appealed to popular imagination. It provided something for everyone. This may account in part for its popularity during the Empire and later. It may justly be considered the first book to reflect and determine the average second-century Roman's idea of history.

It is hard to find a word of praise for this textbook, which was held in high repute in ancient times, in the Middle Ages, and as late as the eighteenth century. Praise such as Joseph Scaliger's, 'un très bel auteur', is no longer heard.[1] The title of the book itself, according to the best MS. available, the Bambergensis, shows in summary the reasons for much of the modern criticism: Epitome ... de Tito Livio Bellorum Omnium Annorum DCC. 'Condensed Livy' says Ronald Syme, who takes Florus severely to task in his book on Tacitus.[2]

He is rarely considered worth mentioning as a source of any importance, and whenever he is quoted, it is always in connection with the same passages: his account of Varus' defeat in the Teutoburger Wald, which is compared to that of Cassius Dio—and sometimes given preference, even by scholars of standing.[3] On other occasions he is compared to Velleius Paterculus, especially with reference to his markedly rhetorical descriptions, but here again opinions differ as to their their respective merits.[4] The best known

---

[1] *Scaligerana*, ed. Des Maizeaux (Amsterdam 1740), II, 377.

[2] R. Syme, *Tacitus* (Oxford 1958), II, 503. Cf. P. Zancan, *Floro e Livio* (Padua 1942).

[3] F. Koepp, *Die Römer in Deutschland*, Monographien zur Weltgeschichte 22 (Bielefeld and Leipzig 1926³), 23, indicates Ranke's preference for Florus' account of the battle in the Teutoburger Wald to that of Cassius Dio. In more recent research, however, the scales are tipped in favour of Cassius Dio; cf. A. W. Byvanck, *Nederland in den Romeinschen tijd* (Leiden 1943), 110 (with bibliography). F. Millar, *A Study of Cassius Dio* (Oxford 1964), 91, offers very little of importance for our purposes.

[4] Cf. for example J. Wight Duff, *A Literary History of Rome in the Silver Age* (London 1927), 89, who favours Velleius Paterculus. J. Lana, *Velleio Patercolo o della propaganda* (Università di Torino, Pubbl. d. Fac. di Lettere e Filosofia, vol. IV, fasc. 2, Turin 1952).

passage in his work, which is often quoted, is that comparing the history of Rome to that of the individual—childhood, adolescence, maturity, and old age. The statement that always follows the quotation, that he borrowed it from Seneca Maior, certainly deserves more thorough investigation.[5] Finally, whenever Trajan is discussed by modern authors, a passage is referred to in which the emperor's reign is very favourably presented.[6]

These four points show, *grosso modo*, that Florus is not always considered a third- or fourth-rate source, but is actually accorded some attention for his own ideas. Nevertheless, to my knowledge no scholar has ever regarded this author as a representative of the rhetorical history of the *second* century (not even in his praises of Trajan). This is all the more remarkable when one takes into account that our sources for that period are very meagre. The inferior quality of this work, for which, I confess, I can muster no admiration, is probably the reason that people have rarely asked themselves what was typical of the second century in this book. In spite of Florus' ineptitude he may very well be representative for his time, since the third-rate author often constitutes a better source for his own period than those who occupy the lonely positions

---

[5] Florus' 'organic' historical view from Prooem. § 4 ff. is generally linked with Lactantius, *Inst. Div.* VII 15,4; *Hist. Aug., Vita Cari* 2; Amm. Marc. XIV 6,3. In addition to references to these passages in the older literature (see *Mnem.* XVIII (1965), 368, note 4) we should mention here: C. Tibiletti, 'Il proemio di Floro, Seneca il Retore e Tertulliano'. *Convivium*, NS 3 (1959), 276 ff. I. Hahn, 'Prooemium und Disposition der Epitome des Florus'. *Eirene* 4 (1965), 21-38. F. Vittinghoff, 'Zum geschichtlichen Selbstverständnis der Spätantike', *HZ* 198 (1964), 529-574, esp. 558. Garzetti, 'Floro e l'età adrianea', *Athen.* 52 (1964), 148. R. Häussler, 'Vom Ursprung und Wandel des Lebensaltervergleichs', *Hermes* 92 (1964), 313. A. Demandt, *Zeitkritik und Geschichtsbild im Werk Ammianus*, Diss. Marburg (Bonn 1965), 138, 201. R. Syme, *Ammianus and the Historia Augusta* (Oxford 1968), 137. F. Paschoud, *Roma Aeterna* (Neuchâtel 1967), 62, note 141. M. Fuhrmann, 'Die Romidee der Spätantike', *HZ* 207 (1968), esp. 536, note 22. C. G. Starr, *The Awakening of the Greek Historical Spirit* (New York 1968), 139. S. Mazzarino, *Il pensiero storico classico II*, 2 (Bari 1966), note 55: l'intuizione del tempo nella storiografia classica (pp. 412-461). For the position in Lactantius it is interesting to consult H. W. A. van Rooijen-Dijkman, *De Vita Beata, het zevende boek van de Divinae Institutiones van Lactantius*, diss. Leiden 1967, 109 ff. Compare also the searching analysis by P. Jal in the Introduction of the first volume of his edition (Paris 1967), p. lxix ff.

[6] Prooem. § 8, cf. Julian, *Caes.* 327 d. Syme's acid remark, Tacitus, I, 218-219, occasioned by this praise is based on his sceptical attitude towards Trajan as an emperor ('he could think of nothing nobler than a war of conquest').

at the summit. Mediocre textbooks such as Florus' Epitome—and not only the mediocre ones—are of the greatest assistance in understanding a particular period. I do not feel called upon to salvage Florus' honour, but I am certainly interested in the extent to which he represents his time. He is, moreover, entitled to our attention because of his influence upon Ammianus Marcellinus and Orosius, Festus and Jordanes, Malalas, and numerous mediaeval historians. He was also very probably translated into Greek, and therefore had some influence in Byzantium.[7] Later, the great humanists and philologists praised him. In the Netherlands alone six editions of his works were published between 1638 and 1674.[8] This has all influenced our view of much of Rome's history: even after one hundred and fifty years of critical work, many of the political leaders of the Republic are still presented in authoritative handbooks exactly as they were portrayed by Florus and his successors. It is not, for instance, Appian's picture of Marius that has become the accepted one, but Florus' inaccurate description of this important figure as a man of humble origin, *nobilitati semper inimicus* —a statement that is simply incorrect for this respectable burgher, this *eques*, who, making use of the ways available to him, amassed a huge fortune before he ever entered politics.[9] On the other hand, scholars in Eastern Europe are more inclined than those in the West to make much of slave rebellions, gladiator wars, and above all, of Spartacus. It is clear beyond all doubt that the Marxist historians' interpretation is biased, but here again we have a presentation of the facts for which Florus is one of the main sources.

---

[7] S. F. Rühl, *Die Verbreitung des Justinus im Mittelalter* (Leipzig 1871); cf. O. Seel, *Die Praefatio des Pompeius Trogus*, Erlanger Forschungen, Reihe A: Geisteswissenschaften, Bd. 3 (1955), ii.

[8] The chief editions were listed by E. S. Forster in the introduction to the edition of Florus in the Loeb Classical Library, *Lucius Annaeus Florus, Epitome of Roman History* (Ed. 1960), xv. Quotations from Florus in the text are from this edition. See also P. Jal, in his edition of Florus, Introduction p. clxiii.

[9] I 36,13; II 4. Cf. E. Badian, 'From the Gracchi to Sulla', *Historia* 11 (1962), 197-245, esp. 215. T. F. Carney, *A Bibliography of C. Marius*, Proceedings of the African Classical Associations, Supplement Number 1, 1961. See also H. J. W. Verhaak, *Velleius Paterculus en de rhetoriek van zijn tijd* (Diss. Nijmegen, 1954), 48, who discusses Marius' popularity in the rhetoric of imperial times. Marius was supposed to have established a professional army *pro obscuritate generis sui*. The traditional, and incorrect, presentation of the facts among modern historians is based on these rhetorical sources (cf. Syme, *op. cit.*, I, 40).

A further justification for my choice of subject is that the descriptions of historical personages praised by the Roman historians, and later criticized by Christian authors, are not infrequently derived from Florus rather than from Livy. Augustine's condemnation of 'non tam narrare bella Romana quam imperium laudare' [10] was written with Florus in mind. Even though this criticism is in some instances unfair—Florus did not write only in praise of the Roman Empire—it should not be ignored, since it is of great importance in assessing later changes in the appreciation of Roman exampla in a different (Christian) climate of opinion. Investigation of Augustine's work on this point makes it quite clear that he regarded Florus as well as Livy as enemies. The 'sentimental and emotional pagans' (the term is Momigliano's) [11] whom he opposed on account of the potentially dangerous influence of their emotional arguments, used to read Florus' textbook which, being 'pious and ecstatic',[12] was exciting and easy to read. This Christian pastor knew where to find his enemy: there where his religious flock was threatened. If his flock did any reading at all, they would be more likely to read the epitomists rather than the authors whom we consider first-rate such as Livy, Sallust or Tacitus. Oddly enough, it was not until the nineteenth century, and even then it proved no easy task, that a selection took place at last and Livy, for instance, came in for his share of praise and the epitomists were rejected. Yet after the rejection of Florus and those who wrote as he did, similar criticism was often levelled against Livy. This indicated the extent to which the great authors were equated with the writers of text-books: at this time they were all regarded as compilers. A great contrast, as I have pointed out, with the reputation they enjoyed in the sixteenth and seventeenth centuries.[13]

---

[10] *C.D.* III, 19. S. Wight Duff, *op. cit.*, 746, n. 6.

[11] *The Conflict between Paganism and Christianity*, essays edited by A. Momigliano (Oxford 1963), 99, lays undue stress, in my opinion, on the enmity Augustine bore Livy. Werner also rightly points out the influence of the second-rate historians, in connection with *C.D.* 18,21: 'Durch Trogus Justinus ist die Stellung der mittelalterlichen Weltchronik ein für allemal festgelegt'. They largely determined the Christian picture of history. (H. Werner, *Der Untergang Roms*, Forsch. zur Kirchen- und Geistes-geschichte 17, Stuttgart 1939, 214, note 505). Cf. also F. Landsberg, *Das Bild der alten Geschichte in den mittelalterlichen Weltchroniken* (Diss. Basel 1934). Fuhrmann, *art. cit.*, 537 ff.

[12] The words are Syme's, *op. cit.*, 503.

[13] See Seel, *op. cit.*, 78, for the much greater esteem in which the epitomists were held in the sixteenth and seventeenth centuries. See also Seel's edition

Who was Florus and what may be considered typical characteristics of the second century? We do not know whether he is the same man as the poet who wrote during Hadrian's reign, or in which years of the second century he worked,[14] and indeed these facts are of little importance for our purposes. His personality is revealed in his epitome; to this, oddly enough, people have so far turned a blind eye. He represents the spirit of his time to perfection, as will become clear, I hope, from the following traits: his love for the past and the rhetorical style of his rendering, the edification of his readers by means of examples, and his conviction of the relevance of history. Whether they are intended to be followed or avoided, his examples are always uncompromising in intent. He is interested both in Rome's internal affairs and in her foreign relations, although the latter decidedly have his preference; the rapid expansion of the Empire and the internal peace with its concomitant facilitation of travelling aroused general interest in other people, in their way of life and culture. All these impulses and varied interests had one underlying ideal: *homonoia*, the unity of the Empire, the unification of all nations for one single purpose: the glory of Rome.[15] The work of other Roman historians sometimes betrays a trace of uncertainty about the invulnerability of this glory.[16] It will be seen that Florus differs considerably on this score—such doubts are unknown to him.

Florus' comment on the conquered territories, 'It is more important to keep a province than to conquer it', gains special emphasis in the light of the defeats in the East, the failure of Trajan's last years.[17] Here he betrays a typical second-century attitude.

In dealing with Q. Fabius Maximus Cunctator, he smuggles in the contemporary concept of empire, notably by means of a slight but telling alteration in his nickname. Poseidonius had dubbed him

---

of Justin, *praef.* p. xii. Florus' enormous influence on later writers is explained by E. Malcovati, in her edition of Florus, 70; cf. Jal, *op. cit.*, xxix ff.

[14] M. Schanz, *Geschichte der römischen Literatur* III² (1905), 69; Forster's introduction in the Loeb Classical Library, p. x. Jal, *op., cit.*, II, 131 (Appendix).

[15] See my article, 'Religion and Literature in Hadrian's Policy', *Mnem.* 8 (1955), 123 ff. esp. 127 ff.

[16] Polybius was the first who repeatedly drew attention to this (e.g. 29, 21; 38, 21-22). The modern literature is almost impossible to survey. I mention only Werner's summary (*op. cit.*, passim); S. Mazzarino, *La fine del mondo antico* (Milan 1959); Momigliano, *op. cit.*, 2.

[17] I 33, 7: Plus est provinciam retinere quam facere.

'The Shield of Rome' and Plutarch had followed suit. Florus changed it to "The Shield of the *State*', elsewhere to 'The Hope of the *State*'. The Cunctator thus acquired a new function as an example to the second century. His changed nickname is not to be found anywhere before Florus.[18]

The author reveals his remaining intentions in a number of passages. One of these is particularly remarkable. Following the detailed description of the fall of Numantia and before the very brief discussion of Aristonicus and Pergamum,[19] Florus writes, 'In the first place, in accordance with our original plan, we will describe the just and honourable *(pia)* wars waged against foreign nations, in order that the greatness of the daily increasing empire *(imperium)* may be made manifest'. In 130 B.C., the term 'imperium', meaning the Roman Empire (Italy and the provinces), was not yet in use in Roman speech.

This passage is curious in yet another respect. 'Iusta illa et pia bella' is contrasted to civil strife: 'scelera, turpesque et impias pugnas', an antithesis which he introduced here but used nowhere else in his story. He was well aware that the conduct of affairs abroad before 130 B.C. was not always honourable and just: witness the last Macedonian War, the Third Punic War, the destruction of Corinth and the siege of Numantia in Spain; he condemns all these episodes in the strongest of terms.[20] Florus is not alone in his indignation: Appian, for instance, expresses himself almost as strongly on the subject of Spain.[21] Judging by what we know of him from the *Periocha* lib. 48, Livy is a good deal less troubled by ethical scruples. All that the *Periocha* tells us about the destruction of Corinth is the laconic statement that Mummius destroyed the town in accordance with a decree of the senate 'because they did violence to Roman envoys'.[22]

It almost seems as if the unification of the State, as it progressed, caused the wars of the past to be transformed into problems of an ethical nature. It could be no otherwise, now that there were even emperors from Spain. Certain episodes in the past needed to be glossed over, and it became necessary to reinterpret history. It

---

[18] I 22, 27: imperii scutum (a little earlier: imperii spes). In Poseidonios (*FGrHist.*, 87, θυρεόν (Plut. *Marcell*, 9, 7; *Fab. Max.* 19, 4).

[19] I 34 (II 19, 5).

[20] I 30; I 31; I 32; I 34.

[21] App. *Iber.* 13, 76.

[22] Liv. *Perioch.* 52; cf. Eutropius IV 14, 1.

would be shortsighted to dismiss the resulting ethical picture of history, that perfectly met the requirements of a unified Empire, as mere edification. Augustine understood very well that, if his attack upon Rome's past was to be effective, he would have to penetrate the layer of edification to find the hard reality of the historical image of a more distant past. In the second century and perhaps already in the first, the public required a different image than that of stalwart republicans. Conquests had to be re-inter-preted, the old image destroyed. This was a difficult task, in the course of which the works particularly of the second-rate historians inevita-bly accumulated all sorts of discrepancies. One of the most blatant examples of a rationalization after the event is surely the beginning of the systematic exposition in which Florus, just after his discussion of the horrors of Corinth and Numantia—atrocities which he himself actually pointed out—unblushingly went on to say 'Hitherto (130 A.D.) the Roman people had been glorious, illustrious, humane, upright and high-minded' (*pulcher, egregius, pius, sanctus atque magnificus*). It was a concession to the past (similar to that which Appian, the greater of the two, permitted himself in a toast to Scipio Aemilianus) [23] which sounds quite ridiculous after his acknowledgement of the horrors perpetrated in Numantia. Florus knew better. After all, he saw the Syrian War as the beginning of moral disintegration: 'Illae opes atque divitiae adflixere *saeculi mores*'. Was he thinking of his own time, when a humane emperor wrote in a famous letter to his governor of Bithynia that justice should be upheld, even on behalf of the indigenous population, and that 'Informations without the accuser's name must not be admitted in evidence against anyone'? Trajan's words, 'and by no means agreeable to the spirit of the age' (*nec nostri saeculi est*), throw a surprising light on a new age in which, according to the historian, the old mores were re-established. [24] 'The poisoning of wells is an inhuman method which your ancestors did not practise.' Here again we see the humaneness of a more enlightened age (I 35,7).

The use of the term 'Imperium Romanum' in describing the Roman wars in the third century B.C. is no isolated anachronism, but before quoting another instance, I should like to point out that modern historians also refer to the 'Roman Empire' when writing

---

[23] App. *Iber.* 13, 85. On Appian's account, see A. E. Astin, *Scipio Aemiliamus*, (Oxford 1967), 153.

[24] I 47, 8; cf. Plin. *Ep.* 10, 97.

about this early period, and that they also see the Second Punic War in this light. I do not intend to quarrel with this designation. In this context, however, it should be noted that the use of this anachronism implies an interpretation of the past which has its prototype not in Livy's work, but in the textbooks of imperial times: yet another reason not to neglect the epitomists.

Certain wars with foreign powers who had ruled areas which by Florus' time had long been Roman territory, are stigmatized by him as rebellions. This would imply, for instance, that Perseus of Macedonia had been nothing but a rebel, whose insubordination was justly punished: 'Macedonia rursus se *erexit*, Macedones *exurgunt*'.[25]

Another example of the habit of viewing the past through the eyes of the present is furnished by the wars with Mithridates, which thus appear in a curious light. It is not made clear that the issue at stake was the control of Asia Minor and Greece. The war against an Eastern tyrant at once reminds the author of the painful years of Trajan's reverses. This emperor's expedition against the Parthians was an act of defence, as indeed were all wars in the East, in an attempt to strengthen the vulnerable Eastern frontier of the empire. The same motive is now ascribed to the war with Mithridates: the flank of the empire was exposed (*nudum latus imperii*). The author holds the activities of Marius, Sulla and Sertorius responsible for this state of affairs; in other words, civil war had further aggravated the long-standing weakness of Rome's boundary.[26] It is furthermore obvious that Florus was not concerned with the support which Mithridates obtained in Asia and Europe. He states briefly that the king's actions were greatly feared by Asia (*terror Asiae*).[27] No wonder that the actions of the Cimbri, Teutones and Tigurini also reminded Florus of contemporary events. Rome rejoiced at the defeat of the latter in Noricum; this was good news of the liberation of Italy and the salvation of the Empire,[28] which pleased men and gods alike. A feat of arms which took place in 100 B.C. was thus eulogized two hundred years later in terms then commonly used in connection with Trajan's expeditions against the Dacians.

---

[25] I 28, 1.   [26] I 40, 4: nudumque latus imperii ostendebant procul Marius, Sulla, Sertorius.

[27] I 40,8. What it was really like is described by H. Fuchs, *Der geistige Widerstand gegen Rom in der antiken Welt* (Berlin 1938), 7ff, 15f. For the political aspects, see J. Deininger, *Der politische Widerstand gegen Rom in Griechenland, 217-87 v. Chr.* (Berlin 1971).

[28] I 38, 19: Hunc tam laetum tamque felicem liberatae Italiae adsertique imperii nuntium.

For the author himself it was natural to dismiss wars in subject territories as insurrections. Viriathus is simply a *latro*; the account of his behaviour is very biased, and possibly influenced by the activities of the *latrones* of the second century A.D., which even extended as far as Italy. If Florus was influenced by later events, this would serve to increase his topical interest. Similarly, Soviet historians have adduced the *latrones* of Florus' own time as a proof of social unrest in the very period that the so-called bourgeois historians, following in Gibbon's footsteps, are apt to shower with praise. If Florus was in fact thinking of them while writing of Viriathus, then the Soviet historians would conversely be justified in writing about the later *latrones* with Viriathus in mind and, since Viriathus' guerilla war constitutes a significant episode in the history of the republic, make use of him to increase the prestige of the second-century *latrones*. There is no doubt that Viriathus was important to Florus. The details of his account may differ considerably from Appian's far more extensive report but, even though the latter is the more factual, they are alike in their recognition of the ethical implications of their praise of the capable barbarian leader who laid bare Rome's perfidy.[29]

The most conspicuous difference between Appian and Florus, a difference of, to my mind, more general import than the episode of Viriathus, is the emotional quality or, if you like, the romantic atmosphere that pervades Florus' descriptions of savage and un-civilized peoples. A comparison of Appian's and Florus' accounts of enemy tribeswomen and their participation in battle, will make the difference sufficiently clear.

App. VI 12,72 (The Bracari in Spain): 'They are a very warlike people, and among them too the women bore arms with the men, who died with a will, not a man of them showing his back, or uttering a cry. Of the women who were captured some killed themselves, others slew their children also with their own hands, considering death preferable to captivity'.

Florus I 38,16 (The Teutones): 'There was quite as severe a struggle with the womenfolk of the barbarians as with the men; for

---

[29] Viriathus as a *latro*: I 33, 15. It should be borne in mind that λήζω and λῃστής are designations for 'guerilla' warfare and 'guerilla' leader (App. *Iber*. 12, 61 ff.). Appian's praise of Viriathus demonstrated Roman perfidy (12, 69-70); summary of Viriathus' character, 12,75. For *latrones* in general, see chapter IV, p. 143, note 72, below.

they had formed a barricade of their wagons and carts and, mounting on the top of it, fought with axes and pikes. Their death was as honourable as their resistance; for when, after sending a delegation to Marius, they had failed to secure their liberty and to be made priestesses—a request which could not lawfully be granted—they strangled all their infants or dashed them to pieces, and themselves either fell by wounds inflicted by one another, or else, making ropes of their own hair, hanged themselves on trees or the yokes of their wagons'.

The two historians are contemporaries, but Florus is the more aware of what his readers want. Both, however, are part of the same tradition, to which Tacitus also belonged. The picture of the 'noble savage' is decidedly laboured. Descriptions of barbarians were *de rigueur* and made use of the same attributes time and again. And repetition is fatal. 'How savage these Alpine people were, is proved by the action of their women, who, when missiles failed, dashed out the brains of their own children against the ground and hurled them in the faces of the soldiers'.[30] This contains little that is characteristic of the second century; the description, however, has become more mechanical. After all, we have here a literary product that was in great demand and supplied to order. The description of inhumanity, however, needed a counterweight, hence the emphasis on the Roman conqueror who knew his limitations and wisely treated the defeated with moderation—self-control on the part of the conquerors also being a favourite theme.

He condemns unnecessary provocation of the enemy. One of the customs followed by Trajan during or just before Florus' time, was that of erecting *tropaea* in the conquered area. He cannot bring himself to agree with this procedure. His disapproval is expressed in his criticism of Fabius Maximus and Domitius Ahenobarbus, who first initiated this custom during the Gallic campaign in 121 B.C., when they erected a sign on the battle field in commemoration of their victory.[31] This matter deserves further consideration at this point, since the correctness of Florus' statement that the generals of 121 were the first to do this, demonstrates clearly that

---

[30] II 22. See also for references to brave barbarian womenfolk: I 27,6; I 34,14. The wife of Hasdrubal, in the year 146 B.C., is similarly idealised: I 31,17. B. Walker, *The Annals of Tacitus* (Manchester 1952), 225 ff., provides some illuminating remarks on the theme of 'le bon sauvage' in Roman historical writings.

[31] I 37,6.

modern research has never taken our author sufficiently seriously. G. C. Picard's treatment of the subject is typical.[32] In the first place, he mentions a number of legendary examples of *tropaea* in 'foreign' countries from the Aeneid, which, as he himself admits, are not conclusive evidence, but which nevertheless paved the way for further criticism; then he produces numismatic evidence: coins showing Nike and and a *tropaeum*. These images, however, offer no conclusive proof of the presence of such monuments in foreign territory. All Picard's subsequent examples are marred by the same defect. The point is that Florus is concerned with the practice of setting up these *tropaea* as a deliberate provocation, *ipsis quibus dimicaverant locis*. That is why there is no contradiction in his reference elsewhere to Flaminius' *tropaeum* in honour of Jupiter on the Capitoline.[33] Florus' emphatic disapproval of provocative trophies can best be explained in the light of later criticism of the Tropaeum erected at Adam-Klissi to mark the success of Trajan's punitive expedition against the Dacians after the defeat suffered under Domitian.

At any rate, this reasoning keeps our feet firmly on historical ground, based as it is on second-century problems, and provides a more satisfactory explanation than Picard's attempt at interpreting an isolated statement of Florus'. According to Picard, we have here an example of the *inventiones*—investigations which the peripatetic school had made fashionable. This is far-fetched if one remembers that Florus was no trained philosopher. Nor can we regard him, as Picard also tries to maintain, as an opponent of the hubris of generals, tyrants or of Persian customs nor, in this context, as a *laudator temporis acti* (which he undoubtedly was, as he shows at the beginning of his work in particular). Quite possibly, in his time it was commonly felt that 'monuments are dangerous, for they may perpetuate hatred'. If such were the case, this *topos* must have been based on an actual event, for all *topoi* are based on past events, however distant that past may be. But for this passage we need not search very far. Adam-Klissi proves that *tropaea* were recognised as a problem in the second century.

---

[32] G. C. Picard, *Les trophées romains. Contribution à l'histoire de la religion et de l'art triomphal à Rome* (Diss. Paris 1957), esp. 104-107. Doubts about the correctness of Picard's account are expressed in P. Jal, 'Nature et signification politique de l'ouvrage de Florus', *REL* 43 (1965), 358-383, esp. 381, note 12; also Jal's edition of Florus I, 142.

[33] I 20,5 (after the Gauls' defeat).

The above discussion of Picard's arguments was necessary to demonstrate that he and nearly all historians refuse to see Florus as a man of his time. Those who see him merely as an 'abbréviateur de Tite-Live',[34] are blocking their own view; and this view can be fascinating, indeed, as is shown by the above passages, as well as those that follow. Florus is not particularly interested in further conquests. Rome is satiated 'Cappadocia, as well as the territory of the Armenians and Britons, which though they served no practical purpose, constituted important titles to the imperial glory' (I, 47,4).

In the second century, slaves were far less numerous than they were, for instance, in the first century B.C. Clashes with armed slaves were therefore unthinkable, let alone actual wars with slaves. And do we not hear the voice of those opposed to large country estates, the propagandists for small holdings with few labourers per land-owner, in Florus' words 'Bella servilia unde nobis nisi ex abundantia familiarum'? [35]

In spite of this sound judgement, he considers it an indignity that free men should be compelled to fight, to exert themselves, in order to keep worthless individuals in order.[36] Indeed, even the help of slaves, called in for the Second Punic War, must be considered a disgrace to Rome and to their leader, even though they proved themselves *virtute Romani*.[37]

The difference between Livy and Florus may be seen from the following (that is, if we may take the *Periochae* to reflect Livy). According to Florus, Andriscus, the man who was popularly known as Philippus, son of Perseus, and was in command of the Macedonians in the last war, brought shame upon Rome, not because of his success but simply because of his humble origin.[38] No trace of this shame is to be found in the *Periocha*. Florus regards the popularity of the gladiators, originally defeated enemies, as a means of pandering to popular taste and, consequently, as dishonourable.[39]

There are two ideas which, even though they are not necessarily typical of second-century attitudes, were certainly common among

[34] Picard, *op. cit.*, 104.
[35] I 47, 10.
[36] II 7, 1: Quis aequo animo ferat in principe populo bella servorum?
[37] I 22, 23 and 30.
[38] I 30, 3-5.
[39] I 47, 10.

the bourgeoisie of the time (particularly among the more prosperous
and influential): (1) gladiator games are not in keeping with
traditional sobriety; (2) they are a stain on Rome's reputation,
because she once had to muster all her strength against these people
as their revolt constituted a serious threat.

Florus derives some consolation from the fact that the enemies
of Rome also fell victim to the splendour and luxury which are a
danger to all men. Not even Hannibal escaped this danger. At a
time when, thanks to his victories in Italy, the occupation of Rome
lay within his grasp, he allowed himself to be tempted by the comfort
and luxury of life in Baiae: from then on his fate was sealed. It
does not seem to matter to Florus that it was only in the first
century B.C., and not two centuries earlier, that Baiae was first
mentioned by Varro as a centre of wealth. This should hardly
surprise us: nor is he well informed about the contemporary
position of Athens, which was, in Florus' time, at the peak of her
fame. During the Mithridatic wars Athens was plagued by famine;
Florus rhetorically calls the town *frugum parentem*, possibly with
Demeter of Eleusis or even a vague memory of a tragic chorus at
the back of his mind.[40]

Is it justified simply to brand him as being rhetorical here, or is
there more to it? An affirmative answer to this question can only
be provisional and would require a more extensive investigation
into the position of Athens in the literature of the second century.
We know that Athens—as indeed all of Greece—originally had a
strong tendency to regard Mithridates as a liberator. Possibly
Florus wrote in accordance with a tradition defending Rome,
claiming that the greatest city of Hellas was doomed to starvation
and destruction without the protection of the Empire. It was undoubtedly in keeping with Hadrian's spirit to improve the ties
with Athens. No wonder, then, that Florus writes with evident
satisfaction that it was Athens who requested Rome for aid before
the last encounter between Rome and Macedonia: 'the Senate
resolved to grant help to such illustrious suppliants'. No wonder,
either, that Rome was willing both in the schools and in the textbooks to denounce the destruction of Corinth as an outrage. Thus
was Hellas won.[41]

---

[40] I 22, 22. Varro, *sat. Men.* 44 (Buecheler), Cicero, *Pro Caelio* 15; *ad. Att.*
I 16; *ad fam.* IX 2; 12,1. On the healing springs, Lucr, 6, 748. See also on the
history of Baiae, J. H. d'Arms, *Romans on the Bay of Naples* (Cambridge, Mass.
1970), esp. 42 f.

[41] I 40, 10: frugum parentem; I 23,5: Placuit senatui opem tantis ferre

The second book (which starts with the Gracchi and confines itself to internal Roman affairs, and briefly discusses the wars at the borders only after describing the battle of Actium) contains hardly any direct indications of those characteristics which might be considered typical of the second century. But that is not surprising, either. The denunciation of Antony's behaviour is taken for granted in the standard histories, while the inevitable praise of Brutus and Cassius belongs to the traditional view permitted and possibly proclaimed by many emperors, even by Augustus. Reasoning along the lines laid down by the ancient senatorial code of honour, Florus deplores the fact that they did not crown their heroism by committing suicide. The Ides of March 44 B.C. were recorded in history as a warning: *Sic semper tyrannis*. Those emperors who tolerated this point of view were able to avoid the appearance of absolute power, which could be extremely dangerous for them. Distinguished senators who kept portrait busts of Caesar's murderers in their homes were the friends of Pliny the Younger—as loyal a servant of the emperor as they. Admiration for the killers of tyrants was no more than a game, politically harmless and hence permissible. Furthermore, it had educational value and was therefore a desirable attitude to take in rhetorical history textbooks. This is not, however, a characteristic of the second century alone. Thus, for the greater part of Book II, which concerns the time of the revolution, Florus readily found his material, ordered and time-honoured.[42]

Again it is no coincidence that experiences of Trajan's campaigns may be found woven into the descriptions of the Dacians in the second book,[43] nor that the description of the slaves contains nothing particularly typical of the second century; the decline of slavery made former problems seem unreal.[44] Only the memory of the disgrace, which we discussed above, still clung to Rome.

One would expect to find traces of the Parthian as well as the

---

supplicibus; I 32, 1 (the destruction of Corinth): facinus indignum. For Athens under Hadrian, cf. P. Graindor, *Athènes sous Hadrien* (Cairo 1934).

[42] II 17,10; 18,5; 21,11 (Antony); II 17,15 (Brutus and Cassius). The praise of Pompey also fits in well in this connection, as does the indication *Pompei iuvenes* for younger relatives of the great man (I 41,9). See also in connection with these *legati* of Gn. Pompeius in the war against the pirates in the year 67, C. Cichorius, *Römische Studien* [reprinted Darmstadt 1961], 188. Conversely, Florus criticises Caesar's expedition to Britain: non enim provinciae, sed nomini studebatur (I 45, 19).

[43] II 25, 12.

[44] II 7 ff.

Dacian wars, particularly towards the end of the work. But again we are disabused: Crassus' defeat was due to his breach of faith; the Parthians themselves had wanted an alliance. Appian, according to whom Pompey did not wish to fight the Parthians without the sanction of the Senate, gives us a different picture.[45] Perhaps Florus' selectiveness is in itself significant here: he mentions only Crassus, whereas Appian also refers to Pompey. The former possibly lays such emphasis on the horrors of the past as a warning to the present, and this would also be in keeping with his emotional, moralistic style. However, as we said before, these points may be no more than mere indications.

He has a markedly childlike attitude to the war tactics of Eastern peoples, expressed chiefly in his respect for the elephant as a military weapon. Pyrrhus, the First (not the Second) Punic War and Antiochus III give him occasion to expatiate on the subject of fighting elephants. They inspire his finest rhetoric. When at last the Romans themselves take to using these animals against the Allobroges and other Gallic tribes, this to him is satisfaction indeed. Curiously enough, he has not the slightest notion of the actual fighting methods of other peoples. The elephant's reputation as 'the tank of antiquity' dies hard, even though Tarn, who believes that this concept was introduced by modern historians, contests it convincingly. Nevertheless, it was historians like Florus who transformed elephants into weapons of attack, whereas in reality they were used as a defensive screen, a kind of rampart, behind which the cavalry could prepare its attacks unseen. Florus knows nothing of all this. To him the elephant is a hunted animal. He knows it only in tormented fury, aroused by governors and their retinues, closely resembling that of the formidable barbarians (*immanitati gentium pares*).[46]

---

[45] I 46 (Crassus); I 40, 31 (Pompey). App. *Mithr*. 106 (Pompey).

[46] Elephants: I 13,13, 17,28 (Pyrrhus); I 18,28. Here it is very clear that the hundred elephants captured in the First Punic War are regarded as comparable to the results of a hunt: magna praeda, si gregem illum non bello, sed venatione cepisset. I 24,16 (Antiochus); I 37,5 (against the Allobroges).

W. W. Tarn, *Hellenistic Military and Naval Developments* (Cambridge 1930), 95 ff. The statement that elephants were never used again after the battle of Thapsos (Tarn, 100) is in contradiction to Amm. Marc. 24,6, 8. See the comments of M. F. A. Brok, *De Perzische expeditie van Keizer Julianus volgens Ammianus Marcellinus* (Diss. Leiden 1950), 155, in which the prevailing idea of the elephant as a 'tank' was adopted. But it is possible

The most important change to appear in the historical image of
Rome after Polybius was prompted by the experience of conquest.
The aging Polybius certainly doubted whether Rome's power would
last for ever. Yet in his historical narrative itself he sounds pre-
dominantly optimistic. One quotation may serve as an example:
'After they had beaten the Carthaginians in the above-mentioned
war (i.e. against Hannibal), and when they considered that the
greatest and most important tasks in the attainment of world
power had been accomplished, then the Romans were sufficiently
emboldened to stretch out their hands and cross over to Greece and
Asia'. But Polybius admired Demetrius of Phaleron, who also
predicted the downfall of conquerors because the wheel of Fortune
turns relentlessly; he also admired Scipio Aemilianus, who was
aware of the instability of Rome's power even as Carthage burned,
and wept for her future.

Florus had no such mixed feelings. In the first place his attitude
is based on the position of the conquered party: 'after the conquest
of Carthage no nation felt ashamed of being conquered'. The victory
of Rome is a blazing fire that spreads rapidly, a mountain torrent
that sweeps everything before it.[47] Sometimes mere accident
coincides with the will of the gods: 'quodam casu, quasi de industria
sic adgubernante fortuna'.[48] And when the balance of fate happens
to raise up one of Rome's opponents, he says: 'At this point the
breeze of Fortune veered somewhat, but only in order to provide
more evidence of the Roman valour, the greatness of which is more
often put to the proof by misfortunes'.[49]

The unceasing warfare waged by Rome is due to the will of the
gods lest, in peace time, the weapons of the Romans rust and fall
into disuse.[50] No less than three times do Castor and Pollux show
their support; at lake Regillus they joined in the fighting, and after
the defeat of Perseus and of the Cimbri they announced the victory
in Rome.[51] Time and again the weather gods are kindly disposed

---

that the Persians put elephants to quite different uses than did, for instance,
the Seleucids six hundred years before. Cf. I. Opelt s.v. Elefant, in *RAC* IV
(1959), esp. col. 1011 and 1022 (uncritically).

[47] Polybius I 3,6; cf. I 32,7 (cf. also Walbank's comments); Florus I 23,1;
post Carthaginem vinci neminem puduit.

[48] I 24,1.

[49] I 18,32.

[50] I 19,2.

[51] I 5,4 (lacus Regillus); I 28,14 (Perseus); I 38,20 (Cimbri).

towards the Romans.[52] Even the statue of Apollo in Antioch broke into a cold sweat, filled as the god was with apprehension for the safety of his beloved Asia.[53] So inevitable is Rome's victory, that Perseus is mocked for his visit to the holy island of Samothrace, 'relying on the well-known sanctity of the place, as though temples and altars could protect one whom his own mountains and arms had been unable to save'.[54] Macedonia thus fell *quodam fato*,[55] and Mithridates met the same fate because Pompey was one of Fortuna's favourites.[56] Florus was quite quite aware that Macedonia had once been a great empire,[57] and he was equally aware of Pompey's inglorious end; to his mind this was also Fortuna's doing.[58] He regards many of the reverses suffered by the Romans as due to either the gods or Fortuna.[59] As always in the case of writings that are rife with platitudes and rhetoric, one should not venture to assess the religious content, nor weigh what is true and what is false. This question cannot be decided.

But, once he has studied this epitome, the reader will have no doubts about one question which can be answered: Does Florus, too, think that the power of Rome is temporary? The answer is short and sweet: he does not. Even after his discussion of certain horrible episodes in the civil war his confidence in the future of Rome is unshaken. It is no coincidence that his work ends with the deification of Augustus, that second Romulus who is worshipped and honoured both as the son of a god and as a god in his own right. The comparison with the ages of man is discontinued, for *praeter spem* (so perhaps he had had his doubts), the senile Empire was reborn as a young man.[60]

A textbook, we are told, should be 'positive'. Florus did not disregard this requirement. His faith remained ostensibly unshaken, and to this he owes his fame.

---

[52] I 24,17; I 38,15. Even the moon favours Rome, I 40-21.

[53] I 29,3.

[54] I 28,9.

[55] I 30,1.

[56] I 40,21.

[57] I 23,2.

[58] II 13,51. A. Nordh, 'Virtus and Fortuna in Florus'. *Eranos* 50 (1952), 111-128, gives a useful list (though with few comments) of the places where Florus refers to these concepts.

[59] One example out of many: Crassus' defeat by the Parthians is a punishment by the gods of Rome's violation of a treaty (I 46,6).

[60] I 1,17 (Romulus); II 34,66 (Augustus); cf. *Prooem.* 3ff (the stages in the life of man).

CHAPTER TWO

AURELIUS VICTOR I

It is a great pity that we shall never know Emperor Julian's opinion of Sextus Aurelius Victor. It would have been interesting to know why the Emperor ordered this *scriptor historicus*, whom he had first met in Sirmium, to come to Naissus in 361 to take up the governorship of Pannonia Secunda. Equally, we should have liked to know Theodosius' reasons for promoting him, an African provincial and the son of a poor man lacking the advantages of an aristocratic education, to the prefecture of the city of Rome in 389. He evidently had an excellent record, and his promotion enabled him to take his place in the highest circles of the empire as a *vir clarissimus*. Perhaps both emperors agreed with Ammianus Marcellinus' comment: a man of exemplary sobriety.[1]

There are many gaps in our knowledge of his personality and career. The details given in his work, which comprises some fifty pages in the Teubner edition,[2] are scarcely supplemented elsewhere.[3] His modest book, however, has more to offer than one would suppose from the unanimous judgement formed by modern writers; we may well term him neglected. In all fairness, it is easy to see why his book has attracted so little attention. It does not exactly represent an artistic or historical high water mark in Roman literature and, besides, he is overshadowed by Ammianus. Nevertheless, the fact that the latter commends him, and moreover refers only to his

---

[1] Aurelius Victor. *De Caes.* 20,5: rure ortus tenui atque indocto patre. A good modern characterization is that given by C. G. Starr: 'Aurelius Victor, Historian of Empire', *AHR* 61 (1955-'56), 574-586. Ammianus Marcellinus 21,10,6: Ubi Victorem apud Sirmium visum, scriptorem historicum, exindeque venire praeceptum, Pannoniae secundae consularem praefecit, et honoravit aenea statua, virum sobrietatis gratia aemulandum, multo post urbi praefectum. Dessau, *I.L.S.*, 2945: veterum principum clementiam sanctitudinem munificentiam supergresso d.n. (= domino nostro) Fl. Theodosio pio victori semper Augusto, Sex. Aur. Victor, v.c., urbi praef., iudex sacrarum cognitionum, d.n.m.q.e. (= devotus numini maiestatique eius).

[2] Edited by F. Pichlmayr (1911), revised by R. Gruendel (1961, 1966²).

[3] In addition to the literary text and inscription mentioned in note 1 he is referred to in: Hieron. *Epist.* 10,3; Joh. Lydus *De mag.* 3,7; Paul Diac. *Hist. ling.* 2,18.

historical work and to no further important details of his successful
career as a public servant, is not without significance.[4]

Modern studies tend to fall into two categories. One emphasizes
his shortcomings—the lacunae in a short summary are easy enough
to pick out. But when, as in this case, an author himself announces
his work as a collection of *historiae abbreviatae*, such criticism is
somewhat facile. O. Seeck may be regarded as representative of this
first group of critics. He writes of a 'paltry summary' of the work
of earlier writers, whose only merits were that they possessed a
lucid and simple style, lacking, however, in any scholarly or artistic
value. In spite of these inadequacies, he continues, by dedicating
his work to Julian, this author was immediately appointed Consularis of Pannonia and, even under Theodosius, prefect of Rome,
even though he too (like Themistius, who also held important posts)
was a pagan.[5] His reasoning teems with statements that are,
to say the least, doubtful. In the first place, there is no proof
that Aurelius Victor summarizes any earlier author.[6] Secondly,
Aurelius Victor's style is far from simple and lucid—comparison
with his contemporary, Eutropius, who possessed these admirable
qualities to a marked degree, shows this most clearly. Victor does
not care in the least about simplicity and lucidity, but in fact tries
to combine the scholarly and the artistic in his manner, although
it must be admitted that he (all too) rarely succeeds. Thirdly, there
is no connection between this little book and Emperor Julian, and
it was certainly not dedicated to him: the suggestion that the
governorship of Pannonia Secunda was a reward for Victor's dedication of his work to Julian is a figment of Seeck's imagination.
Finally, the difference in preferment between pagan and Christian
officials that Seeck suggests was almost negligible in the fourth

---

[4] Starr was the first to place him within a broader framework of fourth-
century Roman historical writing: 'In his incisive direct approach he far
surpasses most of his contemporaries' (art. cit., 584).

[5] O. Seeck, *Geschichte des Untergangs der antiken Welt*, IV, 193: 'Sextus
Aurelius Victor, ein Afrikaner niedrigsten Standes, überreichte 361 dem
Julian eine Sammlung ganz kurzer Kaiserbiographien. Zum grössten Teil
war sie nicht mehr als ein dürftiger Auszug aus den Werken früherer Schriftsteller; ausser einem schlichten, klaren Stil lässt sich ihnen weder wissen-
schaftlich noch künstlerisch irgend ein Vorzug nachrühmen. Trotzdem
wurde der Verfasser für diese Dedikation sogleich zum Consularis Pannoniae
ernannt und stieg unter Theodosius sogar zum Stadtpraefecten von Rom auf,
obgleich auch er Heide war'.

[6] For more detailed discussion of this matter, see pp. 28, 32, 43, 54f., 92,
109ff., 116ff., 124, 156, 187, 198.

century, so that the position to which Theodosius raised him need certainly not surprise us.[7]

Although considerable advances have been made since the publication of Seeck's famous book, his first observation continues to exert an influence on modern research. Victor the man is considered of less importance than his source(s). At this point we should stop to examine a theory which merits our attention, and which has, indeed, been occupying scholars for close on a century— namely that of Enmann's historian. In an article dating from 1874, which still makes interesting reading, Enmann postulated a common source for Aurelius Victor, the *Epitome de Caesaribus* and certain other short histories of emperors. His name being unknown to us, this author has since been named after his discoverer.[8] Epigones have since attempted to consolidate or weaken this theory with varying degrees of success. Enmann himself did not adduce his hypothetical historian as an exclusive source, but the more fervent of his admirers went further and considered all fourth-century *abbreviatae historiae* as having a single source, while his more moderate followers gave the abbreviators more freedom than did the father of the theory himself. This historian, manufactured in 1874, continues to make his presence felt in the literature of today.[9]

---

[7] Victor 42, 17-19 appears rather to indicate that the author had more sympathy for Constantius than for Julian. He compares the position of Julian as Caesar with that of Tiberius and Galerius under Augustus and Diocletian, respectively. J. A. Straub, *Vom Herrscherideal in der Spätantike* (1939), 56-57, rightly says: 'Die Beispiele sind deshalb gewählt, weil sich Julian widerrechtlich seit seiner Usurpation das Auspicium anmasste, das den beiden andern als rechtmässig erhobenen Augusti (nach ihrer Erhebung) zustand, und weil sich Aurelius Viktor in der schwebenden Auseinandersetzung für Konstantinus entscheidet'. Cf. n. 305: 'Als Caesares hatten Tiberius und Galerius grössere Erfolge unter den Auspicien ihrer Augusti errungen; so auch Julian. Aber da er nun sich anschickte, sich ein eigenes Auspicium anzumassen, sieht Aur. Viktor, durch das Beispiel der beiden andern gewarnt, besorgt in die Zukunft'.

[8] H. Enmann, 'Eine verlorene Geschichte der röm. Kaiser und das Buch *De Viris illustribus urbis Romae*', *Philologus*, Suppl.-bd. IV, 1884, 337-501.

[9] A. Alföldi, *A Conflict of Ideas in the Late Roman Empire*, Oxford 1952, 98: 'About the middle of the fourth century a little work, composed of short biographies of Emperors, came into being. It is not in our possession today, but, in the decades following, a whole series of authors, mostly senators, pirated it; in the main they seem to have taken over its material, adorned it with their own flowers of style, and then presented it under their own names. Of this company was Sextus Aurelius Victor'. R. Syme, *Ammianus and the Historia Augusta* (Oxford 1968) also alleges that Victor and Eutropius used a common source and he says (106), 'the "Kaisergeschichte" must stand

At this early stage it seems expedient to summarize the conclusions of the present study:

1. there is no evidence to show that Victor used one source only as his sole point of departure;
2. Victor's work itself offers no support even for the more moderate view that the author used one main source and other, secondary, sources;
3. the differences between *De Caesaribus* and the *Epitome* are so great as to preclude any grounds for considering even these as having a common source.

To my mind J. H. E. Crees provides the most valuable discussion of this matter.[10] In connection with the fourth-century writings on the Emperor Probus, Crees turns to the historians 'Vopiscus' (*H.A.*), Aurelius Victor and Eutropius and remarks, 'though it seems certain that our writers used common sources, there is no need to narrow this down to a single source'.[11] He rightly considers the most important element of correspondence between the authors to be the chronological framework within which the events are individually placed, and he believes that this may form the actual basis; he thus obviates any mention of direct dependence. However, we shall see that it is precisely in structure and in his arrangement of his work into periods that Victor differs from his contemporaries.

A more positive evaluation is to be found in more recent research,[12] particularly with reference to passages formerly quoted only to indicate Victor's unreliability and ignorance. Nowhere is the favourable change in the attitude of scholars more clearly illustrated than in their treatment of those passages (19,1 and 20,1-4) where the author confuses the emperor Didius Julianus, who was killed by Septimius Severus, with the jurist Salvius Julianus, and

---

as a valid postulate because of Victor and Eutropius'. A. Chastagnol, however, speaks of 'la très hypothétique et trop commode histoire impériale d'Enmann' (*Bonner Historia-Augusta Colloquium* 1964/65 [1966], 56).

[10] *The Reign of the Emperor Probus*, repr. Rome 1965 (1st ed. 1911), esp. 70-71. He supports his argument with an amusing comparison: 'We should not, for example, consider it remarkable if upon consulting three text-books of English history we found the author in each case asserting that Queen Anne died in A.D. 1714, and that she had many children, who all died young'.

[11] J. H. E. Crees (*op. cit.*, 70).

[12] W. Hartke, *De saeculi quarti exeuntis historiarum scriptoribus quaestiones*. Diss. Berlin 1932. E. Hohl, 'Die H. A. und die Caesars des Aur. Vikt.', *Historia* 4 (1955), 220-228.

observes that the murder of this learned emperor only harmed the
murderer's reputation in the eyes of posterity, whereas the *gratia
doctarum artium* survives, unaffected by murder. It is greatly to the
credit of R. Laqueur that he identified this remarkable mistake
in the work as an error peculiar to the author. As is so often the case,
here, too, we become better acquainted with the man and his
working methods through his errors. In **19,1** he expresses his uncertainty as to whether the Emperor should be identified with the
jurist: 'At Didius (an Salvius?) Julianus fretus praetorianis ... ad
insignia dominatus processit'. He then interpolates a description
from which it appears that Victor has answered the question 'an
Salvius?' affirmatively. 'He was a member of a distinguished
family, outstanding in the field of urban law.[13] For he was the
first to create order out of the chaos of edicts which the praetors
were wont to issue in great numbers and without order. From
this it is sufficiently clear that learning alone is not enough if
the character does not help to restrain desires; for he, who taught the
people a better, though hard way of life, himself stooped to a crime,[14]
which under the terms of his own edict merited the death penalty'.

The historical account is resumed, prefaced by the words: *Neque
cupito tamen potitus diu*. For Severus avenged the murder of Helvius,
overthrew Didius and had Helvius deified by senatorial decree.[15]
Subsequently Victor's attention is again drawn to Didius (whom
he regards as identical with Salvius Julianus) and, evidently in
criticism of Severus, refers to the measures taken against the
writings of the presumed jurist-emperor, followed by a eulogy of
civilization and a denunciation of Severus and his followers.[16] Only
in this connection, however, for he goes on to praise Septimius
Severus, a compatriot, in a passage in which he also reveals his own

---

[13] The words *ius urbanum* in this passage clearly mean 'the law of the
praetor urbanus'.

[14] He had had the opposing emperor Helvius Pertinax killed: 18,2:
Milites impulsore Didio iugulavere. A survey of Didius Julianus is to be found
in G. Alföldy. *Die Legionslegaten der römischen Rheinarmee*, Epigr. Studien 3
(Köln-Graz 1967), 38. For further discussion of this passage, see p. 45, below.

[15] 20,1: Helvium senatus consulto inter Divos refert. Cf. Eutr., see p. 152.

[16] 20,1-4: Salvii nomen atque eius scripta factave aboleri iubet; quod
unum effici nequivit. Tantum gratia doctarum artium valet, ut scriptoribus
ne saevi mores quidem ad memoriam officiant. Quin etiam mors huiuscemodi
ipsis gloriae, exsecrationi actoribus est, cum omnes, praecipueque posteri,
sic habent illa ingenia nisi publico latrocinio ac per dementiam opprimi non
potuisse.

African origin.[17] It is characteristic of Victor to recount the good
and the bad about both Didius and Severus. There is no reason
whatsoever for Laqueur to doubt the authenticity of his dualistic
observation on Didius. In my opinion there is equally little occasion
to do so in the case of Septimius Severus. For this reason I do not
agree with Laqueur when he ascribes Victor's praise of Severus to
an African source.[18] The black-and-white characterization is typical
of many of his 'sketches', including those of Augustus, Nero, and
Constantine.

It is possible, although proof will never be forthcoming, that the
author's blunt and wayward style is linked with his wish to do
justice to the discreditable as well the creditable incidents in the
lives of his subjects. Any writer who wishes to combine the irreconcilable aims of giving a condensed history of an emperor with
that of the moralist pointing out good and bad, would need the
mastery of language and style of a Tacitus to realize this ambition.
Such gifts, however, are unique, and Victor possessed neither. What
concerns us particularly here is that, in the description of Septimius
Severus, it would be incorrect to ascribe one line of reasoning to
Victor (the confusion between two people, Didius and Salvius and

---

[17] 20,5-8: Quo bonis omnibus ac mihi fidendum magis, qui rure ortus tenui
atque indocto patre in haec tempora vitam praestiti studiis tantis honesti-
orem. Quod equidem gentis nostrae reor, quae fato quodam bonorum parce
fecunda, quos eduxerit tamen, quemque ad sua celsos habet. Velut Severum
ipsum, quo praeclarior in republica fuit nemo; quem quamquam exacta
aetate mortuum iustitio elogioque lugendum sanxere. struentes illum iustum
nasci aut emori minime convenisse. Scilicet quod corrigendis moribus nimium
postquam ad veterum innocentiam quasi mentium sanitatem pervenerant,
clementem habuere. Ita honestas, quae principio anxia habetur, ubi conti-
gerit, voluptati luxuriaeque est. Cf. Carthage indicated as *terrarum decus*
in 40,19.

[18] This is the only point where I disagree with R. Laqueur's otherwise
convincing exposé (in *Probleme der Spätantike*, Stuttgart 1930: 'Das Kaisertum und die Gesellschaft des Reiches'; esp. 25-27: Exkurs 1: 'Die geistige
Bildung des Aurelius Victor'). Another view is expressed by A. D. E. Cameron
(*CR* 1965, 21), who believes that the words *an Salvius* were added by a copyist,
since Victor knows very well that the name is Didius (18,2: impulsore
Didio foede iugulavere [Pertinacem]). In 20,1, however, it appears that
Victor is again writing of Salvius (Salvii nomen atque eius scripta factaque
aboleri). Hence our author himself must have been uncertain as to the
correct name, which may have been caused by the use of two different sources
and by a vague memory in his own mind of two similar names. The words
an Salvius? may express this uncertainty. Cf. R. Syme, *Ammianus and
the Historia Augusta* (Oxford 1968), 107: 'a peculiar error all of Victor's own'.
But see A. D. E. Cameron in *Hermes* 92 (1964), 374, note 5.

the resulting censure of Severus), and to isolate another (culminating
in the praise of this same emperor, his compatriot, *quo praeclarior
in republica fuit nemo*), to be regarded as a reflection of memories
of the emperor treasured in Africa, where he was born. To my mind
both facets of the story stem from Victor's own interpretation and
mirror his insight into the complexity of the human personality.[19]
To sum up: thanks to Laqueur we have learned to recognize one
passage as authentic, even though it rests on a confusion of identities.
On further consideration, moreover, we make bold to suggest that
that which Laqueur regards as an addition based on African memories also originated with Victor himself. This view is also based on
Victor's habit, to be observed elsewhere, of presenting both the
favourable and unfavourable aspects of a question. To distinguish
between two versions which may be traced to different sources is,
I feel, based on an oversimplification of the whole question of
sources. This important matter will necessarily exercise us repeatedly in the course of this study. Victor's subtle, though crudely expressed, assessment of Severus and others is his personal contribution to Roman history writing.

It is customary both for former harsh critics and for those who
judge his modest talents more favourably to discuss his treatment
of Didius Julianus and Severus. Studies such as those of Starr and
Alföldi further stress certain passages which place him in his own
environment. This, like Laqueur's study, is an improvement on
the derogatory attitudes of the past. The passages quoted show
that he was a senator and a cultured man. He is proud of his
senatorial rank, but in moderation. I cannot agree with Alföldi that
he is 'brimful of senatorial arrogance'. To be sure, he deplores
the fact that senators are excluded from military command (as
under Gallienus: 33, 33-34). He is especially critical of the senate in
the third century,[20] and his criticisms are characteristic particularly
of a man who belongs neither to the hereditary nobility, nor to the
emerging rural aristocracy, nor to the military leaders.[21]

---

[19] Here Victor succeeds in achieving something in which Tacitus, driven by
ira or *studium*, failed: Tacitus' examples do not grow, but are either good or bad
from the outset with their innuendoes and biased interpretations. See my
Benaderbaar Verleden (Leiden 1952), 23, and 'Caesar 2000 Jahr nach seinem
Tode', in *Caesar*, Wege der Forschung, Band 43, Darmstadt 1967, 423.

[20] See Victor 37,5. Also 37,7: The senate lacks the power to install a ruler:
incertum an ipso cupiente per desidiam an metu seu dissensionum odio.
Cf. Alföldi, *Conflict*, 105.

[21] See on this Starr, *art. cit.*, 580.

The same reserve necessary in the case of his supposedly senatorial attititude, should be observed with regard to another widespread modern interpretation of Victor's views. According to this interpretation Victor is a spokesman in a 'Kulturkampf' waged by fourth-century pagans, who had become aware of themselves as a group. We must be careful in using the concept 'Kulturkampf'. In its most extreme sense the term denotes a struggle between pagans and Christians,[22] but it should be stated forthwith that Victor betrays no trace of such a struggle. It is as if the great controversy between pagans and Christians does not exist for him. This makes it more probable that Victor belonged to the peace-loving intellectuals who condemned emperor Julian's sometimes intolerant attitude in this struggle.[23] In this respect he is spiritually akin to Ammianus Marcellinus who openly criticized Julian, whom he otherwise admired, for his policy.[24] At the same time, this historian is full of respect for culture,[25] and the same goes for Victor. But such respect cannot be denied in Christian authors. If there is any question of a 'Kulturkampf', it is rather in the sense of a closed front of pagans and Christians together in an 'age of anxiety'.[26]

The defence against barbarism is a recurrent theme in Victor's work. Augustus is praised for his interest in cultural affairs (1,5); the period following the first imperial dynasty is therefore considered ill-fated (9,12) and the general cultural background of the Julio-Claudian emperors stands out as a valuable example (8,7-8). The fact that the 'establishment' makes no distinction between the civilized and the uncivilized, the competent and the incompetent (*mixtique bonis indocti ac prudentibus inertes sunt*), horrifies him. A passage added to the description of Constantius II contains outright condemnation of the latter's rather unselective methods of appointing subordinates (42,24). But what is most serious in his eyes is the fact that these people, who think only of their official

---

[22] See J. Straub, *Heidnische Geschichtsapologetik in der christlichen Spätatike. Untersuchungen über Zeit und Tendenz der Historia Augusta* (1963); cf. A. D. E. Cameron's discussion of this work in *JRS* 55 (1965) 240; R. Syme, *Ammianus and the Historia Augusta* (Oxford 1968), 212-213.

[23] For instance, Julian's notorious edict on education. See C. J. Henning, *De eerste schoolstrijd tussen Kerk en Staat onder Julianus de Afvallige*, Diss. Nijmegen 1937.

[24] Ammianus Marcellinus 22,20. 7; 25,4, 20.

[25] e.g. 14,6. 1; 21,10. 8; 30,4. 2.

[26] The expression is taken from the title of Dodds' book, published in 1965.

position and use their functions in order to amass a fortune, exploit their social inferiors. Their power is no true authority (*nomen potentia vacuum*) and as officials for the supply of food they rob the population (*annonae specie rapax*). Thus the officials harshly oppress the lower classes ('insolens miseris').[27] Here we can see the social awareness, new in his time, of a man *rure ortus, tenui atque indocto patre.*[28]

The brief psychological characterization which Victor sometimes adds to his description often makes his sketch unique. An example is the description of Gallienus who deprived senators of the right to exercise military command; he carried out this severe and daring measure, which does not appear to befit a *socors*, 'for fear of his own indolence'.[29] But how often does it not happen that a weakling does something 'tough' in order to vindicate his position and goes to extremes, as Gallienus does here, and in the process arouses opposition which is not conducive to the healthy development of the state. For this treatment is considered as *proprii ordinis contumelia*; moreover, such behaviour on the part of the emperor was most undesirable at a time in which the *commune Romani malum orbis* rather necessitated universal co-operation, including that of the Senate.

Now if Victor regarded this modest biographical work in the light of a moral obligation, then his task was, in the last analysis, no small one. His task was that of every historian: to bring the *fides rerum gestarum*, the truth of history, to light. His account claims to be reliable. For only on the basis of the truth of history (which inspires faith in history) are the good rewarded and the bad punished, only then is man's pursuit of virtue not in vain.[30] Perhaps modern man tends to make too heavy demands on himself and others: one must uphold one's moral standards, irrespective of the result. And it is hard to practise ethics with no knowledge of an ultimate reward. Perhaps skilful manœuvring with absolute norms has made us intolerant of human weaknesses and too much inclined to despise the 'reward of virtue'. Victor lived at a time when merit, including that of upholding moral values, claimed its just reward. The

---

[27] 9,12.

[28] 20,5.

[29] 33,33-34.

[30] This is in connection with the deification of Gallienus, which Victor condemns. 33,25-28: Quis etiam aliquanti ... Divum dixere. For Starr's translation, see Ch. III, p. 56.

question is whether any period can ever absolutely reject this reward, a question that Victor never asked himself. Rather, he consciously regarded the moral judgement expressed in his historical work as an end in itself. The senate capitulated and approved the apotheosis of Gallienus by Claudius II: Victor disagreed. Far from being an arrogant senator, he was a historian conscious of what was due to senatorial dignity.

To refer any discussion of the question of originality of the Father of History to an 'Ur-Herodot' is a reprehensible proceeding. However, the standards by which we judge the great historian should not be lowered in judging the less great. Of course, it must be admitted that a less original mind will tend to be more derivative than a brilliant and original scholar, which Victor was by no means. But I am not prepared to deny him his laurels, not even in favour of Enmann's historian, so long as I have no shred of evidence that certain valuable characteristics of his work are not his own.

There is another element in his work which may very well be original and for which he is even significant—namely, his arrangement of the periods of imperial history. The division into four periods, which determines the composition of his work, is not to be found in any prior source, and all speculation as to a predecessor has proved futile. Moreover, it should be remembered that his structure had a very great influence. Histories of the imperial era are still being written according to a scheme which ultimately derives from Victor. There is therefore ample justification for a closer look at his classification of imperial history.[31]

The history of Rome after Augustus falls into four stages: the first century until Nerva, with a significant break under Claudius; then the good times which ended with Alexander Severus; third came the period of the 'soldier emperors' of the third century, starting with Maximinus; and finally a new era was ushered in by Diocletian.

Victor was aware that freedom was lost under Augustus. As he pithily put it, *mos Romae incessit uni prorsus parendi*.[32] But this obedience could take various forms, the emperors' clementia could make life bearable, as could their respect for the *docti*.[33] Victor distinguishes two intervals in the first period: Claudius' rule and

---

[31] Cf. Starr, *art. cit.*, 578.
[32] 1,1.
[33] 1,5.

the Year of the Four Emperors. The crisis under Caligula had changed much. Claudius was first proclaimed emperor by the soldiers, not by the senate: *Ita Romae regia potestas firmata, proditumque apertius mortalium conatus vacuos a fortuna cassosque esse.* A very home-grown piece of wisdom: the impotence of human effort in the face of the arbitrariness of fate. But his subdivision of the Julio-Claudian period is nevertheless correct. Modern biographers still (or should I say, again?) refer to the transition after 41 A.D. in this way.[34] For him, the Year of the Four Emperors marks the end of the *principes* of culture and education. Precisely this (secondary) division in his work is strictly personal, in keeping with his respect for education and learning—a respect we have mentioned before, 'All those emperors whose lives I am briefly discussing, and particularly the *gens Julia* (the *Caesares*, literally!) had been so formed by learning and oratory that their extraordinary gifts would certainly have overshadowed their small faults, if all their mistakes, with the exception of Augustus', had not been too great'.[35]

Victor does not deny that a sovereign should possess a good character: *mores* are more important than cultural background. A *summus rector* [36] should possess both. If this is not possible, Victor prefers *auctoritas* based on *elegantia* and *eruditio*, rather than that based on *mores* alone. This shows conclusively that the *mores* which he so much enjoys discussing, hold a relative value for him. Victor glances backwards and then looks .... to the future.

At the time of Nerva's accession, the first major interval, the links with Italy were broken (Victor gives him the cognomen Cretensis).[37] But as in ancient times in the case of Tarquinius

---

[34] For instance, A. D. Momigliano, *Claudius: The Emperor and his Achievement*, 1934 (repr. 1961), Introduction, xv.

[35] 8,7-8.

[36] The term (8,8) was first used for Nero in 5,4; rector gentium.

[37] There is nothing to be found on this subject in the monographs by R. Paribeni, *Nerva* (Rome 1947) and A. Garzetti, *Nerva* (Rome 1950); nor in D. Kienast, 'Nerva und das Kaisertum Trajans', *Historia* 17 (1968), 51-71, who uses the most recent literature. One may recall *Narniensis* (Epit. 12,1) and thus emend Victor's text (cf. R. Syme, *Tacitus* [Oxford 1958], 576 note 1). I hesitate to apply this textual alteration (as indeed do the editors of these abbreviaria). Galba and Nerva had much in common. The former called himself a descendant of Pasiphae (Suet. *Galba* 2), so perhaps Nerva claimed similar ties with Crete. Cf. for similar pretentious analogies M. P. Charlesworth, 'Flaviana', *JRS* 27 (1937), 54. A. Stein

Priscus, a non-Roman, so in imperial times foreign origin did not detract from the positive qualities of a sovereign. On the contrary: the foreign rulers were better than those born in Italy. And Victor liked to stress this tendency and even turned it into a general rule: *Ac mihi quidem audienti multa legentique plane compertum urbem Romam externorum virtute atque insitivis artibus praecipue crevisse.*[38]

Alexander Severus made an effort to continue the line which had run from Romulus to Septimus Severus. It was thanks to Alexander that the empire did not fall as a result of Heliogabalus' excesses. After him, however, all restraint was lost. Those who found their way to the throne were not just provincials, but simply barbarians. Their ideal was no longer to build an Imperium through conquest, but to oppress their subjects. There was no longer any distinction between the good and the bad or the noble and others. Victor is embittered about the consequences of these changes: widespread confusion, lack of order, usurpation of functions by people devoid of any knowledge of government. Thus blind fortune, when given a chance, drives mortals onward, a prey to their desires. The barrier of *virtus*, which formerly offered protection, disappeared. No wonder, for the corruption of the *bonae artes* had already set in.[39] And those who were now in power were among the lowest in origin and ability.

The arrangement in periods is, admittedly, somewhat facile, and shows all rulers later than 235 in a sombre light; the author's further treatment, though, sometimes appears inconsistent. He praises Claudius II and Aurelian,[40] Tacitus, Probus and Numerian. But here Victor is concerned with the evils of the proclamation of emperors by the armies, and not by the senate. This is intolerable to him, as we can see from a curious statement which, although it refers to the murder of Probus, has a more general significance: later (i.e. after Probus' death) the power of the soldiers grew, and the authority and right to choose an emperor was denied the senate

---

(*P.I.R.*[2], nr. 1227) simply assumes that the text is corrupt: 'oppido Narniensi genitus (*Epit.* 12,1) *Cretensis* Vict. Caes. 12,1 absurde corruptum'. See p. 110ff. for Victor and the Epitomist on Nerva.

[38] 11,13.

[39] 24,9: Quo ne confestim laberetur, Alexandri fuit. Abhinc dum dominandi suis quam subigendi externos cupientiores sunt atque inter se armantur magis, Romanum statum quasi abrupto praecipitavere, immisique in imperium promiscue boni malique, nobiles atque ignobiles, ac barbariae multi.

[40] Victor 34,35, esp. § 12 and § 36; 37; 39,13.

until his own time. It is not certain whether the members of the senate themselves agreed to this procedure out of apathy or fear, or in order to avoid civil war.

Similarly, it looks as if Diocletian, another emperor proclaimed by the soldiers, also failed to bring about any change. Nevertheless, the year 284 marks a new era,[41] even though Victor does not admire Diocletian unreservedly [42] any more than he does Augustus. That he had no illusions about him is shown by the way in which he describes how Diocletian, fully aware that the future would bring civil war and destruction, celebrated his jubilee and then abdicated.[43] It is therefore impossible to consider this final episode as a fourth, new period. The Empire, then and from time to time later, enjoyed periods of good administration, but these were no more than breathing-spaces in a history of terror, the most striking aspect of which is its continuity.

CALIGULA AS AN EXAMPLE OF VICTOR'S INDEPENDENT TREATMENT OF HIS MATERIAL

In drawing comparisons between the contemporaries Eutropius, Victor and the writer of the *Epitome,* one should be careful to choose examples from among the *shorter* biographies. For it is here that affinities will come to the fore most distinctly. The longer biographies concern more important emperors who presumably also attracted more attention in the literature, particularly if their rule marked a constitutional or political transition (especially to the historian looking back on the period). It is no coincidence that Gallienus, Diocletian and Constantine, for example, are given more attention than others: they were of greater importance than many others and their influence is noticeable long after their respective periods of rule. Less fastidious chroniclers of scandal had different standards, since they were interested particularly in emperors whose personal lives had attracted attention—especially for their loose morals and rejection of generally accepted values. But in the case of the Julio-Claudian and Flavian dynasties, fourth-century morality or imagination could do little more moralizing or inventing than Suetonius had already done. For lessons in good moral conduct

---

[41] Esp. 39,8 and 15.

[42] 39,46.

[43] 39,48: ubi fato intestinas clades et quasi fragorem quendam impendere comperit.

examples of a general nature sufficed. It would be incorrect to attempt to trace these generalities back directly to a written source. In all national histories there are standard views on historical persons and their conduct, and so it was in imperial times. There was a general picture, sometimes vague, sometimes sharply defined, but its contours were seldom if ever derived from one particular work, let alone from an historical work. The schools did much to preserve oral traditions, and rhetoric and exercises in memorization kept examples alive.[44]

Senator Eutropius needs no more than sixty words to sketch a general picture of Caligula. He sees a climax of horror in the trio Tiberius, Caligula, and Nero,[45] culminating in the damage to the empire perpetrated by the latter. The trinity of greed, cruelty and lust recurs again and again. Caligula's incest with his sisters, mentioned both by Victor and in the *Epitome*, but in more detail, lends the story of his life a personal touch. Nor is his violent death forgotten. Independently of all the writings about him, this was how Caligula lived on in people's memories: as the arbitrary, repulsive potentate who dishonoured the imperial purple for three years, and lived for his unbridled whims and passions alone. But to search for a source for this general picture is, again, methodologically unsound—quite apart from the fact that it is futile.

What does Victor make of all this? In his own personal style, so very different from that of Eutropius' few lucid sentences, he devotes eight times as much space to this emperor. The general background is the same as that indicated by Eutropius, but with one major difference: Victor describes the emperor's progress from bad to worse. There are few or no parallels for this image in surviving writings. The static idea that this emperor remained true to his monstrous self throughout dominates ancient histories concerning him. Victor did not depart materially form this approach: he explains the difference between the first months of his rule and the much longer period of terror as initial camouflage on Caligula's

---

[44] See for instance, the *Sententiae Hadriani* (under the name of Dositheos, a bilingual school textbook). Cf. H. I. Marrou, *Histoire de l'éducation dans l'antiquité*, Paris 1948, 356 and 547, note 18.

[45] VII 11,1: Sed Tiberius ingenti socordia imperium gessit, gravi crudelitate, scelesta avaritia, turpi libidine. VII 12,1: Secessit ei C. Caesar, cognomento Caligula ... sceleratissimus ac funestissimus et qui etiam Tiberi dedecora purgaverit. VII 14,1: Nero, Caligulae avunculo suo simillimus, qui Romanum imperium et deformavit et minuit .... 15,1 execrabilis ab omnibus ...

part. But he did notice the disparity between the early and later years of his rule.[46] (Compare this with his psychological insight into Nero, who went from bad to worse after the first 'wise' years of rule.)[47] Here we must observe that neither Suetonius nor Cassius Dio makes such a distinction in the emperor's governmental conduct. Suetonius does see a difference between his actions as *princeps* (relatively good) and his monstrous crimes, but this distinction (which he does not, by the way, sustain) does not imply a chronological break within his period of rule.[48] Cassius Dio refers to 'his good deeds, which deserve praise' and then to 'acts which met with the censure of all alike';[49] again, this is no more than a method of ordering the facts, not a chronological arrangement. To my knowledge, only Philo writes of a complete change of character;[50] this element also indirectly enters Josephus' picture, although the latter extends his good period of rule to two years.[51] Philo blames the change on the illness which set in six months after the emperor's accession.[52] It is to my mind unlikely that Victor was familiar with Philo's theory which, as has rightly been observed,[53] is disproved by the facts which Philo himself presents. In fact, there is no support

---

[46] His mode of expression betrays the difficulty Victor has with this development in personality: 3,7 and 8 give a confused impression: diu immania animo ita pudore ac parendi specie obtexerat uti merito vulgaretur neque meliores famulos <neque atrociorem dominum> illo fuisse. The words in parentheses do not fit in with his thinking *at this stage*. The contrast between the *famuli* and the *dominus* arose later, but the following passage is concerned with a time in which Caligula still conducted himself as a servant of the state. § 8 is a panegyric on his good relations with the people, senate and army (with a linguistically excellent, and constitutionally completely acceptable *variatio sermonis*: ad populum, inter patres, cum militibus), and of resistence against the *delatores*. § 8 <uti talia ingenia recens solent> also contains a consideration *post eventum*. Only in § 9 does his fury find expression: Sed repente caesis primum vario facinore innocentium paucioribus tamquam beluae hausto sanguine ingenium exercuit. The words are reminiscent of Tacitus and, if *sed* were to be replaced by *nam*, would fit perfectly with the end of § 6. The untidiness is a proof of the genuineness of this man, who knew and wanted to do more than he could convey as a writer.

[47] R. Pichon rightly points this out, *Histoire de la littérature latine*, Paris 1930[12], 789: Hactenus quasi de principe, reliqua ut de monstro narranda sunt. Cf. E. Mary Smallwood, *Philonis Alexandrini Legatio ad Gaium*, Leiden 1961, 169.

[48] Suet. *Gaius* 22.

[49] Cass. Dio 59,9 and 10.

[50] *Leg. ad Gaium* 13, cf. 67 and 73; Comm. Smallwood, (esp. p. 168).

[51] *A.J.* 18, 256.

[52] The same interpretation is to be found in Charlesworth in *CAH*, X, 656.

[53] Smallwood, *op. cit.*, p. 168.

to be found in any other source either. Suetonius and Cassius Dio, who are generally mentioned together (as sources available to the fourth-century historians) certainly taught Aurelius Victor nothing in this respect.[54] Nor can Philo's reasoning (based on Gaius' illness) have influenced Victor's view.

Tacitus' comment, *immanem animum subdola modestia tegens*, refers to the situation in 33 A.D. and corresponds to the words *incredibili simulatione* in Suet. 10,2.[55] A similar idea of the suppression of evil characteristics is expressed by Victor, as we have seen (note 46), but his expression of it, *denique nactus potestatem ... anni mensibus egregia ad populum inter patres, cum militibus gessit* etc. (§ 8), is stylistically unique in its most successful and historically correct series of propositions. Here Victor surpasses many of his known contemporaries such as Eutropius or the Epitomist; many modern scholars would maintain that such praise should rightfully be accorded the unknown author from whom Victor may have borrowed his positive judgement. Even in this case it remains to his credit that he included it in his short sketch, while others did not.

The modern view, which is much too favourable towards Caligula,[56] may be traced to the Epitomist rather than to Victor. After all, the modern view is based on the fact that one of the innovations advocated and effected by Caligula was the concept of a consistent absolute monarchy. This theory is strengthened by *Epit.* 3,8: *Primus diademate imposito dominum se iussit appellari.* Victor does not go so far and approaches the truth more nearly: *dominum dici atque insigne regni nectere capiti tentaverat* (cf. Suet. *Gaius* 22,2).[57]

---

[54] W. Steidle, *Sueton und die antike Biographie*, Munich 1951, 75, rightly says on the matter of Suetonius' opinion: 'Von einem positiven Regierungsbeginn des Kaisers kann man also nur sehr bedingt reden, es kommen vielmehr nur infolge anders gearbeiteter Wirkungswünsche die schlechten Eigenschaften noch nicht zur Geltung'. Suetonius' words 'nec servum meliorem ullum', refer to Caligula's behaviour before his accession, and what follows, 'nec deteriorem dominum', to his behaviour as emperor (c. 10-12).

[55] *Ann.* VI 20; cf. 45,5; 48,4.

[56] J. P. V. D. Balson, *The Emperor Gaius*, Oxford 1934 and R. W. Davies 'The "Abortive Invasion" of Britain by Gaius', *Historia* 15 (1966), 124 ff. P. Lambrechts, 'Caligula dictateur littéraire', *Bull. de l'Institut historique belge de Rome* 28, 1953, 230-232. P. Bicknell, 'The Emperor Gaius' Military Activities in A.D. 40', *Historia* 17 (1968), 496. E. J. Phillips, 'The Emperor Gaius' abortive invasion of Britain', *Historia* 19 (1970), 369-374.

[57] Recommended in this connection, J. Straub in *RAC* II (1954) *s.v.* 'Caligula', Col. 827-837, 832.

In the case of Caligula, the length of the biography is one of the factors which determine the difference between Victor and the *Epitome*; yet this apparently significant difference (Victor's biography is four times as long as the *Epitome*), is far from decisive. The life of Trajan, to give but one example, is of roughly equal length in both works. The composition and the facts, however, are so different that there can be no question of derivation or of tracing to the same source or sources. Let us examine this question in greater detail.

Trajan

All modern discussions of this emperor point out the scarcity of the material available to us.[58] The *Epitome* makes it clear that a considerable body of literature must have existed. What this author says should, however, be viewed with certain reservations since it occurs in a passage full of praise.[59] Nevertheless, it is quite clear that Trajan constituted an example which was frequently referred to in the second and third centuries, since his wars, and especially the unfortunate expedition against the Parthians, influenced the subsequent politics of the Empire, and were discussed by rhetoricians and schoolmasters for the edification of succeeding receptive generations.

The picture that Victor and the *Epitome* present obviously has certain elements in common. In the first place, there is the emperor's non-Italian origin. The fact that this statement occurs at the beginning is not surprising. Neither the statement itself nor its position in the passage provides any indication of derivation. Derivation could only be suspected if their rendering of the facts of Trajan's origin corresponded. Even then one would have to consider the possibility that so factual a statement made by various authors would present similarities, without necessarily justifying the conclusion that we are here concerned with derivations from one and the same source. However, this possibility does not require further consideration because the difference between the two writers

---

[58] *inter alios* J. H. Thiel, 'Trajanus', *Kon. Ned. Akad. van Wetenschappen, Akademiedagen VIII*, 1955, 15-43.

[59] *Epit.* 13,2: Iste talem se reipublicae praebuit, qualem vix aegreque exprimere valuerint summorum scriptorum miranda ingenia. Eutropius also (VIII 5,3) refers indirectly to two traditions concerning Trajan: Adeo in eo gloria bonitatis obtinuit, ut vel adsentantibus vel vere laudantibus occasionem magnificentissimi praestet exempli.

is already quite striking in the first paragraph. Victor is businesslike and clear, the Epitomist loses himself in a show of learning.

<table>
<tr><td align="center">Victor 13,1</td><td align="center">Epit. 13,1</td></tr>
</table>

Victor 13,1	*Epit.* 13,1
Namque Ulpium Traianum Italica, urbe Hispaniae, ortum, amplissimi ordinis tamen atque etiam consulari loco, arrogatum accepit dedit.	Ulpius Traianus, ex urbe Tudertina, Ulpius ab avo dictus, Traianus a Traio paterni generis auctore vel de nomine Traiani patris sic appellatus, imperavit annis viginti.

Ex urbe Tudertina is a piece of scholarly virtuosity which leaves everyone at a loss; the ridiculous suggestion of Traius and Traianus as alternatives belongs to the same kind of armchair scholarship. And it is significant that what should have been the main statement, namely, Trajan's non-Italian origin, is not even mentioned. Victor, on the other hand, supplies the correct information besides mentioning (he is, after all, a senator) that this emperor already belonged to the *ordo senatorius*.[60] Viewed against the background of third-century usurpers, whom Victor so severely condemned, Trajan is entirely in order; and in view of his own background, Victor has the sweet satisfaction of being able to bask in the reflected glory of this *optimus princeps*.

Quite naturally and in accordance with the rules of rhetoric, both authors round off their passage concerning Trajan's origin with a general statement, of very different import. Victor praises the emperor's unique fame in peace and in war, the Epitomist writes that even the greatest historians were hardly able to describe his merits. However, after this introduction, our two authors part company. Victor rightly pays attention to Trajan's foreign policy,[61] military data which are entirely lacking in the *Epitome* except for one very general observation (*diligentiam in re militari*). Victor also devotes more attention to his public works in Rome, while the *Epitome* only refers to the thermae of Sura in connection with his

---

[60] One might consider his father, who was the first of his line to be admitted to the rank of senator; consul and governor of Syria and Asia. See M. Durry, 'Sur Trajan père', in: *Les empereurs romains d'Espagne*, Paris 1965, 45-51.

[61] 13,3 and 4. In passing, we should note his geographical blunders in this context (in § 3, Indum instead of Tigrim. His reference to Sardonios is still unexplained).

friendship with Licinius Sura.[62] Victor, however, mentions the *cura annonae* and the *cursus publicus*; he presents a summary of contemporary events: Anatolius' actions in Illyria, and the Emperor's support of the *pistores*. All this is history, if short and incomplete. The inevitable personal anecdotes are limited to two examples which, and this is no coincidence, illustrate Trajan's friendship with the highly placed Licinius Sura and Sextus Attius Suburanus. And these friendships, this confidence, redound to the emperor's credit, even today. No wonder that his conduct appeared 'exemplary' after a period of imperial extravagance and arbitrary dictatorship. Victor's choice from the wealth of anecdotes is to the point, illustrative and, as far as we know, original. The Epitomist on the other hand has little to offer. He explains away the emperor's relationship with his friends: Sura was no more than a favourite, *cuius studio imperium arripuerat*.[63] Moreover, he needs a rhetorical stopgap to conceal the lacunae in his treatment of the material.[64] Instead of giving details of the emperor's actions he gives the standard eulogy on his life and character which occupies the greater part of his meagre study, and includes (pedantic as he is) a superior observation on the emperor's poor schooling and mediocre oratory.[65] But let us not be too hard on him: he does point out certain details overlooked by Victor: his legislative activities,[66] and also natural disasters and building regulations,[67] and the unique burial ceremony.[68] It is perhaps characteristic of him that he finds it necessary to mention *prodigia*, interpreted as divine signs in favour of the emperor's accession. Here, too, Victor differs: it was beneath his dignity to point out a connection between divine rule and imperial power, even though he was far from sceptical of omens. Victor's concern was what modern research still regards as historical pro-

---

[62] *Epit.* 13,6; see also Cass. Dio 68, 16,1 Cf. *R.E.*, *s.v.* 'Attius' (28). Plin. *Epist.* IV, 6,10 (Sherwin White's Commentary, p. 410).

[63] *Epit.* 13,6.

[64] *Epit.* 13,7: De quo supervacaneum videtur concta velle nominatius promere.

[65] *Epit.* 13.4, 8. Victor, being a man who holds tradition high, does mention the same points, but inconspicuously, in the beginning of the life of Hadrian: eloquio togaeque studiis accommodatior (14,1). These words were kept so general that the reader need not even notice an important contrast with his predecessor.

[66] *Epit.* 13,10.

[67] *Epit.* 13,12 and 13.

[68] *Epit.* 13,11. Cf. Eutr. VIII 5,2.

blems: the war against the Parthians and the succession. Nowhere
does the difference in quality between the two writers stand out
more clearly. The Epitomist is completely silent on these subjects.
Victor gives a biased version, particularly of the Parthian war, but
the text, unfortunately, is decidedly cryptic. This much, however,
is certain: he does not regard the emperor's return as a defeat, but
as compliance with the wish of the senate.[69] The correctness of
this version was already questioned in antiquity, and indeed other
views crop up repeatedly. But Victor's point of view, based on
senatorial tradition, was always loyal to the Optimus Princeps.
This loyalty is just as sincere as the statement which follows—
that Hadrian was chosen as Trajan's successor by the emperor
himself.

Indeed this loyalty emerges the more strongly through Victor's
statement, in that it was due to this choice that divided rule *avant
la lettre* became a fact during Trajan's lifetime.[70] It is surely a false
picture of history, in conflict with all that we know of Hadrian's
succession. Nevertheless, it cannot be denied that the historical
perspective of contemporary events since Diocletian shows Trajan's
successor in an anachronistic light. This account forms the climax
of a laudatory version of an historical reality, a version that may
be noble, but is certainly incorrect. The fourth-century historian
wished to give Trajan credit for every virtue, including that of
sharing the responsibility of ruling the Empire, though he is far
from being servile, as his last words on the subject show. Here he
refers not to the *adoptio in extremis* version, but to that according
to which Plotina falsified Trajan's will.[71] Victor says as much,
laconically and without further comment. Perhaps he himself found
it difficult to accept the traditional view of the legitimacy of
Hadrian's claim. If so, we will never know for certain, though his
treatment of Hadrian, which is noticeably less favourable than that
of Trajan, would seem to indicate such an attitude.

To sum up, our conclusion must be that Victor is far superior to

---

[69] Victor 13,11; rogatu patrum Italiam repetens morbo periit grandaeva
aetate ascito prius ad imperium Hadriano civi propinquoque.

[70] Victor 13,12: Abhinc divisa nomina Caesarum atque Augusti indoctum
que in rempublicam, uti duo seu plures summae potentiae dissimiles cognomento ac potestate dispari sint.

[71] Victor 13,13. Quamquam alii Plotinae, Traiani coniugis favore imperium assecutum putent, quae viri testamento heredem regni institutum
simulaverat.

the Epitomist in every respect.[72] Their work has hardly anything
in common in composition or as to the information given. Victor's
version cannot be denied a certain degree of originality, even though
he may have derived his view of the (in his opinion) greatest
emperor from someone else. Most important of all from the historical
point of view is that he reconciles the emperor's actions towards
the end of his life and senatorial intervention. Furthermore, he
attempts to conceal the fact that the emperor neglected to provide
a successor by crediting him with the division of rulership, which
did not become an established fact until 150 years later (the episode
of Marcus Aurelius and Lucius Verus may be disregarded with
impunity).

Finally, a warning is in order against one particularly pernicious
procedure of modern history writing: that of denying Victor the

---

[72] This does not mean that the Epitomist is of no importance. Chapter 13
contains two remarkable statements, and a third is to be found elsewhere
in his work.
(i) 13,2: scriptorum miranda ingenia, which indicates the existence of a
much larger circle of writers than those known to us. There is no reason
to doubt the truth of this: it is easy to be sceptical if one considers the
words quoted as a rhetorical exaggeration. In this case, however, the
question will remain unanswered why the Epit. applies this technique
in this particular place (and nowhere else) or rather, 'adopts' it as the
hypercritical searcher for sources or stylistic purist would say.
(ii) 13,10: the reference, which also occurs elsewhere, to signs heralding
Trajan's arrival in remedium tantorum malorum. The Epit. probably
has Theodosius, with whom the work ends, in mind here. The author
himself compares Trajan and Theodosius, and even shows a preference
for the latter on ethical grounds (Epit. 48,10). Both were preceded
by 'many tyrants'. The words per multos atque atroces tyrannos
certainly apply to Theodosius' predecessors (these may also be predecessors in a more distant past, i.e. the third century), but they also
apply to Trajan. Especially if one remembers the senatorial tradition
which regarded emperors denied the consecratio as tyrants. Among
Trajan's predecessors four had been refused the consecratio: Tiberius,
Caligula, Nero and Domitian (see Eutr. VII 11,1; 12,4; 15,1; 23,1 and
6). Out of a total of ten emperors this number is not inconsiderable.
(iii) The role played by Trajan's wife, Pompeia Plotina, is referred to in a
unique way (not mentioned elsewhere) in connection with procuratores
in the province (Epit. 42,21). The Emperor did not intervene in the rule
of the senatorial provinces until late. This is also known from other
sources, notably the Letters of the Younger Pliny. The statement that
Plotina advised him to intervene is new, but not impossible. Its truth
was accepted by L. Homo, Le Haut-Empire, 434. H.-G. Pflaum, Essai
sur les Procurateurs équestres sous le Haut-Empire romain (1950), 54 ff.,
rightly points out the enormous influence Trajan had on the development of the procurators, a development later attributed to Hadrian.
Epit. 14,11 (op. cit., 58).

doubtful credit of this (incorrect) view of history in favour of some imaginary anonymous author. In short, no author before or after Victor is known to share his views. They do, however, fit the character of the provincial, who found an outlet for his need to idealize even the weakest traits of one emperor, a provincial like himself. And yet .... he does not entirely lose sight of the responsibilities of the historian, which he states so impressively elsewhere (see above). He also includes an interpretation that differs radically from his own—with no further comment.

Victor is not alone in his favourable judgement. At least one of his contemporaries is even more appreciative of Trajan's reign— namely Eutropius.[73] If there was one senator in the fourth century who upheld the honour of his class, it was he.[74] This is why, though he does not forget to mention that during the rule of this emperor one senator was condemned, his terminology is, in fact, approving.[75] Whether his statement is correct or no is beside the point. It paves the way for higher praise: *ob haec per orbem terrarum deo proximus nihil non venerationis meruit et vivus et mortuus.* Thus Trajan is the only man whose last remains are buried within the city.[76] All this appears to arise from a courtier's mentality, but this is to do Eutropius an injustice. His deep admiration is amply justified by the expansion of the Empire. He devotes two chapters to a record of these triumphs. Eutropius is not plagued by doubts concerning the correctness of this expansion policy. On the contrary: his criticism of Augustus' successors is centred on the fact that although they defended the Empire they did not 'nobly expand it'.[77] Eutropius' fear of invasion, which emerges from his emphasis on the *miliaria* [78] constitutes the background against which one must understand his comparatively detailed account of the conquests. And it is quite in keeping with this attitude that his beautiful

---

[73] Eutr. VIII 1; 2,4-6; 8; 10; IX 8; 5.

[74] The words 'brimful of senatorial arrogance', used by Alföldi for Victor (*Conflict*, 98), apply rather to Eutropius, the aristocrat and stylist, than to the *homo novus* who wrote so laboriously, and never forgot his humble origins.

[75] Eutr. VIII 4: Nihil non tranquillum et placidum agens adeo ut omni eius aetate unus senator damnatus sit atque is tamen per senatum ignorante Traiano.

[76] VIII 5,2.

[77] Romani imperii quod post Augustum defensum magis fuerat quam nobiliter ampliatum (VIII 2,2).

[78] See Chapter IV, p. 120.

picture is not marred by any reference to the failure of Trajan's expedition in the East. He simply states laconically, 'Having gained great fame in war and peace, he died near Seleucia in Isauria on his return from Persia'. *E Perside rediens*—nothing could be more neutral and innocent. One may wonder why the fear of invasion did not here, too, induce him to deliver a warning inspired by the true course of events. Presumably he felt that nothing should mar the perfection of this inspiring *exemplum*. The description of this period was not to end on a false note, in order to affirm the truth of the well-known benediction proclaimed at later imperial successions: 'More fortunate than Augustus, better than Trajan'.[79]

There was no need for Eutropius to keep silent about Trajan's return from the east, but it was more politic to mention this fact in connection with his successor, whose reputation in senatorial circles (including Victor) was not so good—indeed in certain respects even doubtful. For instance in the passage on Hadrian (which is no more than half the length of that devoted to Trajan) we read that he apparently wished to diminish his predesessor's fame in war and therefore, actuated by jealousy, withdrew the troops from the east: *Traiani gloriae invidens*.[80] A cruder, more dishonest approach is hard to imagine. But, once again, when investigating the mentality of an historian, the historical accuracy of a statement is not the point at issue. The fourth-century senator is frankly biased and his object, that of summing up history for the ignorant, obliges him to make use of 'myths'. Otherwise he runs the risk of not being understood.

Ever since the time of Hadrian himself,[81] Hadrian's 'guilt' or 'innocence' with respect to the change in imperial military policy had been a vexed question. Fronto had already openly sided with Hadrian. Certainly he calls Trajan *summus bellator*, but the admira-

---

[79] VIII 5,3.

[80] VIII 6,2; cf. Festus, Chapter V, p. 205.

[81] Traiano suam potiorem gloriam in sanguine militum futuram de ceteris eius studiis multi coniectant, nam saepe Parthorum legatos pacem precantes dimisisse inritos. Fronto, p. 198 in ed. M. P. J. van den Hout, *M. Corn. Frontonis Epistulae I* (1954). The identity of these *multi* escapes us; surely they were inspired by Hadrian's autobiography, a reflection of which is to be found in *SHA* 1, 10,2; there Hadrian is greater than Trajan, and on a par with Augustus in government matters and military insight. In general Fronto is favourable to Hadrian, with whose pacifist policy he agrees (v. d. Hout, p. 195, line 11 ff.: Quin provincias manu Traiani captas variis bellis ac novo constituendas omittere maluit quam exercitu retinere). On the other hand, Fronto respects Trajan but does not admire him (v. d. Hout, p. 24, line 20 f.).

tion that he demonstrates in discussing Hadrian is lacking in the
case of Trajan's policy of peace. His criticism of the fact that the
emperor sought amusement by frequenting the theatre is unworthy
(Galen says the same about Marcus Aurelius) and so is the almost
inevitable reference to his addiction to drink: *et praeterea potavit
satis strenue*.[82] In keeping with this narrowmindedness is the allusion
to Trajan's jealousy of the successes gained by his generals, and
to the murder of Parthamasiris.[83] However, two generations after
Fronto the calumnies about Trajan amounted to no more than the
'desire for fame' of which Cassius Dio writes.[84] All these statements
must have been largely based on that mysterious work, Hadrian's
autobiography, which is occasionally mentioned but of which we
hardly ever encounter a trace.[85]

Discussions as to whether or not Trajan's eastern policy was
justified are endless and fruitless. In this respect the modern
historian is certainly in no better position than the *multi*, referred
to by Fronto, or the fourth-century abbreviators. The evaluation
of Trajan's policy is still a moot point, and the arguments remain
the same as those of the Roman historians, often worthless or very
prejudiced in either direction. It is not my intention to choose sides
in this conflict; I merely wish to adduce one piece of evidence, not
because it happens to be *pro Traiano*, but because in the welter of
encomiums and scandalous rumours it is the only solid statement;
made, moreover, by the most distinguished historian of Trajan's
own time, Flavius Arrianus. He says that the Emperor considered
that every effort should be made to persuade Osroes (King of the
Parthians) to avoid war.[86] It is quite possible that Arrian was

---

[82] p. 214 (v. d. Hout), Galen VI, 405 (Kühn).

[83] p. 199 (v. d. Hout). Cf. F. A. Lepper, *Trajan's Parthian War* (Oxford
1948), 7.

[84] 68, 17,1: δόξης ἐπιθυμία.. Cf. Lepper, *op. cit.*, 191 ff. Pflaum, *op. cit.*, 107 ff.
In the *Epit.* (48,10: Illa tamen, quibus Traianus aspersus est, vinolentiam
scilicet en cupidinem triumphandi) we find the same accusations as in
Cassius Dio (68, 7,4 and 17,1) and later again in *H.A. Hadr.* 3,3 and *Sev.
Alex.* 39,1.

[85] It is tempting to accept the suggestion P. Jal makes in his 'Nature et
signification politique de l'oeuvre de Florus', *REL* 43 (1965), 358-383, esp.
379, namely that the terms in which Florus' pacifism is expressed are
Hadrian's own. (Florus I 33,8 and II 30,29). In this connection Jal rightly
refers to *Epit.* 14,10: iactabat palam plus se otio adeptum quam armis
heteros. The sentiment expressed in 48,10 (see note 84) may come from the
same source.

[86] A. G. Roos, *Studia Arrianea*, Leipzig 1912, p. 30 (s. vv. ἀπείρατον,
γνωσιμαχῆσαι), cf. Chapter V, p. 206, note 107.

better informed than Cassius Dio, and that he was not suggesting that this was a purely diplomatic last bid for peace, but simply that he was a better judge of Trajan's attitude than contemporary or later critics. At all events this explanation would correspond to the views of the emperor Julian, who knew the East all too well. He termed the war against Decebalus a war of aggression, but that against the Parthians a defensive war.[87] In view of Julian's bantering tone in these conversations one would be inclined not to take this opinion too seriously, were it not for the fact that it is so much in agreement with Arrian's authoritative account.

COMPOSITIONAL PROBLEMS

Septimus Severus

There are hardly any chapters in which Victor takes more trouble to interlard his historical account with moral comments than c. 19-20, in which he discusses the reign of Septimus Severus: his fellow countryman must be placed in a favourable light. Equally, nowhere do his limited talent and clumsy presentation stand revealed so clearly as here. Since much has already been written on the subject of his limitations,[88] a short list may suffice here. There is the confusion of the emperor Didius Julianus and the jurist Salvius Julianus, who lived two generations earlier,[89] the observation that Septimius Severus was *legatus* of Syria when he was proclaimed emperor (he was in fact governor of Pannonia Superior), the confusion between Septimus' victory at Lyons and Constantine's victory at the Pons Mulvius (also to be found in Eutropius VIII, 17). The sequence of the military exploits mentioned is not without flaws; the King of Osroene is called the King of the Persians;[90] Pescennius Niger was defeated at Cyzicus, which should be Issus.[91] The list is

---

[87] *Caes.* 328 A.

[88] M. Platnauer, *The Life and Reign of the Emperor Septimius Severus* (1918) and J. Hasebroek, *Untersuchungen zur Geschichte des Kaisers Septimius Severus* (Heidelberg 1921). T. D. Barnes, 'The Family and Career of Septimius Severus', *Historia* 16 (1967), 87-107.

[89] See above p. 22ff. Eutropius, however, says that they were related (VIII, 17).

[90] 20,14ff.

[91] Correct in Cassius Dio, 74,7,1 and Herodian 3,4,2; the same error occurs in Eutr. VIII, 18, who, incidentally, is better informed on the subject of Niger than Victor. Cf. Hasebroek, *op. cit.*, 61; R. Syme, *Ammianus*, 104ff. (who holds the traditional view of the 'common source').

incomplete, and not characteristic in itself of the author (whose sources, once again, cannot be traced).

The very clumsiness of the presentation, however, will allow us us a clearer insight into the author's personality. In the first place, the chapters suffer from the two irreconcilable tasks the author sets himself: on the one hand that of extolling Didius Julianus, whom he takes for Salvius Julianus, as a man of *bonae litterae*, and hence to condemn his murderer (Septimius Severus), but on the other hand to glorify the latter, who is a fellow countryman, without condoning the crime. One could hardly imagine that this presentation would cause difficulties for the modern historian, to whom a differentiated picture is the chief requirement of a good historian. He even goes so far as to regard the almost unanimous glorification in the sources of a sovereign like Trajan with suspicion.[92] An author writing for the masses has to generalize; this has always been the case, and so it was in the fourth century A.D. Although Tacitus was capable of subtlety, albeit reluctantly and with difficulty, few other Roman historians possessed that faculty—least of all the African *homo novus* Aurelius Victor. Before we analyse him further, however, a possible misunderstanding must be eliminated. The crudeness of his praise and censure, which are sometimes haphazardly juxtaposed, should be regarded as quite distinct from the possible use of more than one source. It is an intrinsic element in the author's presentation, as will appear from the following.

Didius Julianus

The introduction is not promising. The bloody murder of 'Aulus' Helvius Pertinax took place *impulsore Didio*.[93] But subsequently it is the turn of the murderer himself, and in this context he makes the afore-mentioned erroneous identification with the jurist. His life and actions show with sufficient clarity that 'learning

---

[92] See J. H. Thiel, *art. cit.*, 22ff., who rightly objects to the exclusively favourable judgement of the emperor on psychological grounds. R. Syme, *Tacitus* (Oxford 1958), e.g. 36ff. and 495, is much more severe in his judgement, suspicious as he is of all emperors who restricted the power of the senate. Curiously, a study of Trajan is lacking in the collection of studies on *Les empereurs romains d'Espagne* (Paris 1965), presumably on account of the scarcity of the literary sources (at least, in comparison with the surviving literature on Hadrian).

[93] c. 18,2: Eum milites, quis exhausto iam perditoque orbe satis videtur nihil, impulsore Didio foede iugulavere. For the reactions of the populace, see Z. Yavetz, *Plebs* and *Princeps* (Oxford 1969), 5.

alone is not enough if the character does not help to restrain desires; for he, who taught the people a better, though hard, way of life, himself stooped to a crime, which under the terms of his own edict merited the death penalty'.

The transition shows some subtlety. The distinction between *ingenium* (character) and an extensive knowledge of the law, *iuris urbani praestans scientia,* is neatly made. People can understand this, history has enough examples to show of great men of gross or immoral habits, and primitive morality is soon satisfied: 'However, he did not long possess the power he craved'.

We are here offered a sketch of a minor emperor, the details of whose life were not so varied and numerous as to confuse the author. Moreover, his judgement is clear-cut: praise for the jurist and censure of the *ingenium* that gave rise to *saevi mores* (20,2). Julianus' reputation among later generations rests chiefly on the former. Victor, who had himself gained fame through his writings, says triumphantly: *Tantum gratia doctarum artium valet, ut scriptoribus ne saevi mores quidem ad memoriam officiant.* The best of Julianus lived on after him.

And yet this conviction, derived from history and personal experience, should also determine his judgement of his fellow-countryman Septimius Severus, who had had Julianus killed.[94] However, this is not so. One would expect Victor to have made a similar distinction between Septimus' cruel deeds and valuable writings,[95] but he cannot permit himself to do so, mainly because not all the deeds of this emperor were cruel; indeed Victor finds much to praise in his relatively long period of rule, moreover he is happy to do so for his compatriot. It is interesting to see how he tries to reconcile his partiality, his historical evaluation and his moral condemnation.

In the first place he underlines his condemnation of Julianus' murder in an Tacitean passage: 'Indeed, such a death is even a source of fame for the victims, a curse upon the murderers, for all—and in particular later generations—maintain that those great talents could not have been suppressed except by crimes and madness fostered by the state'.[96]

---

[94] End of c. 19: missique (of course by Severus) qui fugientem insequerentur, apud palatium Romae obtruncavere.

[95] Victor does mention the emperor's autobiography. In 20,22, he expresses a favourable opinion of his literary work (idemque abs se texta ornatu et fide paribus composuit), which is not shared by Cassius Dio 75,73 or Herodian 2,9,4 (it is shared by *H.A. Sev.* 18,6).

[96] 20,3; cf. Tac. *Ann.* IV 35.

Subsequently, the eternal value of literary achievements inspires him to conclude that these products of the mind also deserve confidence, a confidence which must, as a result, be transferred to the authors of these works, the *boni*, among whom Victor also counts himself. This is perhaps the most frequently quoted passage from the *Caesares* (which is incidentally seldom quoted for its own sake): '(therefore one must have confidence in the judgement of all good people and also of myself), since I grew up in the country, the son of a poor, uneducated father: in my time I have come through my pursuit of literature to live the life of a nobleman'.[97] The observation that North Africa brought forth but few talents, but that those who came from there and distinguished themselves rose to the highest offices, brings us back to the subject of this caput: Severus. However, if we follow the train of thought, the link is most infelicitous. The entire digression on the permanence of the exponents of *bonae litterae*, who cannot be silenced but live on in the memory of posterity, was written in honour of Septimius' victim. And the latter's autobiography was not apparently of such merit as to outweigh the cruel murder of his adversary in the struggle for power. Had this been the case, Victor would not have failed to make use of this opening to rehabilitate his imperial compatriot.

The train of thought may be reconstructed as follows: (1) Julianus was a man of letters whose fame remained undiminished throughout the centuries, and was indeed enhanced by his violent end; (2) I myself improved my social status by the same study of letters—which was all the more difficult for me because of my parentage and provenance; (3) this native land brought forth few talents, but those few were indeed most remarkable; (4) the most striking of these is Severus himself *quo praeclarior in republica fuit nemo*. Here we must point out that the example fails in many respects. In particular, because Severus was definitely not of low birth, but a scion of a consular family on his mother's side;[98] he was by no means outstanding as a man of letters, even though Victor describes him as *philosophiae, declamandi, cunctis postremo liberalium deditus studiis*.[99] Moreover, with all due respect, Victor was not to be

---

[97] 20,5 cf. for instance C. G. Starr, *art. cit.*, 574-586. See above, p. 19 and 27. For the second half of this translation, I am indebted to Peter Brown's *Augustine of Hippo*, London 1967, 21-22.

[98] T. D. Barnes, *art. cit.*, 87 ff.

[99] 20,22.

compared with the emperor he admired. The latter, when letters and the law failed to satisfy his talent and ambition, found a quite different way to achieve fame.[100] Victor's argument is rendered even less tenable in the following passage (20,6) by its lack of logic: 'quem (Severum) quamquam exacta aetate mortuum, iustitio elogioque lugendum sanxere, struentis illum iustum nasci aut emori minime convenisse'.[101]

To begin with, there are difficulties in connection with the form in which the text has survived. It is clear that this passage contains a well-known saying about Septimius, later included in his *vita*: 'illum aut nasci non debuisse aut mori, quod et nimis crudelis et nimis utilis reipublicae videretur'.[102] If one considers this 'bon mot' in its context, it would seem to have its origin in the emperor's autobiography in which he defended himself against the allegation of cruelty. Later, when this allegation was discussed, the senate declared 'that Severus either should never have been born at all or never should have died, because on the one hand he had proved too cruel, and on the other too useful to the state'.[103]

On the basis of the passage in the *vita Severi*, Victor's text may be read as follows: 'illum aut nasci aut emori convenisse'.[104] Corbett's suggested alteration (*eloquio* instead of *elogio*)would seem to be an improvement. The saying in question is reported not as an epitaph, but as part of a funeral oration which was in turn part of the *consecratio*, here indicated by the word *iustitium*. Naturally a speech of this content cannot be considered historical: Severus' sons would not have tolerated such criticism so soon after his death. Senatorial

---

[100] For his career, see T. D. Barnes, *art. cit.*, *passim*.

[101] The text is that of Pichlmayr-Gruendel. Instead of *elogio* Corbett reads *eloquio* (*Scriptorium* 3 [1949], 254 ff.).

[102] *Vita Sev.* 18,6-7.

[103] Translation by D. Magie in the Loeb edition.

[104] Already suggested by Arntzenius (1733); *aut nasci aut emori* constitutes a unity. Arntzenius, who prefers *qui* to *quem*, adheres to *quamquam*. In that case it should be argued that Victor makes a distinction between the emperors who died by violence, and those who died of old age. However, it is absurd to suggest that the latter category of emperors encountered more difficulty in being accorded the *consecratio*, (which suggests *quamquam*). Although it is a hazardous undertaking to try to explain the use of *quamquam* in the text, I should like to suggest the following chain of events. Originally, the text read *quem*, which a copyist changed into *qui*, but in such a way that the original word was still legible. A second copyist, not satisfied with this change, added *quem*, a third read this as *quem quem* and wrote *quamquam*, a fourth overlooked the relative and interpolated *quem* in front of *quamquam*. One could call this process 'tritography'.

tradition (which could be strong, witness the emphasis Eutropius placed upon it albeit not in connection with this particular emperor) had it that the sentiment which was later to find its way into the history books as a 'bon mot', was expressed by the Senate. Perhaps we had better conveniently ignore the words *iustum*, and *quamquam* and reconstruct 20,6 as follows (< > indicates Latin additions to the sequence): 'Velut Severum ipsum <ad sua celsum habet>, quo praeclarior in republica fuit nemo; quem exacta aetate mortuum iustitio eloquioque sanxere <patres>, struentes illum aut nasci aut emori minime convenisse'. (Considering his cruelty he should never have been born, considering his good rule he should never have died).

It is hard to say at which point the saying originated, which occurs in Victor in so mutilated a form. I believe it must have become popular a considerable time after the death of Septimius Severus, when the people had experienced the rule of his sons and successors. In view of their life and rule the pious wish, 'if only Septimius had not died', is perfectly understandable.[105]

Victor's edifying comments are to be found in 20,7-8: 'Scilicet quod corrigendis moribus nimium, postquam ad veterum innocentiam quasi mentium sanitatem pervenerant, clementem habuere. Ita honestas, quae principio anxia habetur, voluptati luxuriaeque est'. I am not certain as to its translation, partly because of the contrast with the earlier reasoning: '(the senators said that) evidently because they considered him all too radical [106] in the restoration of morals, but regarded him as a mild ruler when they had returned to the proprieties of yore. Thus virtue is first con-

---

[105] Th. Birt agrees that the judgement 'it would have been better for him if he had never been born or that he had never had to die' dates from a later period (*Karakterbeelden uit het Rome van den lateren tijd*, translated and edited by Dr. N. J. Singels [1924]). This character sketch, intended for the general public, is one of the best available of this emperor. Birt interprets his epigrammatic judgement as follows: 'Had Severus had sons and grandsons who were like himself, a new era would have begun with him, and he would have gone down in the history of the world as one of the greatest of the great. Now he was no more than a meteor ...'. This is certainly correct, and the saying should be explained as an expression of the feelings of those who had experienced the deeds of his son. The emphasis on his advanced age, *exacta aetate mortuum* (Victor 20,6), *admodum senex* (Eutr. VIII 19,1) (though he was only sixty-five when he died) is perhaps also a consequence of the idea that the end of his reign was the end of everything.

[106] *nimius* as adjective: 'offensive', cf. 8,7 and 11,7.

sidered tiresome, but once it has been established, it comes to be pleasant and agreeable.'[107]

It is difficult to trace back the original point of departure in this final moral tirade. At first, it was asserted that Septimius was a man of contradictory actions, a ruler who was both cruel and mild. Later, the senate expressed its opinion of him, a pithy summary of which survived. In 20,7-8, Victor gives the impression that those who considered the emperor too rigorous (*nimius*) or cruel (*crudelis*) were wrong: the emperor's severity was a moral judgement, which they themselves sorely needed because they had forgotten the old proprieties. What was originally the emperor's fault became the fault of the senate—a twist in the discussion contradicting the judgement of the senate, to which he himself alludes. The words *illum aut nasci ... minime convenisse* convey a (partial) condemnation of the emperor, which is later weakened to *corrigendis moribus nimium* and subsequently becomes an imperial virtue: *honestas quae principio anxia habetur*. Thus Victor treats his illustrious countryman. He cannot save Septimius' reputation without sacrificing his loyalty to the predecessor, whom he identifies with Salvius Julianus.

Septimius' misdeeds culminate in his harshness towards his political enemies. Victor's attitude is most evident in 20,12. A man who had supported Albinus because he lived in the neighbourhood of his camp, was regarded by Septimius as an enemy.[108] The emperor would not listen to reason. When the unfortunate prisoner asks, 'What would you have done in my case?', the emperor answers malevolently, 'I should have had to submit to the same lot which you shall undergo'. This retort provokes the following outburst, couched in the superlatives with which we are familiar when Victor's indignation is aroused. 'Nothing could be worse than these words and this deed.[109] For good and just men must lay the blame for such differences of opinion, however violently they flare up

---

[107] I am somewhat hesitant about this translation, since it has *voluptati luxuriaeque* used in a favourable sense. The combination does not recur in Victor, as opposed to *luxus lasciviaeque* (14,6) and *luxum lasciviamque* (31,2) both of which are used *in malam partem*. However, I believe *voluptati luxuriaeque* must be interpreted in a favourable sense in 20,7, since otherwise Victor's line of reasoning is abruptly cut off. This is never entirely the case, in spite of his 'staccato' way of thinking.

[108] 20,11. Read *quidam hostium* (instead of *hostiam*), a mistake that has survived all editions.

[109] Apparently the sentence was carried out, even though he does not mention the fact.

initially, on circumstances and, constantly spurred by the desire
to protect the citizens rather than plunge them into ruin, they must,
if necessary, suffer the true story <of the hostility> to be falsified'.[110] This is an appeal to the solidarity of the *boni sanctique*,
chief amongst whom is the emperor. He was apparently deaf to such
an appeal and thus, for Victor, became an historical cautionary
example.

The historian did not fail to devote due attention to the emperor's
personal life, either. Rumours on this subject were rife, notably with
regard to the Empress Julia Domna. In view of her infidelity,
Victor regards the emperor's faithfulness as an act of criminal for-
bearance, dishonouring imperial glory. Under these circumstances
marital fidelity 'brings disgrace alike to those of low and high estate,
and it was even worse in the case of Severus, before whom bowed not
only private citizens, individuals or criminals, but empires and
armies, and even evil itself'. The last few words constitute a remarkable comment—a piece of imperial theology which has not,
to my knowledge, been noted by modern commentators. Here we
see the beginnings of the concept of the infallible sovereign who
can do no wrong, which was to gain popularity in the Middle Ages.
It is a curious article of faith for a historian like Victor, who judged
even emperors by his own standards of good and bad moral conduct.
emperial theology is difficult to reconcile with the incorrect
behaviour of the individual emperor. Here the ethics of the exempla
have outlived their usefulness. An emperor who can do no wrong
because (*ei*) *vitia concessere*, can no longer be regarded as exemplary.
The last words of Septimius recorded by Victor would be a good
illustration (if they are historical) of an unsuccessful example:
Cuncta fui; conducit nihil.[111]

The chapter on Septimius Severus contains 'transitions' in his thinking, associations in the mind of the historian, which also occur
elsewhere in his work, but which are particularly striking here.

---

[110] My own reading of 20,12 runs: *Quo dicto factoque durius nihil. Cum
boni sanctique* ... It is remarkable how often the text, particularly of the
moral comment, has survived in a corrupt form. Perhaps Victor's language
was less than suitable for these diatribes, or was his text therefore clumsier
than elsewhere ?

[111] 20,29. Cf. E. Kossmann, 'Over de koning die geen kwaad kan doen',
Historie en Metahistorie, in *"Robert Fruin"*, Lustrumbundel, Leiden 1952,
19-29; this discusses the continued influence of the same idea in the Middle
Ages and later.

Paragraph 23, starting *Legum conditor longe aequabilium,* rounds off one of the more favourable passages (§ 14-22). Nevertheless, Septimius' sense of justice is by no means unquestioned. His behaviour towards his enemies is severely condemned, presumably because the case that Victor discusses concerns a member of his own social class, or at any rate one of the *boni*. And Victor feels that since Septimius, too, is a *bonus,* he should have dealt with the case against this involuntary partisan of Albinus', as a matter between *boni*. The historian considers Septimius' answer to the unfortunate 'enemy' to be excessively severe, the more so as he believed that the *boni*, certainly if one is emperor and thus by definition a *bonus* oneself, should be treated more mildly. Hence, *Quo dicto factoque durius nihil*. But this entire train of thought is in conflict with § 23, Legum conditor longe *aequabilium*, which is evidently, in view of the preceeding paragraphs, intended as praise. One cannot expect an impartial legislator to maintain separate standards for political opponents of a higher class. And that is, in effect, what Victor wants in § 12.[112] The interpretation of the text is not certain, but it is clear, as we have said, that he is here appealing to the solidarity of the *boni sanctique,* to which both the emperor and his anonymous 'enemy' belonged.

The transition from § 23 to § 24 is remarkable. Paragraph 23 indicates what Victor expects of a true ruler: integrity. For all look up to him, and all are subject to him. Indeed, to one who holds this concept of a sovereign, it is fitting that the very vices be in subjection to him. In the list *non privati neque singuli aut flagitiosi, verum imperia et exercitus atque ipsa vitia,* there is a close connection between *privati et singuli* on the one hand, and the subjects implied in the collective nouns, *imperia et exercitus* (empires and armies) on the other; similarly, the word *vitia* refers back to the *flagitiosi*. Thus Victor pays the highest tribute to the ruler: even evil itself is subject to him. But this, too, is hardly in keeping with a ruler who does commit evil, as Septimius repeatedly did. Here we see yet another contradiction which remains unresolved.

---

[112] It is no coincidence, to my mind, that in § 23, after noting the absence of prejudice in Septimius' legislation, Victor touches upon the less favourable aspects of his rule (Julia Domna's behaviour mars the emperor's fame, whereas his character must be above all *vitia*). However, for other interpretations of Julia Domna see Herodian and Cass. Dio. Here again, the search for sources is frustrating; perhaps Marius Maximus may be held responsible for the scandals attaching to Julia Domna (Syme, *Ammianus*, 91).

A number of suggestions have been made to get round this
apparent contradiction. The obvious explanation is that *vitia* must
be regarded as *physical* defects. This theory finds support in *nam
cum pedibus aeger* etc. and, in § 26, in the emperor's question
'Sentitisne ... caput potius quam pedes imperare?' Nevertheless,
this does not satisfy me. The line of reasoning in § 23 and § 24 is,
after all, that Severus' reputation is damaged by the love he continued to bear his wife, even when she was unfaithful. ('Caesar's
wife must be above suspicion'.) This is a disgrace, both for the
humble and those in high positions, and particularly so for the
emperor.

If one introduces the interpretation 'physical defects' here, the
reasoning based on the interpretation 'morally bad', *Quod cum
infimo turpe tum potentibus* etc., is interrupted.

Casaubonus apparently objected to this solution of *vitia* as *vitia
pedum*: he changed *nam* into *iam* and thus eliminated the chief
argument for this interpretation. Anne le Fèvre [113] read *saevitia*
instead of *vitia*, and Casaubonus read *vita*. I do not consider either
of these alterations necessary. However, the former—that of *nam*
into *iam*—has a certain attraction. Yet I adhere to the reading of
nam, because (1) this and similar conjunctions do not necessarily
stand for any logical links in Victor's work, since as many examples
show,[114] conjunctions originally indicating causality have frequently
lost this function in his writings; (2) the possibility that such conjunctions do have a causal function should not be excluded; in
that case the transition in Victor's reasoning, expressed by his use
of *vitia* in the sense of 'moral defects' or, more concretely, 'all
criminals', reminds him (quite apart from this meaning) of a *vitium*
suffered by the emperor, i.e. his *vitium pedum*, his gout. This associa-
ation of ideas, whether deliberate or no on the part of the historian,
could explain § 25. *Vitia* has acquired a double meaning, which it
loses in translation.

---

[113] See for this famous scholar, later Mme Dacier, W. Schmid in *Bonner
Historia-Augusta-Colloquium* 1963 (1964), 126, especially note 11.

[114] Wölfflin demonstrated this for the *Epit.* 5,5: eo namque dedecore
reliquum vitae egit, ut pudeat memorare huiuscemodi quemquam. The use
of *namque* is explained by Suet. *Caes.* 5,6. No similar derivations can be
traced for the later emperors after Domitian. Indeed, in my opinion, it is
quite possible that many causal conjunctions have lost their meaning. See
also Wölfflin in *ALL* 12 (1902), 446. With respect to Victor, I noted, among
others, the following instances: igitur (39,13; 11,1; 14,1; 28,1; 31,1; 36,1;
38,1; 40,1); hinc denique (39,31); idcirco (11,4); ceterum (21,1).

The interpretation of *vitia* as *pedum vitia*, as adhered to by Olivarius, Schott, Sylburg and Gruter, and the ostentatious display of learning contained in their inevitable remark that the word 'occurs in Lampridius' in this sense, can only be regarded as facile.

CHAPTER THREE

AURELIUS VICTOR II

Comparisons and Examples

The historian of imperial times sees the behaviour of rulers in terms of parallels. Even though he has enjoyed but an average education, he has heard of Romulus,[1] and of Caesar, whose actions were compared with those of Alexander.[2] Thanks to the *chronique scandaleuse* he vaguely knows something about Julia, the notorious daughter of Augustus, and her indirect influence on her father's policies, especially in connection with the problems of the succession. He sees history repeat itself in the marriages Diocletian and Maximian arranged for their successors.[3] For such comparisons in time, this moderately skilled historian needed no source to copy. In the first place, his talent is greater than many people will concede, and in the second place, these examples were stock phrases at school and in the conversation of any but the most uncultured.

As Quintilian was among the first to affirm, it is a part of the responsibilities of the *grammaticus* or schoolteacher to teach history. Nevertheless, the thoroughness we expect, and which the most highly rated Roman historians tried to achieve, was lacking. Quintilian, who was, after all, an author of note, says: 'In addition to this (*sc.* the figures of speech) he will explain the various stories that occur: this must be done with care, but should not be encumbered with superfluous detail. For it is sufficient to set forth the version which is generally received or at any rate rests upon good authority'.[4] Which authors he prefers becomes apparent elsewhere, when he recommends Livy for children and Sallust for more advanced students: 'For instance when prescribing for boys, I should give Livy the preference over Sallust; for although the latter is the greater historian, one requires to be well-advanced in one's

---

[1] A.V. 35, 12. Aurelian is compared to Romulus.

[2] *Epit.* 35, 2 (even his unoriginal mind makes its own comparisons, lacking in Victor; the accepted comparisons had apparently become too much of a cliché).

[3] A.V. 39, 25.

[4] Quint. I, 8, 18. *Cf.* H.-I. Marrou, *Histoire de l'éducation dans l'Antiquité* (1955³), 374.

studies to appreciate him properly'.[5] This preference is undoubtedly linked with Quintilian's admiration for Sallust's style, which he praises time and again. However, it cannot be sufficiently emphasized that his admiration is directed not to poetic expressions or forms, but to an old-fashioned manner of writing, which may or may not be poetic in style.[6] It should furthermore be borne in mind that the rhetorical flourishes in the textbooks were cultivated and learned by heart at school. They were then used by all former schoolboys, by older men displaying knowledge acquired in youth, and also by authors of historical manuals writing at a time when possession of a personal style was no recommendation, for no-one could be concerned about an author's style at a time when the empire was threatened by Goths, Alamanni, Parthians and Persians. Writers were more likely to adopt a particular style suited to the prevailing pessimistic mood and to the dangers that threatened. When they realized this, they turned to a past that seemed just as dark, described in terms as oppressive. The works of Sallust struck the right note. His popularity with these historians is different, however, from the grammarians' admiration for his style. For centuries these schoolteachers had instilled his text into the minds of their pupils and this process naturally bore fruit. Any author writing history in the fourth century had the Sallustian mode of expression at his fingertips. It has thus become possible in modern times to correct corrupt passages in Sallust's text by comparing them with that of his less eminent descendant.

Victor was considerably influenced by Sallust, as was already established nearly a century ago.[7] This cannot be said of Livy: his *œuvre* was too long. In this respect, however, Florus exactly met the requirements of a later, more superficial generation, which required its information to be presented more concisely. The author of *De viris illustribus* was also popular and his similarity to Florus is sometimes striking. Their mental resources and command of the facts were roughly equal, though these gifts were marred by the limitations of formal education. Mutual borrowing need not be considered, much less the anonymous source postulated by Enmann.[8]

---

[5] Quint. II, 5, 19; both quotations in the translation by H. E. Butler in the Loeb Classical Library; *Quintilian*, vol. I, (1953).

[6] See R. Syme, *Sallust*, (1964), 258.

[7] E. Wölfflin, 'Das Sallustianische im Stile des A.V.', *Rh.M.*, 29 (1874), 285 ff. Th. Opitz, 'Sallustius und A.V.', *Fleckeis. Jahrb.*, 127 (1883), 217.

[8] Wölfflin's comments on this matter have never been taken seriously

The Epitomist, in speaking of *summorum scriptorum miranda ingenia* [9] and Victor, in defining the aim of historical work with such assurance that Tacitus could hardly have improved upon it,[10] go much further than a mere imitation of the style of their predecessors. Notwithstanding their numerous shortcomings and modest talents, they range themselves in a tradition which considers the writing of history a pragmatic undertaking intended (though the writer may sometimes despair of the result) to demonstrate that evil is punished and good is, or should be, rewarded. Whether this actually happens and whether justice really will triumph is a burning question that also exercised the less gifted. Many modern historians are inclined to rate Tacitus so highly, precisely on account of his obvious doubts, that they can no longer regard him as a moralist, a category modern arrogance has taught them to despise. They are thus contemptuous of authors like Victor, who is over-moral. An unfair judgment, to be sure. Victor, too, has his doubts, but nevertheless sees his task clearly.

'If faith in history did not stand in the way—for history does not allow the good to be deprived of the rewards of fame nor permit the evil to secure eternal noble repute—virtue would be sought in vain: for deification, that unique and true honour, could be granted through influence to the bad and impiously withheld from the good'.[11]

It is not always possible to demarcate the stylistic influence an author has undergone and his own experience as a writer, which often only needs *color Sallustianus*. Nor should this surprise modern students who have learned not to regard style as inseparable from form, and not to distinguish form from content. The credit for demonstrating the untenability of the distinction between form and content usually goes to the most recent philological, linguistic, and historical research. This is not, however, altogether correct. It is perhaps one of the greatest merits of E. Wölfflin, primarily a philologist, that, as early as 1874, he professed to be neither able

---

enough by later scholars. See "Das Breviarium des Festus", *ALL* 13 (1904), 84 on the personality of the epitomists; 88 on the errors that occur when they quote from memory, and not from 'sources'.

[9] *Epit.* 13, 2.

[10] Victor 33, 26. For Tacitus' indirect methods of passing an ethical judgement, see *Ann.* XVI, 25. For Tacitus as used by Victor, see Wölfflin, *Rh. M.*, 29 (1874), 302 ff.

[11] The translation is that of C. G. Starr, *art. cit.*, 585.

nor willing to make this unfortunate distinction in Victor's case. In the first place, in his excellent article, he pointed out how closely the style of Sallust is linked with that of Victor. One might even say that this style has become Victor's own. Wölfflin then contended that his originality is not confined to a free use of Sallustian flourishes, but that in many respects he has his own way of interpreting historical facts. He is known as Sextus Aurelius Victor *Afer*:[12] perhaps he is more African than Sallustian, in style as well as in composition. It is no coincidence that African Carthage is praised as the best of countries, and the 'African Tribe' naturally occurs in the chapter on Septimius Severus.[13] Research into this subject is still in its initial stages, but it is clear that to divorce form from content in this instance can only be injurious. Sallust's African heir is one single character; and the style makes the man. History is not left to tell its own tale, a technique dictated by the *grammatici* and known as *enarratio historiarum*.[14] This mode of presentation is far too dry for him. Whether he is imitating Sallust, or whether he is being consciously African, Victor never lets history speak for itself. No, the author is in charge and writes as it were with his heart's blood. This applies above all to his moral pronouncements,[15] but also to his own experience.[16]

Historical *exempla* turn history into something of value for the present. This is why all historiography is biographical; even when it is intended to be chronological, the biographical element is very often present. For a correct understanding of the *compilatores*, inasmuch as they reflect their own time, the biographical aspect is almost all that need be taken into account.

In the following, we shall discuss the *capita* devoted to Nero, Hadrian, Caracalla, Philippus Arabs, Gallienus and Diocletian. These have not been selected arbitrarily, but because it is precisely in these chapters that Victor's moralism, which underlies the importance he attaches to *exempla*, is most apparent. Comparison with the Epitomist and others may be enlightening in this respect and make our delineation of Victor stand out in some relief.

---

[12] His name is given thus in the Brussels manuscript.

[13] 40, 19: *decus terrarum*, i.e. Carthage. Esp. 20, 6: 'quod equidem *gentis nostrae* reor, quae fato quodam bonorum parce fecunda, quos eduxerit tamen, quemque ad sua celsos habet'.

[14] See H.-I. Marrou, *op. cit.*, 375.

[15] E.g. 9, 13; 11, 9; 19, 3.

[16] E.g. 5; 14; 20; 28; 39; 40.

NERO [17]

'It was thus clearly revealed that age is no barrier to virtue, which is easily perverted when character is corrupted by vice; when virtue is abandoned, it seems to be a law of youth that vice re-appears more destructive than before'. Victor's own experience is revealed here, presented as the experience of previous generations— a presentation characteristic of *exempla*. He goes on to state that *licentia* is a vice which threatens people of all ages; this is the generalization, another indispensable feature of the *exempla*. Crimes committed at an early age can not be explained on the score of youth alone. On the contrary, as the first five years of Nero's reign show. Here he makes a surprising point that deserves our attention. One might expect the elderly moralist to adduce Nero's youth as an easy explanation of his later reprehensible behaviour and way of life. Not so Victor. Virtue has nothing to do with age: *neque aevum impedimento virtuti esse*. In conclusion, however, the historian finds that once scruples have been set aside, young people are more inclined to commit acts of *licentia* than their elders. *Ce n'est que le premier pas qui coûte*.

We may thus distinguish four elements of the *exemplum* which may (though not necessarily) determine its effectiveness: (1) wordly experience: *satis compertum est*; (2) the generalization—moral decay is a common danger: *facile mutari*: (3) the element of surprise—in this instance inspired by the case of Nero: youth is no excuse for evil; (4) the conclusion—once committed, evil is easily repeated; and young people are particularly likely to fall a victim to evil, because of the *lex adolescentiae*.

This cautionary example furthermore makes it clear that the *ingenium* of man is not initially fundamentally corrupt. It is circumstances that spoil the character: *corrupto per licentiam ingenio*.

Victor returns to this subject in 5,10, where he puts it as follows: vices invade the spirit, *ubi mentem invaserint vitia*. *Mens* is here more or less synonymous with *ingenium*, the term he uses in 5,3. The text here is hopelessly corrupt.[18] He must undoubtedly mean

---

[17] Victor 5, 3. The translation followed here and sometimes elsewhere is that E. C. Echols, *Sextus Aurelius Victor's Brief Imperial Lives*, Exeter, New Hampshire, 1962. Cf. F. A. Lepper, 'Some Reflections on the "Quin-quennium Neronis" ', *JRS* 47 (1957), 95-103. O. Murray, 'The "Quinquennium Neronis" and the Stoics', *Historia* XIV (1965), 41-61.

[18] The most satisfactory version is: *nequaquam verecundiae externa satietate humanius datur. Verecundiae*: dat. fin. (cf. vitio datur); *externa sa-*

that crimes are initially committed against strangers (*externi*), but eventually, when evil has become a habit, it is turned towards one's own family: *ad extremum in suos agit*. The *peccandi consuetudo* has reached its climax in Nero's matricide. This passage should be translated thus: 'When vices have laid hold of the mind, shame is no longer a barrier when one is sated by crimes committed outside one's own family. On the contrary, when evil becomes a habit, it will inevitably be directed against one's nearest relatives, because it casts about for ever novel and therefore more pleasing objects'. The message of Victor's home-brewed wisdom is clear, however corrupt the text: the wrongdoer goes from bad to worse.

Although Nero has always appealed to the imagination, his name occurs surprisingly seldom in Victor's writings. Emperor Otho is painted in the same dark colours by Victor, they are one of a kind: *Neroni quondam criminose familiaris*.[19] This is remarkable, because the writers of *breviaria* might justly assume that Nero's name was familiar even to the most ignorant of their readers. The reason why it nevertheless occurs so rarely is probably that his successors provided more than enough cautionary examples for the historian's purposes. Reference to Nero was superfluous—horrors were rife. Needless to say, Victor's presentation of Nero gives rise to a particularly distorted image in certain respects, owing to his rough chronological division of Nero's reign.[20] It is not my task to demonstrate this, but one ought to realize that so unsubtle a piece of work entrenched itself in the minds of later generations particularly through the medium of the textbooks, the *breviaria*.

The reign of this emperor marks the end of an era, as the signs

---

tietate = *externorum satietate* (for *externus* see 2, 1); *humanius* = *clementius*, *urbanius*. Walter's solution (see addenda in the edition of Pichlmayr), is unsatisfactory.

[19] Victor 7, 1: Nero is mentioned quite neutrally as the one who gave Vespasian his orders in the Jewish war, *quod Neronis iussu susceperat*. 27, 7: *lustri certamine, quod Nero Romam induxerat*, is no more than an indication, prior to his Persian expedition. However, it is impossible to see what Nero is supposed to be doing here: his *lustrum* can hardly be identical to the opening of the temple of Ianus. Victor is reminiscent of *Res Gestae Aug.* 13, of its imitation by Nero (Suet. *Nero* 13, 2) and Vespasian (Oros. 7, 3, 7; 19, 4 from Tacitus). Cf. K. Latte, *Römische Religionsgeschichte* (1960) 298, note 1. In itself 27, 7 is clear. In the spring of 242 Gordian opened the temple of Ianus, before marching against the Persians (Eutr. IX, 2, 2; *vita Gord.* 26, 3).

[20] A typical example is given by G. C. Picard, 'Néron et le blé d'Afrique', *Les Cahiers de Tunésie* (Tunis, Faculté des Lettres) IV, (1956), 163-173.

had presaged. Not surprisingly, the historian here follows Providence. In his work Victor, too, marks a caesura after caput 5, and the extent to which this division is determined by moral considerations is significant. Divine portents and the historian's chronology are both inspired by Nero's behaviour. Had this been less controversial, both portents and chronological divisions would have been unnecessary.

The Epitomist does not indulge in ethical reflection, unless the fact that he withdraws into prudish silence, *ut pudeat memorare huiuscemodi quemquam* (§ 5), be considered as such. But he cannot resist mentioning the most lurid details. Life was stronger than principles.

HADRIAN

In dealing with Hadrian's relationship with Antinous, Victor exercises considerable restraint. He refrains from comment on their intimate relationship. Still, in common with all moralists throughout the ages, Victor, speaking as an older man, contends that the young are, in general, particularly susceptible to what they know to be wrong. 'We shall pass over the question (i.e. of Hadrian and Antinous), although we view an intimate relationship between a person of weak character and a person considerably different in age with suspicion'.[21]

Considering his attitude towards homosexuality, which he roundly condemns,[22] Victor could not have been more reticent. B. W. Henderson writes in this connection of 'the more charitable Aurelius Victor',[23] but the truth is rather that the good example which Hadrian generally set by his conduct was spoiled by this stain on his historical image, at least in Victor's eyes. Other doubtful actions of this emperor's are barely touched upon, if they are mentioned at all. He does not, for instance, mention the murder of the *consulares* at the time of his accession to the throne. He apparently prefers the official version of the succession, according to which Trajan had chosen his successor himself, although he is quite aware of the view that Plotina arranged the succession

---

[21] 14, 9.
[22] See below, p. 70,72.
[23] B. W. Henderson, *The Life and Principate of the Emperor Hadrian*, (London 1923), 133.

and secured dominion for her favourite nephew. To the official version he adds those details most favourable to Hadrian.[24]

The manner in which he describes the apotheosis of Hadrian, however, is most striking. In the first place, he ascribes the emperor's cruelties towards the end of his life to the fact of his last illness. Subsequently he places the senate's opposition to Hadrian's *consecratio* in a different light than does, for instance, Eutropius: 'Senatus ei tribuere noluit divinos honores, tamen cum successor ipsius T. Aurelius Antoninus Fulvius hoc vehementer exigeret, etsi universi senatores palam resisterent, tandem obtinuit'.[25] One can still, so to speak, hear the echoes of resistance.

Victor, 14,13-14: 'At patres ne principis oratu quidem ad Divi honorem eidem deferendum flectebantur; tantum amissos sui ordinis tot viros maerebant. Sed postquam subito prodiere, quorum exitium dolori erat, quique suos complexi, censent quod abnuerant'.

It seems like a miracle: suddenly they are there again, the relatives and co-senators who had been thought dead. The *vita Antonini Pii*, in discussing the manner in which this emperor came by his cognomen, tells us how this version of the story originated. One explanation is, 'quod eos quos Hadrianus per malam valetudinem occidi iusserat reservavit'.[26] The meaning of this is clear. What Hadrian, racked by illness, might do in his derangement was undone by his successor.

Eutropius is more severe and less easily reconciled. It is unlikely that he believed that which his contemporary Victor took for granted. But then, Victor, and not Eutropius, was the man of the *exempla*. We can only conclude that Victor also allows favourable examples to remain simple whenever he can. Only in this way can history really 'teach', by being uncomplicated.

The Epitomist's description of this emperor is less favourable than Victor's. It is he who says that the emperor drove his wife Sabina to suicide, *prope servilibus iniuriis*.[27] He also gives more, and more sensational, details of the emperor's death. On the other

---

[24] 13, 12-13; cf. above, p. 38.

[25] Eutr. VIII, 7, 3.

[26] *Vita Antonini Pii*, 2, 4; cf. *Vita Hadr.* 24, 5 and 25, 8. One may speculate whether Antoninus swore an oath to protect senators which coincided with their miraculous return. For this oath in general, see Cass. Dio 75, 2, 1; cf. A. Birley, 'The oath not to put senators to death', *CR* 12 (1962), 197-9.

[27] *Epit.* 14, 8.

hand, however, it is he who coined the expression that characterized Hadrian once and for all: *varius multiplex multiformis.*[28]

CARACALLA [29]

This is a somewhat colourless *vita*, of roughly equal length in both Victor's and the Epitomist's versions. Both authors find it necessary to expatiate on two matters that are, in our eyes, trivial: the emperor's name and the relation in which Caracalla and Geta stood to Julia Domna.[30] In precisely the same way, in a modern popular history, would those juicy details be given which stick in the mind and thus become the common property of a considerable number of readers.

Cassius Dio [31] was the first to discuss this emperor's name: καί τινα ἰδίαν ἔνδυσιν βαρβαρικῶς πως κατασκόπτων καὶ συρράπτων ἐς μανδύης τρόπον προσεπεξεῦρεν, καὶ αὐτός τε συνεχέστατα αὐτὴν ἐνέδυνεν, ὥστε καὶ Καράκαλλος διὰ τοῦτο ἐπικληθῆναι, καὶ τοὺς στρατιώτας μάλιστα ἀμφιέννυσθαι ἐκέλευεν.

The name obviously intrigues Victor as well, and he has his own idea about it—*indumenta in talos demissa.* The allusion contained in the last three words is missing in Cassius Dio. A further remarkable detail, moreover, that Caracalla received this robe as a gift from the people, is, as far as we can judge, Victor's own invention. I venture to doubt whether it is intended ironically. The question of whether the emperor was called after the garment or the garment after the emperor may hark back to an early reference to this 'fashion' launched by the emperor. The *Epitome* further improves upon this, likewise in the style of a textbook, but the additional information it imparts is rightly considered an independent statement.[32] Namely, that the emperor compelled the people of Rome to wear this mantle in his presence, at court.[33] We may be brief on the subject of the *Historia Augusta*, since its references to this detail and other historical data which Victor communicated

---

[28] *Epit.* 14, 6.

[29] Good modern summary by J. Straub in *RAC* (1954), *s.v.*

[30] In this connection the history of Papinian might also be discussed; it is not, however, sufficiently characteristic for our purpose, hence its omission.

[31] 79, 3, 3.

[32] J. P. Wild, 'The Caracallus', *Latomus* 23 (1964), 532-536, esp. 535.

[33] *Epit.* 21, 2: 'At cum e Gallia vestem plurimam devexisset talaresque caracallas fecisset coegissetque plebem ad se salutandum indutam talibus introire, de nomine huiusce vestis Caracalla cognominatus est'.

to Eutropius were derived from these two (or from the tradition upon which they based their work).[34] The *Epitome* cannot be dated with any precision and it may therefore be of a later date than, and influenced by, the *Historia Augusta*. However, the explanation occupies such a unique position in tradition, that this is most unlikely.[35]

The second, notorious, issue is the death of Geta and the relationship between Caracalla and Julia Domna. The fratricide is common knowledge, but nowhere is it mentioned in terms that warrant the assumption of verbatim borrowing.

Cassius Dio [36] gives the shattering words of the son murdered in his mother's arms: μῆτερ μῆτερ, τεκοῦσα τεκοῦσα, βοήθει, σφάζομαι. This phrase properly belongs to a type of historical tradition that is generally apocryphal. A Dutch historian who discussed many apocryphal 'last words' in history rightly pointed out the effectiveness of some of these.[37] They are in great demand for educational purposes, their moral value is considerable, and they stick in the reader's memory. The same goes for his picture of the empress, who is supposed to have witnessed this assassination: 'Thus she alone, the Augusta, wife of the emperor and mother of the emperors, was not permitted to shed tears even in private over so great a sorrow'.[38] This is melodrama, for readers to revel in. Those who count on its effects have even more in store for the credulous; the empress was Caracalla's stepmother, his real mother being Pacciana Marciana, first wife to Septimius Severus;[39] moreover, Caracalla was said to have conducted an intrigue with her. Before it even found its way into the *Historia Augusta*, this rumour was already recorded by Victor. Feverish fancy was not exhausted with this calumny.

---

[34] Eutr. VIII, 20; *Vita Car.* 21, 7.

[35] For general remarks on Eutropius and Victor in relation to the *Historia Augusta*: W. Reusch, *Der historische Wert der Caracallavita*, Klio Beih. 24 (N.F. 11) 1931; R. Syme, *Ammianus and the Historia Augusta*, ch. vii, 'The *Vita Caracallae*'.

[36] 78, 2.

[37] Other words which stick in one's memory are, for instance, 'Libet plane licet' (Victor 21, 3) and the cynical words with which Caracalla expresses his agreement with the *consecratio* of Geta: 'Sit divus, dum non sit vivus' (*Vita Getae*, 2, 9). See B. W. Schaper, 'Het werkende woord', in the Dutch literary journal *Maatstaf* 1 (1953/1954), 637 ff., 696 ff., 772 ff.; 2 (1954/1955) 24 ff., 400 ff., 871 ff.

[38] Translation by D. Magie, Cassius Dio 78, 2, 6. For a comparison with Herodian see F. Millar, *A Study of Cassius Dio* (Oxford 1964), 150-160.

[39] The *Historia Augusta* is full of this: *Sev.* 18,8; 20,2; *Car.* 10,1-4.

Posterity, in trying to find the reason for the disappointing course
of the lives of the later Severi, had a ready explanation. According
to the scandalmongers, both Heliogabalus and Alexander Severus
were natural sons of Caracalla.[40] Julia Soaemias and Julia Mammaea
were easy victims for this kind of historical fabrication, for no
clear-cut chronological objections stood in the way. In the case of
Julia Domna as Caracalla's supposed stepmother this was more
difficult. Caracalla was twenty-nine years old when he died in 218,
and in the year 189, when he was born, Severus had already been
married to Julia Domna for three years. This fact was so clear that
it could not escape the notice even of historians as inept as these.
However, they rose to the occasion and started the legend that
Caracalla was forty-three years old when he died.[41] The *Epitome*
cannot let this sensational story escape its notice, but it also gives
away its fictitious nature by combining the two versions: 'Hic
Bassianus ex avi materni nomine dictus est ... Fuit impatientis
libidinis, quippe qui novercam suam duxit uxorem'. At the end
of the chapter he returns to the first version: 'Vixit annos fere
triginta'.[42]

Comparisons with Alexander the Great were a favoured topic,
which became popular chiefly, though not exclusively, under the
Severi.[43] Cassius Dio had already paid great attention to this
phenomenon (78,7,8). Even in the *breviaria*, our sole source of information for this period, the expositions are full of hatred and
mockery—estimable pieces of prose.[44] The *Epitome* betrays a lack
of intelligence, but also a certain originality, when the author
remarks on the facial resemblance between Caracalla and the great
Alexander. Perhaps he drew his conclusions from a portrait. Be
that as it may, one should not be too hasty in assuming literary
derivation. The Epitomist noted something which might have been
seen by anyone who had looked at a picture or a statue of the
emperor: 'When he contemplated the portrait of Alexander the
Great, he had himself called "The Great" or "Alexander". The

---

[40] Herodian V, 3,10; 7,3. Cf. *Car*. 9,1. Maesa herself had the bad taste to
spread this rumour during Macrinus' rebellion, in order to further the claims
of her grandson. See also R.V. Nind Hopkins, *The Life of Alexander Severus*,
(Cambridge 1907), 23.

[41] 29 years old: Cassius Dio, 78,6,5; 43 years old: *Car*. 9,1.

[42] *Epit*. 21,2,5 and 7.

[43] *Epit*. 21,4.

[44] A. Bruhl, *Le souvenir d'Alexandre le Grand et les Romains* (Paris 1930).

insincere words of flatterers encouraged him to go so far as to walk around with a stern face and with his neck turned to the left shoulder—a posture he had noticed on the portrait of Alexander. And he was convinced that in this way he looked exceedingly like him'. There is a world of difference between Cassius Dio and the Epitomist: two centuries of decline in the writing of history. And yet, the past is sometimes evoked more vividly by looking at portraits than by listening to the reminiscences of soldiers and citizens. Our image of Caracalla as a sovereign is incomplete without Cassius Dio, who is full of regret and annoyance at the emperor's contempt for true culture;[45] but we also need the Epitomist with his modest talent, for he records some of the emperor's outward display and his eccentricity as posterity saw it, and his nickname alone shows that he was fond of striking external appearances.

In curious contrast is a phrase of Victor's: *patiens, communis, tranquillus*,[46] which is hardly in keeping with the author's usual references to women and ambition. The first word may refer to his endurance and is, in that case, in agreement with Cassius Dio,[47] but 'courteous' (*communis*) and 'even-tempered' (*tranquillus*) do not suit the contemporary image of the emperor very well. We do not know the source of this divergent information. It furnishes yet another proof of the way in which the *breviaria* juxtapose un-coordinated details with no attempt at coherence. It is also possible, however, that this originally applied to Geta, *fratem magna eius humilitate despexit* (*humilis* means rougly the same as *communis*), and was later inadvertently transferred to Caracalla.[48]

To sum up our conclusions, we find that we have two short life-sketches that are quite dissimilar, although there are certain parallels. With regard to these, I should like to make the following comments:

(a) It is no more than natural that the name Caracalla provoked a discussion on the question of how the emperor acquired this name. The differences arise in the treatment of certain details.

(b) The Epitomist does not discuss the death of Geta at first, as did Victor in the chapter on Septimius Severus (20). He therefore

---

[45] 78,11,3.
[46] Victor 21,2; contradicts 20,32.
[47] 78,11,3.
[48] Eutropius says 'paulo asperior et minax' (VIII, 20,1).

takes the opportunity of doing so later, in 21,3. He also feels constrained to say something about Geta,[49] very briefly, but with a
surprising twist on the subject of the Dirae, the goddesses of
Vengeance, who temporarily deranged Caracalla's mind.[50] The
discussion of Julia Domna is in accordance with the same traditionally unfavourable attitude, whose origin is sometimes said to be
due to the influence of the 'aretologische, romanhafte Stil' [51]
exemplified by Antheia and Habrokomos in the story by Xenophon
I, 3,2. This explanation is quite unsatisfactory to my mind, since
this 'romanhafte Stil' is nowhere displayed by the abbreviators.
In my opinion, the lessons taught by history, which are best expressed by means of *exempla*, are a factor of far more importance. Julia
was the name of both the daughter and the granddaughter of
Augustus, and it became synonymous with the traditional idea of
a wanton woman. Their namesake, Julia Domna, thus fell a victim
to traditional prejudice. (A similar association of ideas, in this case,
names, may have underlain the notorious confusion between Salvius
Julianus and Didius Julianus, and there is no lack of more modern
examples.) Victor appears to share this prejudice. His view of Julia
Domna is less objective than that of the Epitomist, who contents
himself with a mere allusion to the *cause célèbre*.

One of the first reactions of primitive minds when first confronted
with history is to compare people who bear similar names. For
instance, Victor compares Philippus Arabs with Philippus cos.: *Et
quoniam nomen admonuit, mea quoque aetate post mille centesimus
consule Philippo excessit nullis, ut solet, sollemnibus frequentatus:
adeo in dies cura minima Romanae urbis.*[52] The usurper Marius,
ferri quondam opifex, reminds him of Gaius Marius, *eiusdem artis
auctor stirpisque ac nominis.*[53]

The type of association evoked by a name is far more easily
recognized than comparisons of events; the fact that certain people
bear the same name is self-evident, and our ancient historian who
bases his conclusions on such a fact considers these legitimate

---

[49] Eutropius is very neutral and therefore biased: 'nam Geta hostis
publicus iudicatus confestim periit' (VIII, 19,2).

[50] *Epit.* 21,3: 'Hic fratrem suum Getam peremit; ob quam causam furore
poenas dedit Dirarum insectatione, quae non immerito ultrices vocantur;
a quo post furore convaluit'.

[51] W. Hartke, *Römische Kinderkaiser* (Berlin, 1951), 35.

[52] 28,2.

[53] 33,9 and 11.

precisely on account of the corresponding names. He says as much in both of the latter two cases. Yet hints at earlier events of the same kind as those which the historian is now relating, are seldom if ever recognized as such by the writer himself. This is not surprising. Allusions require more subtlety and a greater knowledge of history on the part of the author as well as the reader than the *breviaria* can claim. The gifts granted Tacitus were denied Victor. For instance, it is possible, though not probable, that the reference to the murder perpetrated by Caracalla contains an implied allusion to another assassination of much earlier date, namely, that of the second triumvirate in 43 B.C.[54]

In this caput, the following details occur either in Victor's work alone or in the *Epitome* alone:

Only in Vict.	Only in the *Epit.*
§ 2 Alamanni, but nothing about the East	§ 3 remorse about the murder of Geta
§ 4 Caracalla and Egypt, thermae, road to Rome	§ 4 comparison with Alexander the Great
§ 5 funeral	§ 6 end of life, in partic. manner of his death

No general conclusions can be drawn from this. The most important point is that the facts mentioned by both authors, as well as those mentioned only by one, were all obviously required reading in schools or improving material to be used as memorisation exercises by teacher and pupil. In verifying the facts given in a schoolbook we should not look for one or more written sources; no more should we in this case undertake this kind of 'Quellenforschung'. The information on which they base their statements is of the same variety as the following laconic dismissal of Macrinus and Diodumenus: 'We have discovered nothing about these men except that they were savage and cruel'.[55] Of course, there was more to be found, as the *vitae* in the *Historia Augusta* show, but Victor considered this single sentence sufficient to characterize them. He reminds me here of the Dutch history teacher who found his own

---

[54] Domaszewski, 'Die Personennamen bei den Scriptores Historiae Augustae', *Sitz.-Ber. Heidelberg*, Philos.-hist. Kl., 1918, Abh. 13,67 ff. Reusch, Klio Beih. 24, 1931.

[55] 22,2: 'Horum nihil praeter saevos atque inciviles reperimus'.

way of summing up his opinion of three English kings: 'George I,
George II, George III: Fool I, Fool II, Fool III'.

The value of his insight and interest is sufficiently shown up by
a number of major omissions: the Constitutio Antoniniana, the
campaigns in the East, the *donativa* bestowed on the soldiers, the
increased taxation and the monetary devaluation, his death near
Carrhae at the hands of Macrinus, then praetorian prefect.

Rostovtzeff points out that the literary sources are biased, but
adds that their unfavourable opinion should not be underrated
since it is corroborated by epigraphical data and by the papyri.[56]
Occasionally Victor departs from this prejudice. In the chapter on
Caracalla, though it is on the whole unfavourable, Victor does make
one attempt at fairness in his use of the words *patiens communis
tranquillus*; he excuses Caracalla's *liaison* with Julia Domna since
he was seduced as a young man by the older woman. And finally,
his condemnation of the murder of Geta is expressed with far less
severity than that of the murder of Papinian; furthermore, he sees
a connection between these two murders. As far as Papinian is
concerned, Victor appears to attach greater importance to questions
of protocol than to fratricide.[57] The behaviour of emperors and
their family does not affect him as nearly as does that of civil
servants, the class to which he himself belonged. Nevertheless,
Victor is sometimes filled with a humane understanding which
mellows his judgement. The chapter on Caracalla is a proof of this.
Eutropius is equally far from seeking sensation; his treatment of
Caracalla is in agreement with Victor's.[58]

A comparison with Herodian's report shows that this author, too,
took a special interest (as did his readers) and wrote his account
accordingly:[59]

1) Death of Septimius and disputes among his sons, with a
   preference for Geta. Plan for the division of power (3,5), intervention in this matter by Julia Domna (chapters 1 and 3). This

---

[56] *Social and Economic History of the Roman Empire* II, 127 (in the
German edition). The literary sources Rostovtzeff means are Cassius Dio,
Herodian and the *vitae* of Caracalla and Geta. The *Epitome* may also be
included in this list.

[57] Victor 20,32.

[58] Eutr. VIII, 20.

[59] Herodian IV, 1-13.

account is interrupted in chapter 2 by the detailed discussion of the apotheosis of Septimius Severus.[60]

2) Geta is murdered, in the presence of Julia. This murder is represented as being the work of Caracalla, whose apology to the *soldiers* is that he acted out of self-defence (chapter 4).

3) Caracalla's speech to his soldiers (chapter 5)[61].

4) Wholesale slaughter of Geta's followers, including the sister of Commodus; rejection of the daughter of Plautianus and the murder of her family. Terror in the streets of Rome (chapter 6).

5) Expedition to Germania, as a diversionary manoeuvre and also in order to recruit a bodyguard from among the 'barbarians'[62] (A.D. 213).

6) Expedition of the emperor to Ister, Macedonia, Thrace, Pergamum (Asklepios), Troy (imitation of Achilles). Sulla and Hannibal praised in connection with sacrifice at the Hellespont. Antioch and Alexandria (chapter 8).[63]

7) Bloodbath in Alexandria (chapter 9).

8) Parthian expedition: Parthicus (chapter 10) (A.D. 216).

9) Negotiations between Caracalla and Artabanos culminating in attack by Caracalla (chapter 11).

10) End of life (12,3). Killed by a servant of Macrinus' with a grudge against Caracalla.

As we see, Herodian's interest is of a very different nature, even though he is sufficiently well-informed about all sorts of piquant details: Caracalla's *liaison* was not with his stepmother but with his own mother; in Alexandria she was mockingly known as Jocasta.[64]

---

[60] For the emperor's apotheosis see in particular E. Bickerman in *Archiv für Religionswissenschaft* 27 (1929), 1-31.

[61] Perhaps the most favourable feature of Herodian's account is that he does not regard the brothers' quarrel as a family matter but relates it to the attitude of the troops toward the two commanders. This must surely be in accordance with historical reality.

[62] This chapter reveals all the traits traditionally considered typical of the tyrant, the chief characteristic being that the cruel ruler no longer trusts his own people, but resorts to strangers, indeed, barbarians, for the protection of his person.

[63] These expeditions are described according to the traditional pattern, in use since Hadrian.

[64] Cf. Reusch (in connection with *Car.* 10,1-3 and Victor 21,3) *op. cit.*, 59: 'Die Geschichte, die Caracalla gleichzeitig fälschlich zum Sohn der Marcia, der ersten Frau des Severus, macht, liegt auch bei Eutrop (8,20),

The *breviaria* rarely credited the emperors with any specific personal attitude to the past.[65] Even if they had any definite ideas about Rome, the emperorship, and their own task, the succinctness required by the form in which they wrote hardly gave the epitomists sufficient scope to discuss them in any detail. Both Cassius Dio and Herodian, however, take advantage of any opportunity to recount the emperor's historical ideas. Herodian (IV 8,5) gives us the following extract from a speech made by Caracalla: ἐπῄνει δὲ καὶ στρατηγῶν μάλιστα Σύλλαν τε τὸν Ῥωμαῖον καὶ Ἀννίβαν τὸν Λίβυν, ἀνδρίαντάς τε αὐτῶν καὶ εἰκόνας ἀνέστησεν (cf. Cassius Dio 78,13,7).[66]

Mildness on the part of sovereigns and generals is not appreciated. In the time of Septimius Severus, Sulla, Marius and Augustus are praised for their harshness and cruelty (ὠμότης), and the mildness of Caesar and Pompey is condemned, indeed it arouses feelings of revulsion. Once again, the historical accuracy of such statements by emperors cannot be verified. However, they indicate a spiritual climate, that is accorded very little attention even in such excellent works as those by A. Calderini and G. Walser - Thomas Pekáry.[67]

PHILIPPUS ARABS [68]

In this chapter, too, Victor's chief concern is with the ethical aspects of his subject. This emperor seized power by violence and had Gordian killed; that was hard to accept. To his credit, however, are his laws against homosexuality, *usum virilis scorti removendum honestissime consultavit*,[69] a *vitium* which, in Victor's opinion, should be eradicated root and branch. Perhaps this also explains his dislike of eunuchs and his condemnation of castration, since homosexuality was common among the eunuchs.[70] Tradition represents a number

---

ausserdem in *Epitome de Caes.* (21,5) vor und ist auch in anderen Stellen (Sev. 20,2; 21,7; Geta 7,3) ins Vitencorpus gebracht worden'.

[65] Trajan is an exception, *De Caes.* 5,2; *Epit.* 5,2. Cf. Lepper, *art. cit.*, 95 ff.

[66] Opinions about Hannibal have always varied greatly, both in antiquity and recently. See the illuminating article by K. Christ, 'Zur Beurteilung Hannibals', *Historia* 17 (1968), 461-495.

[67] A. Calderini, *I Severi. La crisi dell'Imperio nella III secolo* (Bologna 1949), Vol. VI of the Roman history published by l'Istituto di Studi Romani; G. Walser - Th. Pekáry, *Die Krise des römischen Reiches* (Berlin, 1962).

[68] 28. For the celebration of the 1000th anniversary of Rome, see T. Kotula, *Meander* 16 (1961), 69-84.

[69] 28,6 (cf. *vita Hel.* 32,2; *Alex.* 24,4; 39,2). Also in other passages (14,9; 39,46; 41,24-25) Victor severely condemns homosexuality. Cf. also Ammianus Marcellinus (31,9,5), *Epit.* 6 (Galba): *in adulescentes infamis*.

[70] E.g. 5,7. See M. K. Hopkins, 'Eunuchs in Politics in the Later Roman Empire', *Proc. of the Cambr. Philol. Soc.* 189 n.s. 9) 1963, 62 ff.

of emperors as *effeminati*: Caligula, Nero, Otho, Macrinus, Heliogabalus and Gallienus.[71] In the case of Gallienus, the androgynous
representation of this emperor, which owed its existence to, or was
at least stimulated by, his identification with goddesses should
also be taken into account. Victor disapproves of this tradition:
prodigia of androgynous nature are bad omens. This attitude is
apparent in his treatment of Philip.[72]

In Victor's eyes the most important event of Philip's reign was the
commemoration of the thousand years since the foundation of
Rome.[73] He clearly sees a decline in the manner in which this
celebration is held, when he compares the previous celebration with
the behaviour of the Romans during the eleventh centenary, which
he himself witnessed. In 348, one of the consuls was a certain Flavius
Philippus, a namesake of the emperor Philip. The similarity of their
names causes Victor to complain that the eleventh centenary of the
foundation of Rome passed with no celebration: *adeo in dies cura
minima Romanae urbis*.[74] The indifference displayed towards the
city of Rome means no less to this African than a new threat to
the Imperium Romanum.

All in all, Philippus Arabs is pictured in a favourable light. He
showed his concern for the city by building waterworks, thus
supplying the part of the city across the Tiber with water. It can
be no coincidence that this benefit conferred upon the City by the
emperor is mentioned in one breath with the celebration of the
thousandth birthday of Rome: *exstructoque trans Tiberim lacu,
quod eam partem aquae penuria fatigabat, annum urbis millesimum
ludis omnium generum celebrant*.[75] The difference between conditions
one hundred years before and in his own time is somewhat laboured
in this account. We know that Rome was threatened in 248,
perhaps even more so than in 348. Seen from afar, however, past
dangers seemed less serious than those facing the present, owing
to the prevailing attitude of indifference towards military glory;
besides which, in the past, the gods themselves had demonstrated
their involvement with Rome by means of *prodigia*. Apparently
the voice of the gods had relapsed into silence by 348—not sur-

---

[71] H. Herter in *RAC* IV (1959), *s.v.* 'effeminatus', col. 626 (+ bibliog.).
[72] 28,4.
[73] J. B. Pighi, *De ludis saecularibus populi Romani Quiritium*, ed. altera,
Amsterdam 1965, 88 ff., esp. 91. See Kotula, *art. cit.*
[74] 28,2.
[75] 28,1.

prisingly, since as early as 248 they had already predicted the apathy of later generations: 'At that time (that of Philippus Arabs) this (the later indifference) was, it is said, already predicted by omens and monstrosities'. I should like to mention one instance of these in particular. Once, when sacrificial animals were slaughtered in accordance with the law of the *pontifices*, female reproductive organs were taken from the belly of a boar.[76] This the soothsayers interpreted to mean the decadence of future generations and an increase in vices. The connection is clear if one bears in mind that androgynous beings, both human and animal, were regarded as *effeminati*, i.e. as males degraded to the level of female creatures.[77]

Understandably, Victor, whose mind works associatively, links this explanation of the *haruspices* with a measure of Philip's supposedly directed against this 'weakening', namely, the aforementioned prohibition of homosexuality. 'He believed that the predictions would come to nothing, for at that very time, he saw in passing a youth who looked like his son in front of a men's bordello. Then he promulgated the decree (and this was greatly to his credit) forbidding male prostitution'. The prohibition, however, had no effect, and the evil continued up to Victor's time.[78] 'For if circumstances change, people take to worse sins, since men will pursue that which is dangerous and forbidden with more passion'.[79]

All this had political consequences. Owing to the prevailing depravity the *boni* themselves had become tainted, morally degenerate, and therefore politically negligible. Insecure and dissatisfied, the people felt unhappy. As the following passage puts it, 'Furthermore there was another, very different matter, in fulfilment of a prediction made by Etruscan seers. According to this prophecy, the most effeminate elements will never be happy until

[76] The meaning of '*suis* utero *maris*' is clear from the context, even though 'uterus' usually means womb, not belly as it does here.

[77] A. Alföldi, 'Das Problem des "verweiblichten" Kaisers Gallienus', *ZNum.* 38 (1928) 56-203; *RAC, s.v.* 'effeminatus', col. 626. For androgynous creatures, see the commentary by Pease, Cic. *De div.* I, 98,3, (also bibliography). *R.E.*, XXIII (1959), Nachtr. 2283-2296 (P. Händel). The treatment of *prodigia, portenta*, and *ostenta* in modern works is highly unsatisfactory.

[78] There is something to be said for Damsté's suggestion, to read (28,7) *vitium tamen* here instead of *verumtamen*.

[79] From which it could be concluded that homosexuality spread after it had been officially forbidden by Philip. Very clear on this point, *vita Sev.* 34,4, which is, as A. Chastagnol has convincingly demonstrated, dependent on Victor 28,6; *Bonner Historia-Augusta Colloquium* 1964/1965 (1966), 55 ff.; cf. Syme, *Ammianus*, 107.

the *boni* are all but eliminated. But I am convinced that they do not know of what they speak. For who can be happy, even if all goes well, if decency is lost? On the other hand, as long as decency survives, everything else can be endured'.[80]

The remarkable feature of this passage is that, if Victor is right, the *haruspices* placed themselves at the service of a particular group, the *boni*, and delivered themselves not only of an interpretation of the *portentum*, but also of a political commentary with moral overtones.[81] However, it is quite possible that Victor owes nothing of the kind directly to the *haruspices*, but gives his own interpretation of a *portentum* from the past in such a way as to waive responsibility, and may therefore express criticism with impunity. To the morality of the time, the word *beatus* (*mollissimum quemque beatum fore asserebant*) has positive connotations. The implications, therefore, of describing a person of dubious morals (*mollissimus*) as *beatus* are not in keeping with Victor's ethics.[82] To him 'being happy' is not synonymous with a life without problems. On the contrary. All adversity in life can be borne and all difficulties can be dealt with if one is guided by a strong sense of good and evil. This is entirely in agreement with the tradition of the *exemplum*, with which the historian was familiar since childhood. What he says was taught at school, by military leaders, by moralists, pagan and Christian alike, in the same manner. The term *beatus* came to be used to describe the emperors from Constantine onwards.[83] Ever since Cicero, the word had been used in a political sense, denoting a state which is not being torn by factions.[84] The importance that Victor attaches to the correct use of this word should not surprise us. It contains all that he and his contemporaries regarded as the greatest good **for men** and gods, for emperors and subjects, for state and citizens. But, *pudore amisso*, even the lustre of the *beatus* is tarnished.

---

[80] 28,8-9.

[81] There is nothing to be found on the subject of *prodigia* such as those mentioned by Victor in P. Catalano, *Contributi allo studio del diritto augurale* I, Turin 1960.

[82] For the connection between *beatus* and *fortunatus*, see *TLL*, *s.v.* 'beatus', col. 1920, line 22 ff. The link between *beatus* and *aeternus*, which occurs so often in the Christian authors (see P. J. Couvée, *Vita Beata and Vita Aeterna - A Study of Lactantius, Ambrosius and Augustinus*, (thesis Utrecht, 1947), is lacking in Victor.

[83] *TLL, ibid.*, col. 1914.

[84] *De Fin.* I, 58; also *TLL, ibid.*, col. 1913.

No life of Philippus Arabs and of his son was handed down in the
Historia Augusta. Nor have we any knowledge of written sources
that Victor might have consulted. Little was known about him,
and Victor further selected the information he considers of greatest
importance. For this he even dared to defy the *haruspices* with
their misuse of the term *beatus*. He is more than a 'heathen, interested in prodigies'.[85] *Prodigia* must be explained, and for that
Victor had his own code.

The Epitomist has but little to add.[86] He stresses the emperors'
mortality by detailing their deaths. Some abbreviators write at
length on this point; their work is somewhat reminiscent of the
memento mori, though by no means in the Christian sense. Philippus
Arabs was killed. His head was split open above the teeth: *medio
capita supra ordines dentium praeciso*. No textbook, wherever or
whenever it was written, fails to present such details, even though
educationalists have succeeded, in the last few decades, in eliminating many such horrors from school curricula. However, it is not
so long ago that Dutch children learnt in minute detail about the
wounds inflicted on William of Orange at each attempted assassination. Every Dutch schoolboy knows that Count Floris the Fifth of
Holland was killed in the same way as was Philip, according to the
Epitome. The discovery of Floris' grave some years ago in Rijnsburg
confirms the story. Those who have held the skull in their hands
have had the sweet satisfaction of knowing a childhood legend
to be true.

Victor does not mention the fact that Philip was of humble birth
—though he usually likes to mention this detail. Perhaps the commemoration of the thousandth birthday of Rome diverted his
attention from such personal details. The *Epitome* remedies this
omission, and adds that the emperor's father was a *nobilissimus
latronum ductor*. This, too, is an oral tradition remembered, like
many others, even when recorded history is forgotten. The *latrones*
were strong; they appealed to the imagination,[87] especially if they
were *nobilissimi*—which seemed impossible!

---

[85] *Oxford Classical Dictionary*, first edition (1949), 125 (A. H. McDonald).

[86] The only independent contribution of the *Epitome*, which has attracted
slightly more attention, is the reference to the fact that Philip had a son,
which includes the name he used before he became co-regent. See Alföldi,
art. cit.

[87] See also *Mnem.* 18 (1965), 377. Cf. Victor 39,17: 'manu agrestium ac
latronum, quos Bagaudas incolae vocant'; 41,12: 'servili aut latronum

In the *breviaria* we are thus twice confronted with an oxymoron: the *mollissimus* who is *beatus*, and the *latro* who is *nobilissimus*. To Victor, such ideas were abhorrent. They represent a profanation of all he held sacred.

GALLIENUS [88]

Modern research generally agrees that senatorial prejudice placed this emperor in a most unfavourable light, and that no change was to be discerned in this attitude until the studies of A. Alföldi were published.[89] There is no doubt that modern historians have not always treated this emperor fairly. This is because they were far too strongly influenced by the least reliable sources, notably the *Vitae* of the Thirty Tyrants and of Gallienus himself in the *Historia Augusta*. However, before these obscure works came into existence, a modest body of information was compiled (by Aurelius Victor and Eutropius) which should not be disregarded. They are also one-sided; they, too, make great mistakes, but their final conclusions are more subtle than modern critics would have us believe. Alföldi's studies, chiefly archaeological and numismatic, confirm much of the information given by these writers, which therefore deserves a more positive evaluation. Eutropius' summing-up [90] may still be used to conclude any historical exposé of Gallienus' rule: *imperium primum feliciter, mox commode, ad ultimum perniciose gessit*. We shall limit ourselves to the subject that best illustrates these words, and which is, indeed, given special attention by these writers—Gallienus' relations with the senate. It is quite likely that the chapter Victor devotes to him owes its length to his emphasis on Gallienus' exclusion of the senate from military commands, thus breaking the power of this *ordo* and earning the hatred of the senators. Perhaps this hatred was aggravated by the fact that

---

more'. The fear which the *latrones* generally inspired is best expressed in the *Vita Gallieni* 4,9: 'denique quasi coniuratione totius mundi concussis orbis partibus etiam in Sicilia quasi quoddam servile bellum exstitit latronibus evagantibus, qui vix oppressi sunt'.

[88] Victor 33.

[89] Thus A. Heuss, *Römische Geschichte* (1960), 594, referring to A. Alföldi, 'Die Vorherrschaft der Pannonier im Römerreich und die Reaktion des Hellenismus unter Gallienus', in: 25 *Jahre Röm.-German. Komission*, Frankfurt am M., 1930, 11 ff. (= *Studien zur Geschichte der Weltkrise des 3. Jahrhunderts nach Chr.*, Darmstadt, 1967, 228 ff.). For a recent evaluation of the sources, see H. J. Willger, *Studien zur Chronologie de Gallienus und Postumus*, thesis Saarbrücken, 1966, 10 ff.

[90] IX, 8,1.

Rome was losing importance as the centre of government and that the emperor used Milan as a base of military operations; understandably, in view of the activity necessary on the northern front. Perhaps, moreover, the hatred of the *ordo senatorius* was further fanned (although these pagan authors refrain from comment on this subject) by the imperial change of policy towards the Christians, Gallienus' attitude, in contrast to his predecessors, being favourable.[91]

The emotional climate in which this chapter must have been read, is indicated in § 5 by the words *desperatio animi*.[92] The consciousness of decline underlies the manner in which contemporary historians wrote of Gallienus, which is not surprising in view of the military threats presented by barbarians and pretenders.

The installation of a new emperor and the *consecratio* of the deceased had always been undertaken in co-operation with the senate. Under Gallienus all this degenerated to an ignoble farce.[93] As Victor puts it: *ita quasi ventis undique saevientibus parvis maxima ima summis orbe toto miscebantur*.[94] The storm gathered in all quarters, the frontiers were no longer inviolable. There was no remedy for these dangers, and it was certainly not to be found, in the opinion of our historian, in an intermingling of high and low, of small and great. The old maxim, that water can only flow downwards, also applies to social change: equalization can never succeed in raising the inferior to the level of the superior. It is possible that this reflection contains a covert allusion to the relationship obtaining between pagans and Christians,[95] the words *parva* and *ima* are surprisingly apt for the pagan point of view, especially if the pagan casts his mind back one century. However, if the words have been so used, the allusion is so subtle that no modern interpretation to this effect can ever be confirmed.

On the other hand, he is most explicit on the subject of the deterioration of emperors and pretenders as regards their social origin. Emperor Marius,[96] an armourer, *neque etiam tum militiae satis clarus*, represented the lowest ebb. The authority of the state and

---

[91] Cf. L. Homo, *Les empereurs romains et le Christianisme* (Paris 1931), 102, 183.

[92] See p. 97. Cf. *Mnem.* 21 (1968), 266 ff.

[93] Cf. *Vita Gall.* 4,9 and 5,1.

[94] 33,4.

[95] The edict of Gallienus in Eusebius, *H.E.* VII, 13.

[96] 33,9-10; cf. Eutr. IX, 9,2.

all the virtues Rome had stood for had become a mockery. With biting irony the writer sketches the development of history in a comparison between the emperor and his namesake Gaius Marius: 'Hence it was ironically said that it was not at all surprising that one Marius should undertake to restore the Roman state, since that state had been established by a Marius who had been a blacksmith, and the first of that name and family'. This obscure M. Aurelius Marius is thus compared to Gaius Marius, the general of the Republic. That the latter was also a smith is no more than a beautiful thought, a figment of the imagination; that the two Marii were related is likewise a product of the same imagination. This emperor's reign lasted two days. To the associative type of thinking indulged in by Victor (or his 'school'), similarity of names was a sufficient basis for an ironical remark (*ioculariter dictum*). This Marius was regarded as a caricature of an emperor. He was not the only one. Victor's readers included at least one emperor who could profit by the example of his insignificant predecessor. A negative example is still an example.

Victor not only sees the writing on the wall in Gallienus' hostility to the senate, but he regards the increasing power of the civil service as an equally great danger to the State.[97] As an illustration, he selects the function of the *actuarii* in the army. This group of civil servants had developed into a real danger under emperor Victorinus, who had violated the wife of a certain Attitianus, an *actuarius*.[98] 'The power of the combines (*factiones* [99]) of regimental quartermasters (*actuarii*) to which Attitianus belonged grew so great, and their crimes were always crowned with success, because they spared no pains to achieve their ends. People like that are to be found particularly frequently nowadays:[100] evil, corrupt, cunning, politically untrustworthy, greedy, with a natural talent, so to speak, for carrying out and concealing frauds. They control the distribution of corn, and thus constitute a threat to the supervisors of the storehouses and to the fortunes of the farmers as well;

---

[97] 33,13. No parallel for the following passage can be found in the classical literature; it is unique. The translation is in part taken from Echols, see p. 58, n. 17.

[98] For the post of 'army clerk', see A. H. M. Jones, *The Later Roman Empire* (Oxford, 1964), 526, 626 ff. (on this passage esp. 628), 672 ff.

[99] No other interpretation of *factio*, usually department, is satisfactory here.

[100] 'Praesertim hac tempestate' refers to the author's own time.

in addition they have developed the technique of offering bribes to their victims, by whose folly and to whose detriment they have amassed their wealth'.

Eutropius refers to the activities of Attitianus and his *factio* in the following terms: *actuario quodam dolum machinante*.[101] This shows that Eutropius regarded the man with indifference, possibly even with scorn, as indeed he regarded Victorinus: *cum nimiae libidinis esset et matrimonia aliena corrumperet*.[102] Victor, however, takes a different view. His characterization of people of this stamp, *genus hominum ... seditiosum*,[103] shows how near he felt the *factiones* to be to *seditiones*. They owe their influence to the fact that they control the corn supply. Their work involves two groups of people over whom they exercise their reign of terror,[104] (a) the middlemen, *utilia curantibus*, and (b) the farmers or suppliers themselves, *aratores*, and who are summed up as '*his ... quorum vecordia damnoque opes contraxerit*'.[105]

The story of Victorinus' death deserves credence.[106] This was a question of personal revenge, and had no effect on the power of his party. His mother, indeed, continued to wield considerable influence.[107] This would not have been possible in the event of an army mutiny. Army revolts tend to be thorough and have a habit of eliminating the victim's relatives.

We may therefore legitimately ask why Victor mentions the *actuarii* and their destructive influence in this context. The answer is that they threatened the position of the *boni*; a threat that was the more serious since they could influence the army—an avenue closed to the *boni*.

---

[101] Eutr. IX, 9,3.

[102] Cf. *vita trig. tyr.* 6,3: 'a quodam actuario, cuius uxorem stupraverat'.

[103] 33,13.

[104] A different explanation in Jones, *op. cit.*, 628, especially of: *his largiendi quorum vecordia damnoque opes contraxerit*. Jones connects this passage in Victor with the unmistakable popularity of the *actuarii* with the soldiers. This was presumably due to their *largitiones*: 'while regularly bilking the soldiers, they won their goodwill by occasional lavish acts of generosity'. To my mind the passage in question concerns only those in charge of the storehouses and farmers, and not the soldiers.

[105] E. C. Echols' translation (*Sextus Aurelius Victor's Brief Imperial Lives*, 1962) is to my mind correct here: 'They controlled the market, and thus were a threat to those who produced the staples and to the fortunes of the farmers as well'.

[106] There is nothing to be found about the *actuarii* in Hanslik, *R.E.*, *s.v.* 'Victorinus' (1958).

[107] 33,14 cf. Hanslik, *art. cit.*, col. 2078, line 9 ff.

Victor is strongly opposed to Gallienus,[108] whose apotheosis offers a further opportunity to enlarge upon the humiliation of the senate.[109] Although his successor, Claudius II, was responsible, it is as if the man whose death occasioned the *consecratio* were himself to blame.

The consecration of Gallienus [110]

The senators finally consecrated Gallienus, being constrained to do so by Claudius because Gallienus had appointed him as successor.[111] 'The deification was obviously extorted, for as long as there are civilized states, the disgraceful acts of Gallienus cannot be kept hidden, and all the worst types of criminals will be forever considered his match and his equal. Thus do emperors and the best of men, by the glory of their lives rather than by the titles which they seek and obtain, insofar as men may judge, achieve true divinity or are, by the judgment of men, worshipped as gods'.

Eutropius, who defended the honour of the senate to the last, does not mention the consecration. It was bad enough for Victor to have to confess that this sacred ritual had been reduced to a hollow mockery. 'Yes there are even some, just as bad as Gallienus, who have been included among the *divi*, people who hardly even deserved a funeral'.[112] Nevertheless, he has one consolation: truth always triumphs over lies.[113]

Gallienus' wickedness leads Victor to express his deepest sentiments about good and evil, and also to give the fundamental reasons for his historical labours. We therefore have every reason to feel that Alföldi is justified in concluding that Victor's opinion of the emperor is on the whole negative. Generally speaking, this conclusion is correct. But the question is whether his description of the emperor's actions is also negative; and here a curious contradiction emerges. On closer inspection we shall see that no sudden change in attitude has taken place, nor does the despised emperor

---

[108] 35,7: 'quae per Gallienum evenerant'; these words once again demonstrate Victor's dislike of this emperor. For opinions on Gallienus in fourth-century histories, see J. Rougé, 'L'histoire auguste et l'Isaurie au IVᵉ siècle', *REA* 88 (1966), 282-315.

[109] 33,33.

[110] 33,27, 29, 30.

[111] 33,29.

[112] 33,25.

[113] 33,26, for the translation, see above, p. 56.

suddenly appear to be performing good deeds. There is no reversal in the historical exposé. There are, however, contradictions, an acknowledgement of good deeds, which prevent the picture from looking entirely black. A remarkable piece of subtlety, to which the *breviaria* have not accustomed us.

Certainly, as far as the emperor's personal life is concerned, the picture is unfavourable from beginning to end. The successes described at the beginning of chapter 33,[114] are cancelled out by his improvidence in prosperity, though the historian concedes that such behaviour is no more than human.[115] The personal life of Gallienus is incorporated into history in a most sophisticated manner. First *pestilentia* [116] and *desperatio animi* [117] indicate the mood of the time, and then *simulque* introduces the personal element. As always in Victor's work, the link is somewhat tenuous,[118] but it is hinted that the delicate position of the State is also connected with the emperor's behaviour: 'In the midst of all these things (i.e. the afore-mentioned disasters) he remained true to his habit of frequenting taverns and maintaining friendships with procurers and inn-keepers'.[119] And then he propagates that hostile lie about his marital life, which transforms his wife Julia Cornelia Salonina Pipa, a daughter of a Germanic king, into two different people, his legal wife Salonina and his concubine Pipa.[120]

The effect of the emperor's marriage on the riots in Gaul under Postumus is indicated as follows: *qua causa etiam civiles motus atrociores orti*. Presumably we should not take the writer too literally here, either. One thing, however, is certain. We simply do not know the complex reasons underlying Postumus' rebellion. We may not therefore summarily dismiss the possibility of a link between Gallienus' marriage with a German princess and the court fashion of wearing German hair-styles mentioned by the *Historia Augusta* (apparently trivial matters) and the revolt in Gaul.

These first paragraphs of chapter 33 contain serious accusations,

---

[114] It is useless to attempt to establish a correct chronology. Victor is not in the least interested in doing so, and the external evidence is inadequate.

[115] 33,3.

[116] Cf. *vita Gall.* 5,5; Zosim. I, 36; Eus. *H.E.*, VII, 22.

[117] See below, p. 97.

[118] See below, p. 96, n. 176.

[119] 33,6.

[120] See also *Epit.* 33,1; *vita Gall.* 21,3. Stein assumes that there are two people, *RE* xx, col. 1718. Also *RE*, col 2006 *s.v.* 'Saloninus 4'.

but in spite of these Victor is not capable of suppressing Gallienus' achievements with regard to the safety of the State altogether:

§ 1. shows the emperor as energetic and brave: *strenue* and *properans*.[121]

§ 3. *his prospere ac supra vota cedentibus*: *supra vota* suggests that the result was 'unexpected'. This implies not only that the difficulties were so great that expert observers feared defeat, but also that they did not believe that the emperor was capable of dealing with the difficulties that arose after Valerian's ignominious defeat.[122]

The emperor *secundis solutior rem Romanam quasi naufragio dedit*: Goths, 'Parthians', Alamanni and Franks threatened to overwhelm the empire.

§ 8-§ 14. The usurpers within the country, of whom Postumus, Laelianus, Marius, Victorinus and Victoria are named.

§15-§ 16. But the emperor stayed in Rome, held games and celebrated festivals: 'pacata omnia ignaris publici mali improbe suadebat, crebro etiam, uti rebus ex voluntate gestis solet, ludis ac festa triumphorum, quo promptius simulata confirmarentur exercens. Sed postquam periculum propinquabat, tandem urbe egreditur'.

§ 17. This account of events is incorrect: the emperor had already been in Macedonia for some time and was fighting the barbarians there when Aureolus' mutiny broke out in Raetia. Nevertheless, § 17 implies that the usurper was trying to seize power, *excitus . . . socordia tam ignavi ducis*, and that Gallienus, when he defeated Aureolus at Pons Aureoli in the Po valley, had come there from Rome, and not from the front at the north-eastern frontier. At any rate, the fact that Gallienus was capable of defeating Aureolus at all, seems a miracle in

---

[121] Cf. Rougé, *art. cit.*, 228. There is no trace here of the pattern used, for instance, in the treatment of Nero, according to which the good early years are followed by a later period of cruelty.

[122] The insurrections of Ingenuus (mss. Ingebus) and Regalianus preceded the *clades Valeriana* by two years. Victor does not take this into account, but stresses only the restoration of order by Gallienus. For a chronological summary see Besnier, *Le Bas-Empire* I (1947), 176, esp. notes 204 and 205. Walser-Pekáry, *op. cit.*, 28, 41, and others. For a more recent study, in particular J. Fitz, *Ingenuus et Régalien*, Collection Latomus 81 (1966). See below, p. 171.

view of Victor's comments.[123] An emperor who reacts so efficiently certainly does not suffer from *socordia*, indolence. Yet great emphasis is laid upon this characteristic, and it is again referred to in § 33, which is concerned with Gallienus' notorious decision, never repealed, to exclude senators from military commands.[124] This, too, is imputed to the emperor's *socordia*, which seems a curious accusation, particularly since the decision to entrust the functions of military officers to young and untried officers from other backgrounds meant that the commander-in-chief had constantly to be on his guard to maintain his authority. It would have been easier to work with known and trusted staff officers. This step hardly indicates *socordia*, but rather its opposite.

§ 27 ff. Gallienus is finally betrayed and killed. Our lack of information makes it uncertain whether his successor, Claudius II, had a hand in his death, although it seems likely. Victor prefers the version which presupposes the legitimacy of the succession [125] and which furthermore condemns the senate for attempting to be revenged (albeit indirectly) after Gallienus' death.

§ 31. The pattern is obvious and familiar. The new emperor wishes to establish the legitimacy of his claim and therefore prevents the usual slaughter of his predecessor's friends and relatives. Victor sides with the new emperor. However, the text is corrupt and therefore requires more detailed explanation. 'But the senate, having heard of Gallienus' death, decided to throw his relatives and henchmen down the Gemonian steps, and it is an established fact [126] that they had their eyes put out by way of punishment, after the *patronus fisci* had been called to the senate-house as a witness'.[127] A cruel comedy is thus enacted. The tormentors of Gallienus' relatives wished to lend their actions the semblance at least of legality.

---

[123] For the history of Aureolus and his earlier services to Gallienus, see Besnier, *op. cit.*, 185.

[124] See H. N. Baynes, *Byzantine Studies*, 174. Cf. E. Albertini, *L'empire romain* (Paris 1938³), 312, note 3.

[125] 33,28.

[126] *satis constat* is used regularly by Victor for emphasis.

[127] *satellites propinquosque* are the subject of *pependisse*. In § 32 they are again referred to as *eorum*. *Oculos effossos pependisse* can be explained by analogy with *poenas pendere*. Instead of *perduci* which is impossible, read Olivarius' suggestion, *perducto*.

Perhaps they fetched this particular leader of the bar, the *patronus fisci*, because he bore Gallienus a grudge and was therefore willing to take part in this farce; it is also possible that he was compelled to do so.[128]

§ 32 and 33. An unworthy collaboration of the senate and the people is to be remarked here. The army, however, had not forgotten its loyalty towards Gallienus; Claudius acted accordingly and stopped the massacre (§ 32). The bitterness of the senate is explained,[129] though not condoned. From the following it will appear that Victor agreed with Claudius, whom he holds in the highest esteem,[130] and the curbing of these acts of vengeance must have influenced his judgement.[131]

Possible Influence of Tacitus

An adequate description of these conflicts, especially those between emperor and senate, required gifts worthy of a Tacitus. Victor had no such talent, but his rendering is more ingenuous and therefore also clumsier than if he had borrowed directly from Tacitus.

We shall discuss paragraphs 23 and 24 in particular, and compare them with Tacitus' *Hist.* 1,12 and *Ann.* XI, 17. In the preceding paragraph, § 22, Victor had remarked that the murderer of Gallienus was not caught, either because the culprit was unknown or because the murder was considered a public service.

§ 23. Then, as an afterthought (introduced by *quamquam*) he says, 'yet moral standards have declined to such an extent that most people will rather act in their own interest than in that of the State and they will covet power rather than honour'.[132]

§ 24. 'For this reason, the true significance of events and names has been distorted since, very often, a man who gains power by means of some crime says, when his victory is established, that the enemy whose defeat was in fact to the detriment of the State, should be called an ousted tyrant.'

---

[128] *Perducto* could indicate the latter.

[129] § 33, by the decision to exclude the senate from military command.

[130] 34.

[131] We shall not enter into a discussion of whether Claudius II is presented in an unfavourable light because he is considered the founder of the dynasty of Constantine. The Greek sources react by favouring Gallienus (e.g. Zon. 12,25) and adopting an anti-Claudian attitude. Modern studies follow them without further definite proof, e.g. P. Damerau, *Kaiser Claudius II. Gothicus* (*268-270 A.D.*), Klio Beih. 33 (N.F. 20), 1934, 45.

[132] Note that a 'murder', even a regicide, is not condemned as such. If in the public interest, it can even bring *gloria* (in the sense of honour).

From this we may conclude that Gallienus was no 'ousted tyrant' and should be seen, at least according to Victor, in a more favourable light. Yet it is dangerous to stretch logic so far for an author who is wont to connect people and events very loosely and somewhat illogically, guided by the association of ideas.

Is there, then, enough similarity between the above passages and Tacitus to allow us to speak of derivation? I wonder.

Hist. 1,12:	Vict. 33,23:
Paucis iudicium aut rei publicae amor: multi stulta spe, prout quis amicus vel cliens, hunc vel illum ambitiosis rumoribus destinebant.	Quamquam eo prolapsi mores sunt, uti suo quam rei publicae magisque potentiae quam gloriae studio plures agant.

Ann. XI, 17:	Vict. 33,24:
Falso libertatis vocabulum obtendi ab iis, quo privatim degeneres, in publicum exitiosi, nihil spei nisi per discordias habeant.	Hinc quoque rerum vis ac nominum corrupta, dum plerumque potior flagitio, ubiarmis superaverit, tyrannidem amotam vocat damno publico oppressos.

One cannot possibly maintain that Victor borrowed from Tacitus in these passages, unless 'borrowing' be granted connotations so vague and unrestricted as to preclude any direct knowledge of the earlier author. Nor does E. Wölfflin, who wrote a most interesting study of this subject, mention these passages.[133] Undoubtedly Victor's train of thought often, as here, corresponds to that of Tacitus. Sometimes, although not here, this leads to a similarity, even of the choice of words, which is somewhat more convincing.
For instance:

Ann. III, 55:	Vict. 35,13:
Nisi forte rebus *cunctis* inest quidam velut *orbis*, ut quemadmodum temporum vices, ita morum *vertantur*.	quod factum edocuit *cuncta* in *orbis* modo *verti*.

---

[133] *Rh.M.*, 29 (1874), 282-308; esp. 302-308: 'Die Benutzung des Tacitus durch A.V.' It would be interesting to compare Victor's attitude with Tacitus', using the searching analysis by A. Dihle, 'Sine ira et studio', *RhM* 114 (1971), 27-43, as starting point. See also above, p. 25.

The train of thought is the same, the congruence, word for word, remarkable. We know from other authors besides Victor that Gallienus severely clipped the wings of the senate. It seems appropriate, then, to compare Victor's description with that in which Tacitus, three centuries before, described a similar humiliation of the senate far more tellingly and with far greater *ira et studium*. One could also compare § 30, a general condemnation of the principle of hereditary succession,[134] with Galba's speech to the senate at the beginning of the *Histories*. It should immediately become clear, however, that such a comparison is useless. These are thoughts which are commonplace, and repeated whenever necessary. Thus it need occasion no surprise to find this pronouncement in the *Historia Augusta*. In none of these cases is there necessarily any question of a Tacitean heritage.

Historical Reliability

There can be no doubt about the historicity of Gallienus' extremely realistic politico-military measure curtailing the influence of the senate. Certain functions were no longer open to the senate; on the other hand, members of senatorial families were given posts which were formerly held by the *ordo equester*,[135] as has been confirmed by epigraphical research. The abbreviator who recognised the importance of this measure, even a hundred years later, deserves a modest mark of esteem.

There are no decisive grounds for doubting the historical accuracy of § 31 and § 32, the account of the reactions of the senate and the reprisals in Rome. Those who contest the validity of this passage reason, apparently conclusively, that Victor's dislike of Gallienus and his partial attitude to the senate led him to gross exaggeration, even to wild fantasies.[136] This criticism is altogether unfounded, in my opinion. The entrance upon the scene of the *patronus fisci* cannot have been 'invented'.

The suggested comparison of Victor 33,31 and Suetonius, *Tib.* 75, 2 is hardly convincing. Nor do the *scalae Gemoniae*, also mentioned in Suetonius, form sufficient grounds for deducing 'imitation'. This spot was always used for executions of the kind.

---

[134] Cf. W. Hartke, *Römische Kinderkaiser* (Berlin, 1951), 142.

[135] H.-G. Pflaum, 'La séparation des pouvoirs civil et militaire avant et sous Dioclétien (et *De Caes.* 33,34)', *BSAF* 1958 (1960), 78-79.

[136] P. Damerau, *op. cit.*, 46.

An explanation for the similarity of the two passages must be sought elsewhere.[137]

Senatorial opposition to the deification of Gallienus is probably historically true. The fact that Eutropius does not even mention the consecration is particularly significant. That the senators gave in, *subacti a Claudio*, is felt by Eutropius to be a disgrace about which one had best keep silent.

All this is in marked contrast to the *Epitome*, which is extremely short and quotes only some gossip—and in utter chronological confusion at that.[138] It records two new 'facts': the existence of a second son, Salonianus,[139] whom Gallienus had destined to be his successor and his descent from 'Pipa', Gallienus' supposed concubine and daughter to the king of the Marcomanni, who gained part of Pannonia by a treaty. Otherwise, § 1 tallies with Victor 33,6; they are also in complete agreement about the circumstances in which the emperor came to his end.[140]

The literary tradition favourable to Gallienus was summarized by Münzer.[141] Its greater accuracy has long been common knowledge to research.[142] This emperor has been characterized as 'ein Revolutionär auf politischem, religiösem, administrativem, militarischem und finanziellem Gebiet',[143] and rightly so. Yet no-one can blame a representative of the social class that was the chief sufferer under this revolutionary for delineating him in terms rather less than complimentary. We have ample reason to regard Victor with respect for seeking once again to defend the hopeless cause of the senate, one hundred years later. Herein, perhaps, if anywhere, lie the essentials of Tacitus' influence.

---

[137] There are elements here of a 'Defixionsformel' (A. Dieterich, *Mutter Erde* [Leipzig-Berlin, 1905], 77. I hope to revert to this subject in another publication.).

[138] For the difficult chronological questions connected with the rebellion of Postumus, see the searching analysis of H. J. Willger, *op. cit.*

[139] Gallienus may have had three sons, see A. Alföldi, *Studien zur Geschichte der Weltkrise des 3. Jahrhunderts nach Christus* (1967), 106 (ref. from *Numism. Chron.* IX [1929]). See also L. Wickert in *RE* xiii, col. 236, 239.

[140] Victor 33,18-20; *Epit.* 33,2.

[141] Münzer in *RE* viii, col. 366, line 44 ff.

[142] Particularly L. Homo in *Rev. Hist.* 1913, 1 ff, 225 ff.

[143] J. Moreau, *Scripta Minora* (Heidelberb 1964), 29. For an unfavourable opinion of Gallienus in military affairs, see below, p. 210 (the *Breviarium* of Festus).

DIOCLETIAN [144]

In *De Caesaribus* the historical focus is increasingly on the relationship between the emperor and the senate. This is most noticeable in the last period he describes. This is not surprising, since this problem was still relevant in the historian's own time. He regards a description of a past three-quarters of a century removed from the time of writing as the best possible mirror for his contemporaries. His treatment of Diocletian is thus |most enlightening if one wishes to gain a clear insight into the author and his intentions.

Senate and Emperor

The first point to strike the reader is the fact that Victor has no illusions about the moral resistance of the senators. He illustrated this earlier, in his life of Probus, and again has much to say about it in his long chapter on Diocletian, which describes emperors who were capable of dealing with circumstances. A cruder contrast than that which he draws between the enfeebled nobility and the energetic military emperors can hardly be imagined. Of course, this black-and-white image is exaggerated, but it cannot be sufficiently emphasized that this is necessary in a textbook. The two quotations which follow show this contrast between the nobility and a series of powerful emperors. 'And, indeed, while they delighted in idleness and trembled for their riches and counted it more important than eternal life to guard and increase them, they themselves have paved the way for the barbarian soldiers to tyrannize over them and their children.'[145] 'It is certain that experience of evils and need makes men efficient and shrewd, whilst, on the contrary, those who have never experienced anything unpleasant and judge every man according to his property and his gold, make a worse show.'[146]

Diocletian 'was the first of all emperors after Caligula and Domitian to have himself publicly called "lord" and to have himself worshipped and addressed as a God'.[147] This is literally untrue; the title 'dominus', for instance, was already in common use at the time of Pliny the Younger. If one considers the title 'Divus', how-

---

[144] 39.

[145] 37,7 Both translations (of 37,7 and 39,27) are by A. Alföldi, *A Conflict of Ideas in the Late Roman Empire* (Oxford 1952), 105.

[146] 39,27.

[147] 39,4.

ever, which Caracalla still used in speaking of the dead,[148] much has changed. Probus used the title as an official 'Selbstbezeichnung' and it was applied with particular frequency to Diocletian and his co-regents.[149] Victor has no intention of joining the ranks of worshippers and the darker aspects of Diocletian's rule are accordingly placed in high relief. For instance, the fact of his humble origin is used to explain his tyrannical behaviour.

'From these things I see clearly that, to the best of my judgement, even the lowest man, especially if he rises high, knows no bounds to his arrogance and greed. That is why, for Marius in the days of our ancestors and for (Diocletian) in this present age, the old ways of life are no longer good enough; for such souls, only just escaped from starvation, who have never known power, are insatiable. And I am astonished that it is the aristocrats who are usually regarded as arrogant, when they really have some right to console themselves with their prestige for those vexations of the patrician families that give them no rest.'[150]

With patent indignation Victor exposes the foolishness of the imperial robes of state: 'he was the first emperor to demand a supply of silk and purple for his sandals, to wear with his gold-embroidered gala uniform'.[151] These details of dress, which are trivial in our eyes, appealed strongly to popular imagination. The impression made by colourful spectacles, resplendent with imperial majesty and grandeur, is well-nigh inconceivable to us. Every time people saw this magnificence it seemed to have increased in pomp. Innovations in all manner of particulars were thus attributed to one emperor or another. The *Historia Augusta* credited Carinus with wearing the above-mentioned sandals, which were introduced by Heliogabalus, whereas Alexander Severus is given the (implicit)

---

[148] Vita Getae 2 (the well-known saying about his brother, 'sit divus, dum non sit vivus').

[149] A good survey is given by L. Koep in *RAC* III (1957), col. 1254 (*s.v.* 'Divus'); for further references see the bibliography of this article.

[150] 39,6; translation by Alföldi, *Conflict*, 100. For emperor Marius, see 33,9 and 11; for Diocletian esp. 39,6.

[151] 39,2. The words of M.P. Charlesworth are worth bearing in mind: 'The King, the ruler favoured of heaven, must be visibly something hieratic, formal and magnificent. How this originated and developed is a matter for historians of religion and folklorists'. *JRS*, 37 (1947), 34-38, esp. 37. The potential acrimony of the discussion about certain details of Roman ceremonial dress, and of that of republican magistrates, and again about sandals in Diocletian's time, is apparent from the differences of opinion between Alföldi and Momigliano (*JRS*, 56 [1966], 24).

credit for abolishing this footwear. [152] It is no coincidence that the same section of this work contains the information that the latter also abolished the title of 'dominus'.

Humble birth offers poor prospects for good government—a curious maxim to come from the pen of a man whose ambition it was to be a good governor (and who was apparently successful, too), but prides himself on his own modest beginnings. Still, inconsistency is a human failing. Time and again his dislike of civil servants of humble origin crops up. He criticizes Constantine for his indiscriminate bestowal of posts of honour instead of reserving them for senators.[153] The terms of Victor's disapproval are worthy of note: *cunctaque divino ritui paria viderentur, ni parum dignis ad publica aditum concessisset.* One can only conclude from this that posts were conferred upon the nobility according to a fixed pattern similar, as it were, to a religious ritual (*divino ritui paria*). His disapproval is the odder considering the high esteem in which Victor holds Constantine. In fact, the historian himself says that he considers this a mistaken policy, more reprehensible in leaders *summo ingenio atque optimis rei publicae moribus,* in which category he places Constantine, whom he continues to call *maximus.*[154] Such subtlety of historical judgement occurs only too rarely in the works of other authors, and represents an attempt at shading in the facile black-and-white image. In so doing he suddenly rises to the heights of Ammianus, when the latter reproaches his greatly admired emperor Julian for raising men of low birth to high estate despite the fact that he, Julian, had previously criticized Constantine for following this policy.[155]

Nevertheless, if we ask ourselves whether Victor succeeds in unifying these nuances in a convincing and historically reliable narrative, the answer must be negative. In this respect he is far inferior to Ammianus, as is shown by the inequality of his judgement of Diocletian and the other Illyrian emperors. Time and again they elicit approval from this senatorial *homo novus.* But he is incapable of reconciling this approval with his criticism of the emperors' dealings with the senate. These are regarded as a blot on the imperial

---

[152] *Vita Cari,* 17,1; *Heliog.* 23,4; *Alex.* 4,2.

[153] 41,20.

[154] 41,22: *post minimum* (= Dalmatius) *maximumque* (= Constantine the Great).

[155] Ammianus 21,10,8. Cf. A. Chastagnol, *La Préfecture urbaine à Rome sous le Bas-Empire* (Paris 1960), 403.

escutcheon, and in no way connected with the rest of their actions, although now and then he even metes out both praise and censure in the same sentence. In this case, their feats of war earn his praise, whereas his strictures apply to their descent which (and this is forever at the back of Victor's mind) renders them inimical to the old families in the senate. This duality is particularly clear in the following passages.[156]

'He (Diocletian) at once made Maximian, his loyal friend, Emperor, who, although only half educated, was a good soldier and kindly'. On Galerius' and Chlorus' elevation to the rank of Caesar, he comments: 'Their native land was Illyricum, and although they had little concern with the higher culture, yet, having grown up between work on the land and the miseries of a soldier's life, they were very good for the State'. More striking still is the following reflection on the same emperors: 'But they had such astonishing natural gifts that, if they had entered on their careers educated, so that their want of polish might not have been revealed, everyone would have taken them for men of the highest distinction. From this it becomes clear that education, elegance, and amiability are qualities absolutely necessary for Emperors, as without them the gifts of nature are, so to say, unkempt or even shaggy and as such are despised, while the same qualities won eternal fame even for Cyrus, the Persian king'.

We can see that his praise remains grudging. While he gallantly concedes the merits of the military emperors, at the same time he cannot resist reaffirming his obsolete code of ethics. For instance, in the following passage, which we have already quoted above, he says: 'It is certain that experience of evils and need makes men efficient and shrewd, whilst, on the contrary, those who have never experienced anything unpleasant and judge every man according to his property and his gold, make a worse show'. However, he immediately goes on to speak of Diocletian and his co-regents: 'Their concord especially teaches us that intelligence and experience in decent military service, such as they brought with them out of the school of Aurelius and Probus, are almost enough to ensure virtue'.[157] It is as if Victor allowed us a glimpse of the hard life

---

[156] See Alföldi, *Conflict*, 104, from which the translation of the following passages (39,17; 39,26; and 40,12-13) has been taken.

[157] 39,26-28 (translation Alföldi, *loc. cit.*); no alteration in the surviving text is necessary.

of a farmer or soldier which he had probably known himself: *ruris ac militiae miseriis imbuti.*

Diocletian and his consorts are of one mind, they are experienced men who have served their apprenticeship under Probus and Aurelian. Small wonder that their common goal and military experience were almost sufficient to restore virtue—almost, but not quite. There was one further requisite, a unity based on deep personal affection for Diocletian himself, an affection that closely resembled religious veneration. Indeed, his colleagues accorded him the respect due to a father, or rather a god, and this was a mark of their unity.[158] In Victor's eyes, the importance of this continued respect is attested by the history of Rome itself, throughout which men of historic stature arose and evoked such reverence. Significantly he writes, *quod quale quantumque sit, ab urbis conditione ad nostram aetatem propinquorem facinoribus patefactum est.* Thus he justifies his recording of historical *exempla* which were a religious inspiration to their contemporaries and continued to serve as such for future generations.

It is understandable that Victor can appreciate Diocletian when his policy coincides with the morality of the *exempla* or, as he puts it, when it is *honestiorum provectu.*[159] Preferment of the *honestiores* was combined with two other measures, namely, the punishment of 'evil' and the safeguarding of religion. He expresses this as follows: *e contra supplicii flagitiosi cuiusque virtutum studia augebantur. Veterrimae religiones castissime curatae.*[160] Neither he nor his readers need any proof for their deeply-rooted conviction that a man who is well born is also, as a matter of course, a man of high moral standing. This conviction was firmly based on an effective, all-pervading, ancient moral code. Although the change in a train of thought is always difficult to pin-point, it is clearly no mere chance that the traditional moral theory is immediately followed by the passage dealing with the building of fortifications and the embellishment of the cities of Rome, Carthage, Milan and Nicomedia. The phrase *Veterrimae religiones castissime curatae* is obviously closer to the preceding words than to the passage they appear to introduce.

---

[158] 39,29.

[159] 39,45. *Honestiores* here means both respectable people of good behaviour and the well-born.

[160] The punctuation in the modern editions is misleading. *Augebantur* does not introduce a new idea. This function is performed by the words *ac mirum in modum*, etc.

As we see, opinions on Diocletian are, to say the least, divided. Julian and Libanius, and even Victor and Eutropius, are on the whole favourably disposed. They dare not attack him openly. In their opinion, the undermining of state institutions or the misdeeds of those in subordinate positions are chiefly to blame for cruel actions and unjust measures. The picture is blurred, not because the author consulted many contradictory sources, but because the complexity of society necessitated numerous administrative adjustments, and the emperor's decisions were not always equally judicious. The consciousness of complexity lived on in the generations of officers and civil servants who peopled the offices. It is here that we must seek the oral traditions on which the *breviaria* are based, and which are their main sources of information. In addition, authors of these condensed histories of emperors and their actions also had their own particular hobby-horse. This may sometimes lend their accounts a certain charm, but it does not facilitate the quest for historical truth.[161]

The problem of sources becomes even more involved since the emperors of the second Flavian dynasty tended to abuse their predecessors. Apart from Eutropius' dedication of his work to Valens, we may conclude that both authors were quite equal to such prejudices. To those who have read Eusebius on Constantine, Victor and Eutropius are a welcome relief. We cannot dismiss the possibility that certain unfavourable passages about Diocletian were based on information given by civil servants and ultimately derived from court gossip, but by the same token, this (hypothetical) course of events is impossible to trace. All these considerations may serve as yet another warning against a dogmatic approach to the problem of sources.[162]

The *Epitome* has nothing further to add save a reference to the death of the usurper Julian [163] (*Epit.* 39,4). All attempts to account

---

[161] The 'Quellenforschung' for Diocletian's time is extremely well discussed by W. Seston, *Dioclétian et la tétrarchie* I (Paris, 1946), 18 ff.

[162] Seston *op. cit.*, 24: 'Ainsi les comparaisons mécaniques de la *Quellenforschung* sont parfois dangereuses. Elles risquent de faire prendre pour des sources anciennes ce qui n'est qu'invention de compilateurs dont le souci est plus de servir une cause que de transmettre des renseignements exacts. Aucun d'entre eux n'est le copiste servile d'une ou de plusieurs sources. Chacun avec les matériaux qu'il prend dans l'œuvre de ses prédécesseurs, compose le portrait qui lui convient, sans se faire scrupule de développer certains détails ou d'en ajouter de son cru, quand ceux-ci facilitent son dessein'.

[163] His activities took place in Africa in 293.

for the meaning of this detail and the scant information contained in a few passages that rake up family histories and speculate on this ruler's death [164] (39,5-7) have proved futile. This Julian must be distinguished from one M. Aurelius Julianus, a military leader in Pannonia, who rebelled against imperial authority under Carinus.[165] Victor is wrong in thinking this Julian a *corrector Venetiae et Histriae* (39,10).

It is almost impossible to summarize the arguments, but nevertheless we must attempt to do so. As starting point one could take *De Caes.* 39,14 and 15. This passage provides the best proof that Victor's assessment of Diocletian's reign is, in the last analysis, favourable: 'ceteris venia data retentique hostium fere omnes ac maxime vir insignis nomine Aristobulus praefectus praetorio per officia sua. Quae res post memoriam humani nova atque inopinabilis fuit civili bello fortunis fama dignitate spoliatum neminem, cum pie admodum mansueteque geri laetemur exilio proscriptioni atque etiam suppliciis et caedibus modum fieri.' These words, written in connection with the amnesty granted by Diocletian, bear witness to a widespread longing for peace. 'It was an unheard of and unexpected circumstance, that during a civil war no one was robbed of his possessions, good name, or function; the population was ruled humanely and sensibly, while exile, confiscation, even death sentences and bloodshed were kept within bounds.' [166] The chief desires of the times find expression in *pie admodum mansueteque*. The population was weary of war, and longing for peace.

THE DECLINE OF A CIVILISATION

The modern sceptic, that *alter ego* of the modern student of history, does not like the word 'decline'. The only criterion he uses to justify its use lies in the opinion of those who lived in the age he is studying. Even though their judgement is not final and pessimism may lead them to depict their own time in the darkest colours, their ideas still retain their value as an indication of the climate of their time and, sometimes, their prejudices.

The further a historian is removed from the time he describes, the less he may be expected to appreciate its spiritual climate. It

---

[164] Cf. below, p. 108.

[165] W. Seston, *op. cit.* 52, gives all the relevant data.

[166] 39,15. *Geri* should be interpreted as *gubernari*, as in 5,2 and *Epit.* 1,29. *Exilio* is preceded by an asyndeton. However it is interpreted, the sentence remains clumsy.

is precisely this, however, that interests us in studying the attitude
of contemporaries or their direct descendants towards the 'decline'
of a particular period.

In writing of the period from 235 to 284, Aurelius Victor is no
contemporary, but sufficiently close in time for his remarkable
comments to merit our full attention. His observations are far from
being an oversimplification of a reality too complex for his simple
mind to grasp. On the contrary, his view of history from 235
onwards as a continuum of turbulence and unrest represents his
considered opinion: military anarchy, territorial losses, continued
absolutism, the disappearance of an élite, the barbarization of the
army, devaluation of the monetary system and the reversion of the
economy to primitive barter. In his inaugural lecture at Heidelberg,
J. Moreau rightly maintained that these phenomena should not in
themselves be regarded as symptoms of the decline of a civilization,
even though they occur simultaneously at a particular period.[167]
Moreover, he is also right in pointing out that the attitude of those
who witness the actual occurrence of these symptoms is probably
more material than the reactions of people, even historians, of a
later date. Thus he distinguishes 'Epochen der Resignation' and
'Epochen der aktiven Auseinandersetzung mit einer Krise'.[168] We
can but agree and above all adduce the measures taken by the
Illyrian emperors as further evidence. Gallienus and many others
were anything but resigned. So much is clear from their military,
political and economic activities.

Victor was well aware of these activities, undertaken not only
by Gallienus and Aurelian, but also by several others. The word
strenue is used to indicate the energy with which they attempted
ro restore the Empire and to give due emphasis to the energy of
military activity at the borders.[169] Otherwise, his prejudices
flourish, particularly with regard to Gallienus but, as does Tacitus in the case of the Julio-Claudian dynasty, he supplies his
readers with ample data to correct the unfavourable image he
projects; indeed, the information he imparts about Gallienus' suc-

---

[167] J. Moreau, 'Krise und Verfall. Das dritte Jahrhundert n. Chr. als
historisches Problem', Heidelberger Antrittsvorlesung, 11. Januar 1961,
Heidelb. Jahrb. 5 (1961), 128-142 (= *Scripta minora*, herausg. v. W. Schmitthenner, Heidelberg, 1964, 26-41).

[168] *Op. cit.*, 31.

[169] 33,1; esp. 39,3 ff.; 39,15 ff.

cesses is in flagrant contrast to the weakness with which he reproaches him.[170]

The question now arises whether Victor is to be reckoned as a traditional historian of decline, one of the many, starting with his own short history and continuing (as Moreau has clearly shown) up to the present, including Alföldi. As a logical concomitant, a second question: Were all those energetic, sometimes successful, attempts at ensuring a renewed blossoming of the state in vain, and to be regarded only as symptoms of decline? The first question may be answered quite simply in the affirmative. Victor's subdivisions in imperial history are the same as those made by the majority of the modern historians; he also shares the forebodings expressed by all modern historians since Gibbon.

The second question can be answered in two ways. To be sure, it can hardly be called an historical error for this long line of historians to speak of decline when they contemplate the countless set-backs and disasters in both internal and foreign affairs. It is, in a sense, all too easy to criticize this point of view. The critic can convincingly expose the widespread misconceptions which tempted later generations, who know the end of the story, to use the word 'decline' without due caution. Victor, however, is a contemporary, be it a pessimist, whose conviction of decline may be summarily dismissed. His peculiar significance here is that he lived and wrote at a time when recovery was still possible. People could still believe in a restoration. The Age of Constantine, which succeeded that of Diocletian, is not yet dead. The battle of Adrianople has not yet been fought, the disintegration which set in after Theodosius could not yet be foreseen. But he knows the ins and outs of the State better than anyone else. He is the second- and third-generation observer and listener. His informants had experienced the fears of the third century. The comparison was obvious, especially for a person who was more deeply involved in the governing of the State than many casual onlookers. There can be no doubt that a great many people had their misgivings about the future. History showed many precedents for comparisons in time.

The prevailing mood is perhaps best exemplified in a well-known figure of the third century, Gaius Julius Saturninus, the son of Philippus Arabs, who refused to take part in the celebrations of

---

[170] 39,16-17. Cf. for a discussion of Gallienus' merits, M. Besnier, *Le Bas-Empire* I (1947), 185.

the thousandth anniversary of the foundation of Rome, *adeo severi et tristis animi*.[171] Out of the mouths of babes and sucklings .....
This Caesar was eleven or twelve years old when he thus censured his father's (forced) gaiety (*petillantis cachinnantem*).[172] The reactions of this precocious child may be seen as a judgement upon Rome.

In following back the line of reasoning, one should not expect any help from written sources. They undoubtedly existed formerly, but any attempt to trace them is doomed to failure.[173] Moreover, the search for sources often obscures the unique, and often original, features of Victor's book. The method nowadays applied by most historians is to take the *Historia Augusta* as a starting point and then work back to Victor. Consequently, details quoted in the *Historia Augusta* in a watered-down form are often overlooked before it so much as occurs to the historian to consult Victor's text. In the case of Gallienus, for instance, modern historians base their work on the *Historia Augusta*, simply because there is more of it; the next stage is that it is also considered of more importance than Victor. As an example will show, both proceedings are equally misguided.

Victor mentions the plague that broke out in the West after raging in the East.[174] At the same time an epidemic raged in Rome, a phenomenon that often occurs when people already have greater worries and morale is low.[175] Victor makes no attempt to pinpoint the epidemic chronologically.[176] The author of the *vita Gall.* places the report in a different context, that of consulting the Sibylline books and the sacrifices to Iuppiter Salutaris,[177] but not a word is

---

[171] *Epit.* 28,3.

[172] E. Stein, in *RE*, X, col. 767 (Julius, 386) treats this passage in a very different way: 'Von Anekdoten über den Kaiser wird uns eine einzige berichtet. Die Epitome des Victor 28,3 erzählt, der Vater Philippus habe bei den Säkularspielen allzu ausgelassen gelacht und der Sohn habe dies Benehmen missbilligt. Dazu ist, ohne dass die Möglichkeit dieses Vorfalles bestritten werden soll, zu bemerken, dass ein solches Verfahren des Vaters in Widerspruch stünde mit dem Bilder des ernsten und eher mürrischen Mannes, das wir uns sonst von Philippus machen möchten'.

[173] See W. Hartke, Klio Beih. 1940, for proof of the desperate situation of the study of sources. His refutation of N.H. Baynes is not very convincing, and requires further comment. See appendix.

[174] The link is not certain. For the East see Zosimus 1,36; Egypt: Euseb. *H.E.* 7,22.

[175] 33,5.

[176] As so often, his dating is vague: *simulque*.

[177] *Vita Gall.* 5,5.

said about the mood of the population. In the *vita*, the event is assimilated to historical fact without any mention of contemporary reactions. But it is precisely these, and people's dejection at the time, that Victor depicts: their *curae graviores*, their struggle for existence and, above all, their *animi desperatio*.[178] With those last two words, *animi desperatio*, Victor has characterized the period he describes, a century before his own, better than anyone else. Even though his time may have known greater security, he correctly gauged the spirit of a time to which he was possibly more sensitive than most because of his own pessimistic view of the past. This affinity enabled him to surpass himself as a historian of the third century by an assessment that is shrewder than is his wont. For he is right in saying that the *desperatio animi* which the energetic emperors could not overcome showed the third century to be a period of crisis. Victor did not share this attitude. He lived in a different era. At all events, he witnessed Diocletian's amnesty, that rare magnanimity on the part of a conqueror towards the conquered. The historian's comment on this event, born, as it were, of the time of Diocletian himself, once again demonstrates his involvement with those who lived under this emperor's rule.[179] He was writing eighty years later, and greater wars were imminent. Illusions and great expectations rather different from *animi desperatio* induced him to depict a future brighter than it was ever to become. He probably lived to see his hopes shattered.

His sombre outlook on life causes him to lay a certain emphasis on sickness and death. The death of most emperors is described in greater detail, including the cause of death, than in any other *breviarum*. Forty-six passages are devoted to the emperors' death, sickness, wounds or senile decay.[180] Here, too, one might imagine

---

[178] See *Mnem.*, 21 (1968), 267 ff. *Desperatio salutis* and *desperatio futurorum* also occur, but the personal touch is lacking. The phrase *desperatio animi* is unique (see *TLL*, s.v. 'desperatio').

[179] 39,15: 'Quae res post memoriam humani nova atque inopinabilis fuit civili bello fortunis fama dignitate spoliatum neminem, cum pie admodum mansueteque geri laetemur exilio proscriptioni atque etiam suppliciis et caedibus modum fieri'. Cf. above, p. 93.

[180] Tacitus treated this subject with great restraint. See R. Syme, *Tacitus*, 189, 343, 388. The Epitomist indulges in even more nauseating detail here than Victor, as does *Exc. Val.* The Christian authors show a preference for the most sensational rendering of the facts. The death of Galerius may serve as an example. *Epit.* 40,4: *consumptis genitalibus*; *Exc. Val.*: Mommsen suggests that *ingenti* should be read as *inguinis* (not in Moreau); Eus. *H.E.*

that his information is drawn from one or more works describing the lives of emperors from the cradle to the grave. No such work is extant, however, and all speculation is therefore fruitless. Of far greater interest is the fact that neither of his contemporaries, Eutropius and Festus, expatiated on these subjects. Their attention was held by other matters, they make a different selection from among the material available. Conversely, it is typical of Victor to incorporate these details. His preoccupation with sickness and death is in keeping with his pessimistic attitude to life and history. His pessimism is not unbounded, though, notably as regards the fate that befalls the good and the bad. Victor is absolutely convinced that evil will eventually be punished and good rewarded, and, being a pagan, he sees justice done on earth and not, as his Christian fellow-Romans believed, in heaven.

The outlook of a civil servant

In imperial histories the most powerful men were each other's mortal enemies. For instance, Caracalla and Geta. The historian takes a moralistic view of these feuds, but he cannot always bring himself to the fine pitch of moral indignation needed to render the account of the murder worth while, by his standards, for future generations. He therefore sometimes employs diversionary tactics. Thus, in the case of the murder of Geta, the reader's attention is is diverted to the murder of Papinian.[181] The historian writes: 'But the sons (Caracalla and Geta) immediately parted company, as if they had been ordered to wage war on one another. Thus it came to pass that Geta, who was named after his paternal grandfather, was attacked and murdered because his gentler nature irritated his brother.[182] Caracalla's victory was rendered even fouler by the murder of Papinian, as students of history [183] claim to know, for they report that at that time he was Caracalla's secretary of State. When he was directed, following the usual custom, to compose as quickly as possible a memorandum which would ensure the support

---

8,13,16 and Oros. VII, 28,12: *Putrescente introrsum pectore visceribus dissolutis.* Cf. J. P. V. D. Balsdon, *Roman Women* (London 1962), 226, note 17. See also below, p. 101 f.

[181] Victor 20, 32-34.

[182] Cf. p. 63. In no way does this account correspond with the description of Caracalla's caracter in 21,2: *patiens communis tranquillusque.*

[183] *memoriae curiosi*, a good term for the pedagogues, who handed down their wisdom from generation to generation.

of Rome, Papinian, in his grief for Geta, said that fratricide is not so easily concealed as committed. These words sealed his fate.' This presentation of the facts is utterly ridiculous: for one thing it is an established fact that Papinian was *praefectus praetorio*; furthermore, Caracalla could never have violated custom and inflicted so grave an affront upon the man who was [Geta's] tutor and close friend.[184]

The *Historia Augusta* clarifies the matter further: Papinian was murdered as an adherent of Geta's; the insult which Victor rejects as unhistorical lies in the fact that Caracalla is supposed to have ordered a *praefectus praetorio* to address a letter explaining the murder to the senate. This letter, which is said to have accused Geta of planning to overthrow his brother, would have effectively screened the fratricide. The accusation was an infamous lie.[185] This ethical consideration, though, is considered irrelevant. What matters to Victor, and to the *vita* based on his work, is that the story is incompatible with the division of duties usual in the civil service. In the words of the *vita* (§ 7), *sed hoc omnino non convenit; nam neque praefectus poterat dictare orationem, et constat eum quasi fautorem Getae occisum.*

It is impossible to trace the source of Victor's information about the duties of any particular civil servant. On the face of it, one would think that, as a civil servant himself, he would be sufficiently familiar with the history of the civil service to know what Papinian was or was not empowered to do. On the other hand, though, the report about the letter drawn up by Papinian may well, in view of the fact that he was *magister libellorum* under Septimius Severus, have had some truth in it.[186]

The above illustrates the punctiliousness of the civil servant. This characteristic, which led to his discovery of an error in the traditional

---

[184] As Casaubonus rightly suggests, one has to see the jurist only as teacher and friend of Geta, not of both.

[185] Cf. *vita Car.* 8,5-7; Victor's text, however, is corrupt, see Reusch, *op. cit.* 53-54. In § 33 *destinare* = to send, cf. 26,6 and 35,9 (*TLL, s.v.* 760, 33 ff.). Cf. 'tarditas in destinandis auctoritatibus', *Cod. Iust.* 1110 (9), 7,2 (TLL, *ibid.* line 52). Cf. also Victor 33,20; 33,28; 40,1; 42,23. The reading *destinando* has little point, *destinanda = destinata.*

[186] *Dig.* XX, 5,12 pr.: *libellos agente Papiniano.* This is why Von Rohden, perhaps correctly, links this phrase with Victor 20,33 (*RE, s.v.* 'Aemilius' 105). Another possible explanation is that the 'ultimate indignity' inflicted on Papinian was his execution by the axe instead of by the sword. For this interpretation see F. Millar, *A Study of Cassius Dio* (Oxford 1964), 152. Clearly, however, Victor did not have this in mind.

version of Papinian's end, presumably helps him to overcome his indignation at the fratricide; for curiously enough, the murder of Didius Julianus is discussed in detail (even though he mixes up Salvius Julianus and Didius Julianus), whereas the murder of Geta is accorded scant attention. This is because, in the first case, there were no inaccuracies in such technical matters as the extent of the powers of civil servants to be rectified, as there were in the second case. Victor's attention is easily diverted from his main subject. As soon as any detail that interests him shows signs of incorrect treatment he is indignant, sometimes even out of all proportion to the moral indignation warranted by the main facts. The moral issue is thus not always his ultimate criterion. In addition to his attention to certain details, he sets great store by a painfully accurate historical record of his milieu. However, to some degree he can take his milieu for granted, which is why we are more greatly struck by the ethical representations interlarding almost every page than by the occasional corrections of details about the civil service woven into his story. Nevertheless, these little touches of punctiliousness are also of historical value.

Generally speaking, most fourth-century civil servants were not very sophisticated,[187] and so we are inclined to over-rate the occasional exceptional instances of culture and erudition. Ammianus Marcellinus is a case in point. He and his circle are always regarded as possessors of a culture greater than was in fact the case.[188] The majority of officers and civil servants were unable to reach even this level. To make too much of stylistic peculiarities recalling the authors of the golden age would be misleading. Certain flourishes of style from Sallust and Tacitus were quoted at school and learnt by heart. They circulated like coins, just as some schoolboys today master an arsenal of quotations—snatches of seasoned wisdom taken from textbooks, and declaimed with spirit by an inspired teacher. No-one reading Victor and the *Epitome* is impressed with any superiority of cultural attainment. Rather, he is struck by the fervour, occasional enthusiasm and constant dedication employed to display the wit and wisdom of the man in the street.

Some years ago, F. Millar,[189] in discussing Cassius Dio, asserted

---

[187] See P.M. Camus, *Ammien Marcellin* (Paris 1967), ch. III, 'La Culture d'un Officier Romain' (51 ff.).

[188] Illuminating comments on this subject in A. D. E. Cameron, 'The Roman Friends of Ammianus', *JRS* 54 (1964), 15-28.

[189] F. Millar, *op. cit.*, 172-173.

that 'The basic stuff of his contemporary history was the general
knowledge of affairs and incidents which any man in public life
would possess'. This statement is entirely correct as regards Cassius
Dio, Aurelius Victor and Eutropius, but there is more to the latter
two abbreviators. To them, not only contemporary history, but
also Roman history as a whole is based on general knowledge. Their
knowledge is superficial, often historically incorrect, full of gaps
and interspersed with anecdotes. The little that has stuck in the
mind is generally but ill-digested to boot. No encouraging perspective to those whose task it is to impart a knowledge of history.

Sickness and death

In the Middle Ages, people's interest in sickness and death, their
fear of an untimely death, of decline and decay, was perhaps greater
than in any earlier period of Western civilization.[190] Pagan antiquity
also took a considerable interest in these matters—as a mere glance
at Seneca will show. The later historians in antiquity shared this
interest, albeit to varying degrees. The difference between Christian
and non-Christian authors is particularly clear there where their
subject-matter coincides. Nowhere are the brevity of human life
and the contrast between wealth on earth and poverty in the grave
more evident than in the lives of sovereigns, and both groups of
authors were exercised by these points. The intensity of their preoccupation, one might almost say, their morbid absorption in the
subject, is nowhere so profound as in the accounts of Christianity
triumphant, which describe the death-struggle of the enemies of
the true faith with indecent gusto. The persecutions must indeed
have been merciless to give rise to such hatred.

Lactantius furnishes an excellent example of this hatred in his
description of Galerius' horrible disease in *De mortibus persecutorum*.
One can understand the aversion of J. Burckhardt who observed,
'Wir wollen den Lactantius in den von Würmern zerfressenen Unter-
leib nach Herzenlust wühlen lassen'.[191] And Lactantius is not even

---

[190] J. Huizinga, *Herfsttij der middeleeuwen* (The Waning of the Middle
Ages), *passim*.

[191] J. Burckhardt, *Die Zeit Constantins des Grossen*, **229**. Cf. J. Moreau's
Commentary, *Lactance, De la mort des persécuteurs* II (n.d.), **385**; Lact.
De mort. persec., **33**. In the following, the question of the authorship of
De mort. persec. is not touched upon. The fact that I follow scholars who
traditionally refer to 'Lactantius' does not mean that I agree with Moreau
(who considers the work to be authentic).

the chief offender. A comparison with Eusebius [192] shows that the
victors vie with one another in including revolting details. It is
significant that two excellent scholars, who wrote on Lactantius
Eusebius respectively, each feel impelled to defend the object of
their study.[193]

Be that as it may, the pagan authors possess a sobriety that
contrasts greatly with the discursiveness of some of the Christian
authors. Between the two extremes we have the *Anonymus
Valesianus* and Orosius.[194] Many believe that the *Anonymus* was
a pagan, and that those passages which correspond word for word
to Orosius (5,20; 29; 6,33; 34) are Christian additions of a later
date. It would seem legitimate to doubt this interpretation since
the passage concerned with Galerius' illness in An. Val. sounds
Christian, though moderate in tone. Orosius is also moderate, but
the differences are too great to warrant the assumption that An. Val.
based his account on Orosius.

An. Val. 3,8: '... morbo ingenti occupatus sic distabuit, ut aperto
et putrescenti viscere moreretur in supplicium persecutionis
iniquissimae, ad auctorem scelerati praecepti iustissima poena
redeunte'.[195]

Orosius 7, 28, 12-13: 'Cumque persecutionem a Diocletiano et
Maximiano missam ipse atrocioribus edictis adcumulavisset ac

---

[192] *H.E.* VIII 16. Cf. R. Laqueur, *Eusebius als Historiker seiner Zeit*,
Arbeiten zur Kirchengeschichte 11 (Berlin and Leipzig, 1929), 92. E. Keller,
Eusèbe, historien des persécutions (Genève 1912).

[193] Moreau, *op. cit.*, 385: 'Comparé a ces versions (Eus. *H.E.* 8, 16,5;
Rufin, 8,16,5, cf. Zonaras 12,34) le récit de Lactance, malgré son ton haineux
et la joie qui éclate dans la description des supplices de l'impie ... est le
plus sobre et le plus encombré de détails légendaires'. J. Sirinelli, *Les vues
historiques d'Eusèbe de Césarée durant la période prénicéenne* (Dakar 1961),
438: 'Eusèbe décrit complaisamment les souffrances de Galère, mais c'est,
comme le preuve l'enchaînement du récit, pour justifier un si total répentir
et une pareille volte-face, pour rendre compte d'une révélation intérieure
assez inattendue, plutôt que pour mettre en évidence la rigueur du châti-
ment. En somme, c'est à la force de la Providence et non à sa sévérité justi-
cière qu'il veut conclure; et ceci est d'autant plus notable que le réalisme
de la description se serait fort bien accommodé d'une remarque sur les
terribles vengeances du Dieu de colère'.

[194] An. Val. 3,8; Orosius 7,28,12-13.

[195] Lact. *De mort. persec.* takes a similar view: 'Sic omnes impii vero et
iusto iudicio Dei eadem quae fecerant, receperunt' (50,8). Once again, no
sources can be indicated, see Moreau, *op. cit.*, I, 43. At most one could speak
of a certain similarity to biblical accounts: Ex. 9,15; Job 2,7; Acts 12,23
(Herod).

postquam per annos decem omni genere hominum exhausit provincias, putrefacto introrsum pectore et vitalibus dissolutis, cum ultra horrorem humanae miseriae etiam vermes eructaret neque medici ultra iam foetorem ferentes crebro iussu eius occiderentur: a quodam medico constantiam ex desperatione sumente increpitus, iram Dei esse poenam suam atque ideo a medicis non posse curari, edictis late missis Christianos de exiliis revocavit. ipse autem cruciatus non sustinens vim vitae suae adtulit'.

The *testimonia* of undisputed pagan origin, notably Aurelius Victor, Eutropius and the *Epitome* are different, more restrained, in atmosphere, more restrained even than that of An. Val.

Vict. 40,9:	Eutr. X 4,1:	*Epit.* 40,4:
Vulnere pestilenti consumptus est.	Mors Galeri confestim secuta.	Consumptis genitalibus defecit.

Eutropius does not even mention the illness, no doubt because of his high esteem for this *vir et probe moratus et egregius re militari*.[196] His attitude, especially as expressed in the first words, is in striking conflict with the Christian view, which has come to dominate the present picture of history to a considerable degree.[197] Eutropius' opinion of Galerius moreover confirms the impression left by his description of other emperors, that he is relatively impersonal. Victor, being a moralist, set an example that might well have been followed by Christian authors. Yet they never did. Nor was he influenced by earlier Christian moralists, such as Eusebius or Lactantius. His values are altogether different from theirs.

Nevertheless, the new moral orientation hardly affected the position of the pagan authors. Emperors approached pagans, not Christians, for *breviaria*. And they complied, though their writings were subdued in tone, and they refused to pander to the tastes in vogue at court and in the Church. The reputation enjoyed by Eutropius is most surprising. He mentions Christianity but once, in criticizing Julian,[198] and otherwise disregards the new religion entirely. He even fails to mention Constantine's 'conversion'.[199]

---

[196] X, 2,1.

[197] See for instance *RE*, *s.v.* 'Maximianus Galerius' (Ensslin).

[198] X 16,3. Cf. chapter IV, p. 167.

[199] This is certainly not for 'lack of ideas', as R. Pichon suggests, *Histoire de la littérature latine*, (Paris 1930[12]), 788.

Finally we may observe that on the whole the anonymous author of the *Epitome* devotes more attention to sickness and death than does Victor. In a number of cases, however, and they are striking enough, Victor is more detailed and more dramatic than the Epitomist.

Concerning the deaths of Caligula, Galba, Titus, and Geta, Victor writes in greater detail than the Epitomist, but the latter is more explicit on the deaths of all the other emperors, up to and including the Severi. After that the situation is again reversed, and the deaths of Gallienus, Claudius II, Tacitus, Probus, Carus and Numerian are more fully chronicled by Victor. The same applies to Maximinus Daia, Licinius and Constantine.

The total number of deaths referred to in the *Epitome* is considerably larger than that in Victor's works. The latter relates the decease of forty-eight emperors, the *Epitome* of sixty (before Jovian), while most of the descriptions in the *Epitome* are more detailed and gorier than Victor's. Moreover, Victor omits the period ending with Theodosius, from which the *Epitome* derived a further six cases. The greater interest in these particulars displayed by the Epitomist is the more noticeable as his reports are generally more concise than Victor's. A case in point is the death of Caligula, which Victor recounts at greater length. In the *Epitome*, however, the entire history of this emperor is extremely short, so that, brief as the description of his death is, it is still relatively longer than Victor's, forming one quarter of the total. Their reports on the death of the emperor Nero are roughly equal in length, though the *Epitome* is again relatively more extensive because the biography itself is shorter.

A comparison of their reports is advisable, but not without first referring to some of the conclusions long since drawn by Wölfflin: (1) as regard the period up to Domitian, the *Epitome* is markedly dependent on Victor (chapters 1-11), except that its Suetonic *flosculi* are not to be found in Victor; (2) on the whole the *Epitome* is influenced by Suetonius rather than by Tacitus, whereas the reverse is true of Victor.[200] Wölfflin is wrong, however, in his general conclusion that, inspired as he is by Tacitus, Victor's work is annalistic in structure, while that of the Epitomist, who follows in the footsteps of Suetonius, is biographical. On the contrary, the pre-

---

[200] E. Wölfflin, 'Zur Latinität der Epitome Caesarum', *ALL* 12 (1902), 445 ff.

occupation of both authors with the circumstances surrounding
the death of an emperor is rooted in biographical interest. Besides,
the chronological presentation of the Annals is lacking in Victor's
work. It is perfectly true that Victor tries to imitate [201] the style
of Tacitus throughout, and not only in chapters 1-11, but this does
not affect his own chronological division of Roman history.

Whenever Victor is not brief, he has something particular to
say.[202] He devotes much space to Caligula, because senate and
civilians were subject to the whims of the emperor and because then,
for the first time, imperial power degenerated to dictatorship.[203]
No wonder that the righteous combined forces—though in vain.[204]

Galba appears at a crucial moment in the course of history;[205] a
man of high rank, but fearsome in his work: *rapere, trahere, vexare ad
foedum in modum vastare cuncta et polluere*.[206] Indirectly the influence of the soldiers is already noticeable—cutting down their
pay was to be Galba's undoing.

Titus was poisoned, but in the *Epitome* he died of a fever: its
author relies heavily on Suetonius. Victor devotes twenty lines,
the *Epitome* fifty, to the life of this emperor.[207]

Whereas the *Epitome* makes much of scandals,[208] including
those of a later period of history for which he could not consult
Suetonius,[209] Victor is more austere despite the fact that he is

---

[201] E. Wölfflin, 'Aurelius Victor', *RhM* 29 (1874), 282-308, esp. 302 ff.

[202] In the following, the point is not whether Victor is historically accurate,
nor to what extent, but to find an explanation for the fact that he enlarges
upon the death of some emperors and not of others.

[203] 3,9: 'cum senatus atque optimi cuiusque multiplici clade terrarum orbis
foedaretur'. 3,20: 'Ita Romae regia potestas firmata proditumque apertius
mortalium conatus vacuos a fortuna cassosque esse.'

[204] 3,13-14: 'His elatus dominum dici atque insigne regni nectere capiti
tentaverat. Qua causa auctore Chaerea moti, quibus Romana virtus inerat,
tanta pernicie remplublicam confosso eo levare'.

[205] 5,17, i.e. Victor's break after the Julio-Claudian period. Cf. p. 29, above.

[206] 6,1.

[207] *De Caes.* 10,5,6; *Epit.* 10,15.

[208] For which reason, many consider his source to be Marius Maximus,
whose anecdotes certainly pleased a public delighting in scandal. Ammianus
Marcellinus thoroughly disliked him.

[209] The most striking example is Hadrian: *De Caes.* 14,12, in contrast
with the dramatic story in *Epit.* 14, 9 and 12. 'Hic morbo subcutaneo,
quem diu placide pertulerat, victus, dolore ardens impatiensque plures e
senatu exstinxit . . . dehinc miserabili exitu consumptus est, cruciatu membrorum fere omnium confectus, in tantum, ut crebro sese interficiendum
ministrorum fidissimis precans offerret, ac ne in semetipsum saeviret, custodia
carissimorum servaretur'.

sometimes more communicative on the subject of the Severi. Both
authors include the story of Julia Domna, the *noverca* with whom
Caracalla fell in love, but Victor writes at greater length,[210] as
indeed he also does about the murder of Geta and Papinian's
attitude towards the imperial murderer.[211] The *Epitome* does not
display the same interest in *bonae litterae*, nor for the social position
of a *praefectus praetorio*. What does interest the Epitomist is
the consequences of the wicked deed: how Caracalla was tormented by guilt and persecuted by the Dirae.[212] Victor does not get
involved in metaphysics. Nor does he tell us that Caracalla was
murdered by a soldier.[213] Instead of all this, he prefers to expatiate
on the morals of the Severi who, like himself, came from Africa.
His account of Heliogabalus also lacks the dramatic detail of the
Epitome.[214] Victor's reasoning, that Alexander Severus' harshness
cost him his life, contrasts with the theatrical version of the course
of events in the *Epitome*, later followed by the *vita*.[215]

In Victor's narrative, the end of the Severi marks the beginning
of a new period.[216] The first emperor to be dealt with subsequently
is Gordian I.[217] Victor's treatment of him is more detailed than that
of the *Epitome*, and this may be related to the break in 24,9. It is more
likely, however, that he wished thus to emphasize the death of a
ruler who attempted to restore the principle of hereditary succession.[218] The same motive may have prompted him to mention
the Decii and the guilt of the soldiers,[219] and to stress the death of
the last son, Hostilian,[220] who died of the plague.

---

[210] *De Caes.* 21,3; *Epit.* 21,5.

[211] *De Caes.* 20,32-34.

[212] *Epit.* 21,3: 'Hic fratrem suum Getam peremit; ob quam causam furore
poenas dedit Dirarum insectatione, quae non immerito ultrices vocantur;
a quo post furore convaluit'.

[213] *Epit.* 21,6: 'apud Edessam secedens ad officia naturalia a milite, qui
quasi ad custodiam sequebatur, interfectus est'. See also Cass. Dio 78,5,2;
Herodian 4,13,4. W. Reusch, *op. cit.*, 50 ff.

[214] *De Caes.* 23,3; *Epit.* 23,5-7.

[215] *De Caes.* 24,3,4,7; *Epit.* 24,4; *vita Alex.* 62.

[216] *De Caes.* 24,9.

[217] The death of Maximinus only in *Epit.* 25,2.

[218] *De Caes.* 26,4; cf. 27,1.

[219] *De Caes.* 29,4-5; *Epit.* 29,3-4 (shorter).

[220] *De Caes.* 30,2. C. Valens Hostilianus Messius Quintus, son of emperor
Decius, *RE, s.v.* 'Messius' (11), col. 1285 (cf. 1273 f.). See also *RE, s.v.*
'Hostilianus', col. 2501 (Stein). Victor is well informed: the senate, for which
Victor had much respect, had recognized Hostilianus as Augustus when his
father and his elder half-brother had fallen. Hostilianus and Gallus were

His account of Gallienus' death is comprehensive.[221] It records a senatorial tradition in such a way as to enable us to reconstruct the official phraseology of a *damnatio memoriae*.[222] Whatever one may think of this emperor and however one may qualify the criticisms levelled against him,[223] the fact remains that the *ordo senatorius* regarded Gallienus as one of its greatest enemies. Victor is its spokesman and thus hands down an age-old heritage.[224]

On the subject of the emperor Tacitus, Victor again writes at greater length than the Epitomist, though the fever which the latter states as the cause of the emperor's death is not to be found in Victor's work. He was appointed emperor by the senate.[225] Good times unfortunately soon came to an end: after his violent death, Florian *nullo senatus seu militum consulto imperium invaserat*.[226] Senate and soldiers, apparent coequals in establishing imperial legitimacy, are by no means equal in importance. It was the soldiers who put Probus on the throne and it was they who killed him.[227] The Epitomist is not disturbed by the dangers threatening the senate, and the ascendancy of the soldiers causes him no uneasiness. He does remember one detail: 'in turri ferrata occiditur'.[228] Victor places the murder, shorn of this particular detail, in a broader context. He sees the murder of Probus as the final confirmation of his suspicions as to whose power will, in future, rule the empire: that of the army.[229]

Augusti, the son of the latter, Volusianus, was Caesar. Eutropius made the three men into two. IX 5: 'Mox imperatores creati sunt Gallus Hostilianus et Galli filius Volusianus. Sub his Aemilianus in Moesia res novas molitus est; ad quem opprimendum cum *ambo* profecti essent . . .' *Epit.* 30; 'Horum (i.e. Galli et Volusiani) temporibus Hostilianus Perpenna a senatu imperator creatus'.

In modern research the 'source' inevitable enters the picture: 'Unmittelbar aus der verlorengegangenen Kaisergeschichte geschöpft', RE, *s.v.* 'Messius', col. 1273 (cf. Hohl, *Klio* xi, 208,224). Evidence for this, however, is lacking.

[221] *De Caes.* 33,19-21, 28,31.

[222] *De Caes.* 33,31: 'Terram matrem, deos quoque inferos precaretur (vulgus) sedes impias uti Gallieno darent'.

[223] See above, p. 75 ff.

[224] For the exact wording of the formula and its interpretation, see A. Dieterich, *Mutter Erde*, 77-78. See also above, p. 86, n. 137.

[225] *De Caes.* 36,1-2; *Epit.* 36,1.

[226] *De Caes.* 36,2.

[227] *De Caes.* 37,2 and 4.

[228] *Epit.* 37,4.

[229] *De Caes.* 37,5: 'Abhinc militaris potentia convaluit ac senatui imperium creandique ius principis ereptum ad nostram memoriam'.

Earlier on, both had made virtually the same observations apropos of the death of Aurelian. The circumstances attendant upon his death were apparently particularly well-known: Eutropius before them had described it and the *Epitome* followed him literally.[230] According to Victor, Carus was a man who committed hubris and overstepped the limits set to man; both the *Epitome* and Eutropius are very brief.

Numerian [231] receives far more dramatic treatment at the hands of Victor than at those of the Epitomist. This emperor's death marked the close of the period of steady decline preceding Diocletian's accession. The sickening details of his end are somehow symbolic. Numerian is murdered by his father-in-law, Aper, and the corpse is hidden as long as possible. 'Sed postquam odore tabescentium membrorum scelus proditum est, ducum consilio tribunorumque Valerius Diocletianus [232] ... deligitur.' Even Eutropius, who deals with the subject of imperial deaths with great restraint, makes an exception for Numerian.[233] For him, too, the tragic history of the last unfortunate emperors culminates in the rule of Diocletian: *Cum Carum Augustum fulmine, Numerianum Caesarem insidiis perdidisset, Diocletianum imperatorum creavit.*[234] Another blow for Eutropius the senator. He no longer felt any desire to mention the *acclamatio* of the senate: if it had survived at all, it had lost the solemnity of the true investiture of an emperor. As so often when the senate's influence was curtailed, Eutropius prefers not to mention it. Victor is more circumstantial and emphasizes Diocletian's status as absolute monarch: *se primus omnium Caligulam post Domitianumque dominum palam dici passus et adorari se appellarique uti deum.*[235]

Finally, in describing the death of Maximinus Daia, Licinius and Constantine the Great, the abbreviators display a number of striking differences.

---

[230] *Eutr.* IX 15,2; *Epit* 35,6; *Zosim.* 1,62. On the other hand, the *Epit.* gives two further details about Aurelian which are not to be found in Victor. Firstly, his encouragement of the consumption of pork (35,7), and a rare confirmation of the fact that the emperor signed official documents in person (37,8, see F. Millar, *JRS* 57 [1967], 12).

[231] *De Caes.* 38,3-4; *Epit.* 38,2 (Carus); *De Caes.* 38,6-8; 39,1; *Epit.* 38,3-5 (Numerian).

[232] Admittedly Victor mentions the death of Carinus, as does the *Epit.*, but Victor does so in connection with Diocletian; here the *Epit.* is more detailed (*De Caes.* 39,11-12; *Epit.* 38, 7-8).

[233] Eutr. IX 18,2.

[234] Eutr. IX 19,2.

[235] *De Caes.* 39,4.

De Caes. 41,1: *Maximinus ad Orientem post biennii augustum imperium* fusus fugatusque *a Licinio apud Tarsum perit.*

Epit. 40,8: *Maximinus apud Tarsum* morte simplici *periit.*

Victor is restrained on the death of Licinius, the Epitomist less
so.[236] In the case of Constantine, their accounts differ though they
are of roughly equal length.[237] They evidently drew their information from different traditional, though not necessarily written,
sources.

The most lasting impression of the pagan authors is their restraint.
This comes to the fore most clearly in the descriptions of the death
of those emperors who have gone down in history as enemies of
Christianity. Their accounts are far removed from the complacency
of the detailed descriptions given by Lactantius and Eusebius. Even
the emperors whose policy threatened the existence of the senate
are not discussed according to the Christian pattern: nowhere is
their violent death considered a punishment of the gods. The
doubtful connection between (political) crimes and a violent death
is nowhere suggested. The pagan historians merely established
matter-of-factly that the political and military game was hazardous
and that the price to be paid for defeat or the displeasure of the
soldiers was death.

The description of the outbreak of plague that occurred during
the reign of Marcus Aurelius offers convincing proof of the two
attitudes.[238] The pagan literature contains numerous references to
this calamity, but none that regard the plague as a form of divine
punishment. Orosius, however, does not scruple to connect the
persecution of Christians in Asia and Gaul with the plague sent by
the avenging hand of God.[239]

THE CONNECTION BETWEEN VICTOR'S *de Caes.* AND THE *Epitome*

In the above passages we have already established that, in their
attitude towards the sickness and death of emperors, the two works
have little in common. This may serve to illustrate the general un-

---

[236] *De Caes.* 41,8-9; *Epit.* 41,7-8; An. Val. 5,29; Oros. 7,28,20-21.

[237] *De Caes.* 41,16: 'excessit, cum id tetrum sidus regnis, quod crinitum
vocant, portendisset'. *Epit.* 41,15-16.

[238] Eutr. VII 12,2; Amm. Marc. 23,6,24; *Vita L. Veri* 8, 1-3; *Vita Marc.*
13,3-6; 17,2; 28,4. Cass. Dio 72, 14,3-4; Herodian 1,12,1-2 (about the new
outbreak under Commodus); Oros. 7,15,5.

[239] For the ordering of the material incorporated in this paragraph I
am grateful to Mrs. L. C. Verhorst-Grützner.

certainty as to the question whether Aurelius Victor and the Epitomist are connected and, if so, how.[240] This problem is, in fact, insoluble, although a number of relevant factors are known. The first eleven chapters are in many ways similar to Suetonius, which is not surprising in itself. Books VIII and IX of Eutropius contain numerous passages which have been copied verbatim by the Epitomist.[241] As for Ammianus Marcellinus, of the two passages constantly cited as indicating derivation, the fist is highly uncertain, the second is of the anecdotal type and may have been handed down in the usual manner *via* school, office, or camp-fire.[242] Nevertheless, we cannot be sure either way, so that the relationship between the two works remains nebulous.

One thing is certain:[243] the *Caesares* and the *Epitome* are entirely dissimilar works, which were both fortuitously ascribed to Aurelius Victor. Scholars have long since agreed that they were penned by two authors, but no consensus of opinion is possible in other respects. Vague suggestions to the effect that Victor is Tacitean, whereas the *Epitome* tends to follow Suetonius, do not help us materially.

None of all this need surprise us: it merely confirms a conclusion that we already know to be inevitable, The compilers of abridged Roman histories relied chiefly on oral traditions and their own memories, Their idiosyncratic approach to the vast heritage of traditional stories led each to go his own erratic way, now following a written source, then remembering a story told when he was a child; and subsequently each author would incorporate individual experiences gained in the course of his career. There is very little point in attempting to discover any consistency in their methods.

In only one instance are we on firmer ground: the case of Nerva. The *Epitome* is noticeably discursive on the subject, whereas Victor devotes no more than a few lines to him. We venture to account for this disparity as follows.

---

[240] M. Schanz, *Geschichte der römischen Litteratur* IV² (Munich 1914), 75, does not give a very clear picture of the state of research at the beginning of this century. This is not his fault, but that of the scholars of the time. We have learned little more since then.

[241] In the Pichlmayr-Gruendel edition, *Sextus Aurelius Victor de Caesaribus*, (1966), nearly all the parallel texts are indicated.

[242] Amm. Marc. 16,12,63; 30,7,2. It has been suggested that these passages are linked with *Epit*. 42,14 (though the connection is uncertain) and 45,2.

[243] Wölfflin, *RhM* 29 (1874), 282.

As we have seen, Victor introduced a major break between Domitian and Nerva.[244] However, in his *exposé* on Nerva, nothing in the material available to him suggests the break to follow. Only Nerva's excellent choice of a successor is stressed. At this point, the Epitomist takes advantage of the opportunity to throw Victor's division into some relief. His method of doing so is significant. There is no doubt that he expatiates on the subject because it is a convenient introduction to the happier period under the Antonines.[245] The questions foremost in his mind are the legitimacy of the emperor,[246] his dislike of the *delatores* under Domitian, and the new safety, the *alimenta*.[247] These are all undoubted gains, but the shadows are present, too, in the fact that the soldiers sometimes prescribed Nerva's actions. Thus, according to the Epitomist, it was they who determined the emperor's attitude towards Domitian's murderers. There is no trace of optimism in this interpretation of the facts. On the contrary, having established this, the Epitomist could no longer indulge in a long eulogy on Trajan. Perhaps he had less faith in the individual sovereigns than Victor. If so, it would indicate a pessimistic outlook on life and a certain sense of historical realism. It is most unlikely that we shall ever have definite information on his *Weltanschauung*. The above suggestion might nevertheless explain the remarkable length of the chapter the Epitomist devotes to Nerva.

Appendix

Hartke's treatment of the *vitae* of Aurelian and Gallienus (see W. Hartke, *Geschichte und Politik im Spätantiken Rom, Unters. über die Scriptores Historiae Augustae*. Neudruck der Ausgabe 1940, 1962) requires some comment.

(1) Hartke states: 'Im Gegensatz zu dem ... Kapitel 39 der *Aurelian vita* lassen sich die Stücke [18.4 ∼ 21,5.9 =A.V. 35.7; 25.6 ∼ A.V. 35.7 ∼ Eutr. 9,15.1; 32.3.4 ∼ Eutr. 9,13 ∼ A.V. 35,3; 34,5 ∼ Eutr. 9,15.2 (Epit. 35,8) ∼ A.V. 35,8 (36,2); 36,3 und 37,1 = Eutr. 9,14 (= Epit. 35,9) u.a.] aus ihrer Umgebung nicht lösen, sondern sind im Zusammenhang verankert.' (p. 24).

---

[244] For the break, see *de Caes.* 11,12-13; for Nerva, *de Caes.* 12 and *Epit.* 12. Cf. Chapter II, p. 29, above.

[245] See Syme, *Tacitus* II, 628.

[246] 'In curiam a senatu gratanter exceptus est' (12,2).

[247] 12,4.

Let us take a closer look at A.V. **35,7** and Eutr. **9,15.1**, to which the *vita Aureliani* **39** is supposed to correspond so well. These passage discuss the temple to Sol.

Eutr.	Vict.	*vita*
Templum Soli aedificavit in quo infinitum auri gemmarumque constituit.	His tot tantisque prospere gestis fanum Romae Soli magnificum constituit donariis ornans opulentis.	Templum Solis magnificentissimum constituit. (later, § 6) In templo Solis multum auri gemmarumque constituit.

The same information is given in three different ways. The mode of expression does not in any way indicate interdepence. The same applies to the reference to the strengthening of the walls of Rome, which precedes the passage quoted above in Eutropius and follows it in the *vita* and in Victor.

Eutr.	Vict.	*vita*
Urbem Romam muris firmioribus cinxit.	Ne unquam, quae per Gallienum evenerant, acciderent, muris urbem quam validissimis laxiore ambitu circumsaepsit.	Muros urbis Romae sic ampliavit, ut quinquaginta prope milia murorum eius ambitus teneant.

Again the words themselves do not as a matter of course suggest interdependence.

Eutropius subsequently discusses Aurelian's military successes, Victor goes on to describe the 'amnesty law', as does the *vita*, although in different terms. The only possibility of linking the three passages with one another is the fact that sometimes, though not always, the events are mentioned in the same order. This similarity of order is not, however, relevant to our present difference with Hartke. For he creates a distinction between statements which may be isolated from their context and those which may not; his observations are based on this distinction, and he contends that the statements made in chapter 39 can be so isolated, while others may not. The difference is a modern construct, and it does not work, at least not in this case. In both sets of passages compared above, the strongest argument in favour of interrelatedness, of the derivation of the *vita* from Victor and Eutropius, or of all three borrowing from yet a fourth author, is based on the order of presentation of facts. Precisely how all this borrowing was performed remains a mystery. The suggestion that the *vita* in this instance drew on Eutropius and/or Victor is plausible, but the fact that Hartke considers Enmann's hypothesis a proved fact ('Enmann's Unter-suchung ist, was das Grundsätzliche angeht, in den festen Bestand der Wissenschaft übergegangen' [Hartke, 44]) is to rate too highly what is, after all, a false premise.

(2) Hartke tries to separate biographical from chronological sources, thus seeking to create some order in the possibilities of borrowing. His idea in doing so (38 ff.) is to establish that the *Epitome* is more biographical in character, while also con-forming to a chronological order (43), whereas Victor tries to maintain or impose a chronological pattern (usually with little success, and insufficient clarity). This, according to him, changes after Diocletian: the *Epit.* sheds its dependence on Victor and Eutropius, selecting an annalistic source in which 'die Anzeichen biografischer Ordnung auf den Epitomator selbst zurückgehen (47)'. This extremely vague statement is of very little use to us. The hypothesis that Nicomachus' *Annals* constitute the source for the end of the *Epit.* may be disregarded with impunity. The idea of an annalistic source with biographical additions concocted by the author constitutes a hypothesis that may be attractive, but for which absolutely no evidence can be adduced.

CHAPTER FOUR

EUTROPIUS

Eutropius the Man

There are many gaps in our knowledge of Eutropius which will be impossible to fill. Modern scholars tend to identify him with a number of high-ranking officials of the same name who worked between the years 360 and 390. Caution must still, however, be observed. According to his *praefatio*, a dedication to emperor Valens, he was a *magister memoriae*. The dedication gives the emperor the titles Gothicus Maximus, so that 369 or 370 would seem to be the most likely date.

The validity of the identification of the historian with the proconsul of Asia in 371, who bore the same name, is most important.[1] If this official is the same man as the historian,[2] a *terminus ante quem* is set for the *breviarium*. After all, had he already been installed in this post, the author would not have failed to mention the fact in his dedication to the emperor. But some doubt remains as to whether the Eutropius known to have been *Asiam proconsulari tunc obtinens potestate* is the same man as the historian. If we assume this to be the case, many of our uncertainties are removed. We are then in a position to know that the historian was suspected of treason and acquitted, but held no more offices until the accession of Gratian. He then held the office of *praefectus* of Illyricum [3] in 380 and 381, and that of Eastern consul in 387. In that case, he should also be identified with Eutropius the friend of Symmachus, who was among the most successful imperial servants of his time.

Marcellus Empiricus mentions a Eutropius who is sometimes, though without a shred of evidence, identified with the historian. The reference to this man states that 'aliique nonnulli etiam proximo tempore illustres honoribus viri, cives ac maiores nostri, Siburius

---

[1] Ammianus Marcellinus 29,1,36.

[2] See A. Chastagnol in *Rev. Phil.* 41 (1967), 85, in which the older literature is listed. Cf. J. Matthews, 'Continuity in a Roman Family; The Rufii Festi of Volsinii', *Historia* 16 (1967), 484-5; esp. 494-5; M. Hauser-Meury, *Prosopographie zu den Schriften Gregors von Nazianz*, 1960, 80, opposes this view.

[3] A. H. M. Jones, 'Collegiate Prefectures', *JRS* 54 (1964), 78-89; esp. 79, about this particular prefecture; cf. Matthews, *art. cit.*, 495.

Eutropius atque Ausonius' wrote about medical matters; this
Eutropius was a *Burdigalensis,* and lived in the middle of the
fourth century.[4]

It is amazing how easily modern scholars are tempted to draw
far-reaching conclusions from an instance of identical names. One
should realize that there is insufficient support in the sources both
for Seeck's proposed identification of Eutropius with Symmachus'
correspondent,[5] and for that with a nephew and pupil of the rhetor
Acacius of Caesarea. Hence the modern scholar who portrays
Eutropius as in the following quotation oversteps the limits of what
can be justified by reasonable arguments. However, his summary
is sufficiently interesting to merit our attention, since it reflects the
communis opinio of many modern students. 'One of these highly
placed contacts was Eutropius, the historian and medical writer of
Bordeaux. Earlier he had held the proconsulship of Asia, but he
had gone into retirement when he was suspected of involvement in
a plot against the Emperor Valens. He then re-emerged under
Gratian, to take his place with so many of his Aquitanian countrymen at the Court. At some time in this period, Eutropius met
Symmachus at Rome, but soon, after the accession of Theodosius
in early 379, he returned to the East with the new Emperor, and
became prefect of Illyricum in the crucial years of campaigning
380 and 381.'[6] How fortunate it would be if we could accept this
biographical sketch as correct. But it is impossible to be sure. As
far as Eutropius is concerned, we still have little other to go by
than his work—the few scraps of external information carry very
little weight.[7]

[4] Marcellus, *De Medicamentis,* pref. (ed. Helmreich, Teubner 1889,1);
cf. *RE* 6, Col. 1520, 'Eutropius' 3. K. F. Stroheker, *Der senatorische Adel
im spätantiken Gallien* (Tübingen 1948), no. 136 (p. 170), rightly does not
identify this Eutropius with the historian, either.

[5] See O. Seeck, *Die Briefe des Libanius zeitlich geordnet* (Leipzig 1906),
434, 151 ff.; H. F. Bouchery, *Themistius in Libanius' brieven* (Antwerp
1936), 253 ff.

[6] Matthews, *art. cit.,* 494-5; R. Syme, *Ammianus Marcellinus and the
Historia Augusta,* 105, note 3, agrees.

[7] Suda: Εὐτρόπιος, ᾽Ιταλός, σοφιστής, τὴν ῥωμαϊκὴν ἱστορίαν ἐπιτομικῶς τῇ
᾽Ιταλῶν φωνῇ ἔγραψε, καὶ ἄλλα. Georgius Codinus, p. 18, ed. Bonn: Εὐτρόπιος
ὁ σοφιστὴς ὁ τῷ προβάτῃ ᾽Ιουλιανοῦ συμπαρὼν ἐν Περσίδι (cf. Eutr. 10, 16.1)
καὶ ὁ ἐπιστολογράφος [Κωνσταντίνου].

Nikephoros Gregoras: ὁ σοφὸς Εὐτρόπιος, ὃς Οὐάλεντι μὲν σύγχρονος γεγονώς,
῞Ελλην δ᾽ ὢν τὴν θρησκείαν ... μνησθήσομαι ἑνὸς τοὔνομα Εὐτροπίου βραχυλογίᾳ
χρωμένου τῆς θρησκείας ἀκοινώτητον καὶ πρός γε διὰ τὸ ἡλικιώτην ὁμοῦ καὶ
αἱρεσιώτην ᾽Ιουλιανοῦ γεγενῆσθαι.

SOURCES

Eutropius' sources involve the same problems as Eutropius the man. Most of the time we simply do not know where he gets his information. The same uncertainty, moreover, arises when Eutropius is discussed as a source for later historians.[8] There are two passages which require particular attention in discussing Ammianus Marcellinus, for instance, and the extent of his borrowings from Eutropius.

(1) Diocletian's *adoratio* is described by both authors in roughly similar detail.[9] Eutropius says: 'Diligentissimus tamen et sollertissimus princeps et qui imperio invexerit adorarique se iusserit, cum ante eum cuncti salutarentur'.

If we compare this passage with Ammianus, we see that the latter places the statement in an entirely different context. He is concerned not so much with court ceremonial, as with the fact that Ursicinus must submit to it when he appears before Constantius; he goes on to relate the origin of this custom, which was probably known to the entire civil service. The possibilities of handing down certain spectacular facts to succeeding generations are often underestimated. Diocletian's *adoratio* was such a spectacular fact. Ammianus has the following to say: 'Diocletianus enim Augustus omnium primus, externo et regio more instituit adorari, cum semper antea ad similitudinem iudicum salutatos principes legerimus'.

(2) Ammianus' account of Diocletian's attitude towards Galerius, after the latter's defeat by the Persians, is likewise sometimes thought to be derived from Eutropius. However, the facts were familiar enough, and are mentioned by Jerome and Festus besides Ammianus and Eutropius.

---

[8] We agree with W. Seston (*Dioclétien et la tétrarchie*, Paris 1946, 23) when he says, 'Il y a trop de conjecture dans les remarques de quiconque étudia les sources des compilateurs du IVe siècle, et le plus souvent les conclusions de la *Quellenforschung* sont trop absolues'. Comparison of a modern discussion of the sources and the survey given by M. Petschenig in *Bursians Jahresberichte* 72 (1892), 20, shows that nothing has changed in the course of eighty years. This is hardly surprising: research on sources involves too many unknown factors. The student should be prepared to admit that derivations in the *breviaria* are likely to remain highly speculative.

[9] See R. Syme, *op. cit.*, 105, with reference to Eutr. IX 26 and Amm. Marc. 15,5,18.

Hieron. *Chron.* 227 c:

Galerius Maximianus victus a Narseo ante carpentum Diocletiani purpuratus cucurrit

Eutr. IX 24:

pulsus ... tanta insolentia a Diocletiano fertur exceptus, ut per aliquot passuum milia purpuratus tradatur ad vehiculum cucurrisse

Festus 25,1:

pulsus ... tanta a Diocletiano indignatione susceptus est, ut ante carpentum eius per aliquot milia passuum cucurrerit purpuratus

Ammianus 14,11,10:

Augusti vehiculum irascentis per spatium mille passuum fere pedes antegressus est Galerius purpuratus

The main point of the description is that Galerius has to submit to this humiliation wearing full ceremonial dress, *purpuratus*, an emphasis that is characteristic of civil servants, who live in a world of insignia. This, in all likelihood, is the source of the four above passages, all of which stress the word *purpuratus*.[10]

At first sight one tends to link Jerome with Festus on account of the words *ante carpentum*, which they have in common. It would be as incorrect, however, to attach too much importance to this as a mark of 'derivation', as it would be to draw a similar conclusion from use of the word *vehiculum*, which occurs in both Eutropius and Ammianus.

It is significant that Helm, according to whom Jerome used Eutropius as a source on many other occasions, dismisses any connection between Jerome and Festus on this. His reasoning, unfortunately, is weak: he maintains that Jerome did use Eutropius, and that no-one could therefore believe that he also consulted Festus as well. To my mind, the other solution, namely, that Jerome's use of the word *carpentum* is fortuitous, is quite possible. Helm's dismissal of this idea, however, obliges him to assume the existence of a 'source' of which, incidentally, nothing is known. I feel that, in this case, the use of a single word should not be considered decisive. All the stories in circulation at the time mentioned a waggon, i.e. *carpentum* or *vehiculum*. The thread tracing both words to a single written source is somewhat tenuous. And if one persists in one's theory of derivation it seems odd that no-one defends the

---

[10] For legislation on the purple, see *RE* 23 (1959), col. 2013 ff. (K. Schneider).

theory that Jerome derived his rendering directly from Festus.[11] Helm is against this, because he does not expect a man working as hurriedly as Jerome to consult the possible sources thoroughly. This realistic attitude is praiseworthy, but should be taken still further. Considering the situation in civil service circles everywhere and in every age, one should assume that there was a lively oral tradition—certainly as regards facts as well-known as Diocletian's *adoratio* and the humiliation of Galerius.

Galerius' victory in the East was equally well known, and could not but affect all those who desired to write edifying histories. Galerius was, of course, extremely suitable as an example of deed humiliation followed by great honours.[12]

Hieron.:	Eutr.:
Galerius Maximianus superato Narseo et uxoribus ac liberis sororibusque captis a Diocletiano ingenti honore suscipitur	pulso Narseo castra eius diripuit: uxores sorores liberos cepit ... ad Diocletianum ... regressus ingenti honore susceptus est

Festus: superato rege Narseo, uxore eius ac filiabus captis ...

I feel that these passages permit of no definite conclusions as to Jerome's dependence, either on Festus or on Eutropius.

The same futile textual comparison has been applied to the *Epit. de Caes.* One example must suffice,[13] the death of the emperor Julian.

Hieron.:	*Epit.*:
Iulianus in Persas profectus .... a quodam simulato perfuga ad deserta perductus ... ab obvio forte hostium equite conto ilia perfossus.	in Persas proficiscitur ... a transfuga quodam in insidias deductus ... ab uno ex hostibus et quidem fugiente conto percutitur

Festus: ... ab obvio hostium equite conto per ilia ictus.

---

[11] R. Helm, 'Hieronymus und Eutrop', *RhM* 76 (1927): 'Der Ausdruck *ante carpentum* und die stärker die Tatsache betonende Ausdrucksweise stimmt zu Festus; aber niemand wird annehmen wollen, dass H. dazu neben E. auch F. eingesehen habe oder dass er zufällig auf dieselbe Fassung gekommen sei'.

[12] For the following see Hieron. 227 ff; Festus 14,6; Eutr. IX 25,1. Also Jordanes, *Rom.* 301; Oros. VII 25,9; *Chron. min.* I 643.

[13] Hieron. 243b; *Epit.* 43,2. See also Helm, *art. cit.*, 301.

We have here a certain degree of 'correspondence' (Helm), which I propose to analyse. The authors of rhetorical school textbooks took great pains to describe the death of Julian in resounding periods. These were learned by heart and often declaimed at school. The correspondence in the above descriptions is paralleled in Continental history textbooks: 'Philippe le Beau took a cool drink and died.' The only connection this has with the use of any particular source is that at some point a school master expressed the facts in terms that subsequently became popular. The terms presumably used at court and in religious circles to describe the death of Julian were taken over by the Establishment a generation later.

It is so easy to be misled by similarities of expression, even when they correspond word for word. In the following instance the phrasing is identical and the facts are mentioned in the same order, but, even so, there is no reason whatsoever to consider direct derivation. This is the description of the death of Caesar Gallus and the insurrection of Silvanus.[14]

Hieron.:	Eutr.:
Gallus Caesar sollicitatus a Constantio patrueli, cui in suspicionem ob egregiam indolem venerat Histriae occiditur.	Gallus Caesar occisus est, vir natura ferus et ad tyrannidem pronior, si suo iure imperare licuisset.
Silvanus in Gallia res novas molitus XXVIII die occisus est.	Silvanus quoque in Gallia res novas molitus ante diem tricesimum extinctus est.

Even a casual glance at the above shows a number of differences. In the first place, Eutropius does not tell us where Gallus died; secondly, he does not give the exact number of days of Silvanus' reign; and thirdly and, in my opinion, most important, Jerome's opinion of Gallus is decidedly favourable, as opposed to that of Eutropius. Here we have a good example to show how little word-for-word correspondence or the same order of presentation of the facts sometimes helps to establish interdependence. The twenty-eight days are also given by Aurelius Victor (42,16) and the *Epit.* (42,10). There is as little reason to consider derivation here as in the case of Napoleon's hundred days, which no school textbook fails to mention.

---

[14] Hieron. 239cd; Eutr. X 13. See also Helm, *art. cit.*, 300.

Ab uno disce omnes: the many studies of Eutropius' sources are listed by Schanz, among others. They are seldom relevant to an understanding of the author as an individual.[15]

TOPOGRAPHY

Eutropius provides at least one complex of data not found in any other summary of Roman history. He repeatedly mentions the number of milestones (*miliaria*) that indicate the distance to Rome.

Very frequently these details are regarded as derivations from some handbook, which assumption is then used to explain away the phenomenon.[16] Now we know absolutely nothing of the existence of such a handbook, but this, of course, does not necessarily mean that there never was one. However, even if it were true that Eutropius used conveniences of this kind, the question remains why he is the only one to supply these details. The answer is most probably that since at this time the barbarian threat to the peace and security of Rome was increasing, a lively interest developed in other situations and periods in which Rome was threatened, and by enemies much nearer to the City. Eutropius catered to this interest. The following nine passages, all of which are concerned with the history of Rome prior to Hannibal,[17] will illustrate this.

I 8,3 Ita Romae regnatum est per septem reges annis ducentis quadraginta tribus, cum adhuc Roma, ubi plurimum, vix usque ad quintum decimum miliarium possideret.

I 15,2 (Coriolanus) Romanos saepe vicit, usque ad quintum miliarium urbis accessit, oppugnaturus etiam patriam suam.

I 17   Sequenti tamen anno cum in Algido monte ab urbe duodecimo ferme miliario Romanus obsideretur exercitus, L. Quintius Cincinnatus dictator est factus.

I 19   Fidenae sexto, Vei octavo decimo miliario (absunt).

---

[15] M. Schanz, *Geschichte der römischen Literatur*, IV² (1914), 77 ff. Eutropius' significance for later generations need not concern us here. His importance for the SHA has been rightly emphasized once more by W. Schmid, 'Eutropspuren in der Historia Augusta', *Bonner Historia-Augusta Colloquium* 1963 (1964), 123-133. Cf. T. Damsholt, 'Zur Benutzung von dem Breviarium des Eutrop in der Historia Augusta', *Class. et Med.*, 25 (1964), 138-150.

[16] E.g. Schanz, *op. cit.*, 78: 'Angaben über Ortsentfernungen von Rom und chronologische Daten können leicht aus Handbüchern entnommen werden'.

[17] Cf. *Mnem.* 21 (1968), 270.

I 20   Statim Galli Senones ad urbem venerunt et victos Roma-
        nos undecimo miliario a Roma apud flumen Alliam secuti
        etiam urbem occupaverunt.

II 5   T. Quintius dictator adversus Gallos, qui ad Italiam
        venerant, missus est. Hi ab urbe quarto miliario trans
        Anienem fluvium consederant.

II 8   Iam Romani potentes esse coeperunt. Bellum enim in
        centesimo et tricesimo fere miliario ab urbe apud Samnitas
        gerebatur, qui medii sunt inter Picenum, Campaniam et
        Apuliam.

II 12,1 Postea Pyrrus coniunctis sibi Samnitibus, Lucanis, Brittiis
        Romam perrexit, omnia ferro ignique vastavit, Campaniam
        populatus est atque ad Praeneste venit, miliario ab urbe
        octavo decimo.

III 14,1 Decimo anno postquam Hannibal in Italiam venerat,
        P. Sulpicio Cn. Fulvio consulibus Hannibal usque ad quar-
        tum miliarium urbis accessit, equites eius usque ad portam.

As we know, under the kings, Roman territory extended up to
the fifteenth milestone. If we bear this in mind, the importance
of Coriolanus' treachery becomes quite clear: he came up to the
fifth milestone, and was therefore almost as dangerous as the Gauls
and Hannibal, who later pushed as far as the fourth milestone.
When the Cincinnati defended Rome, the enemies first came as
far as the twelfth (the Aequi) and later to the fourth milestone (the
Gauls). Similarly, readers are reminded that Rome was saved on
various occasions by members of one and the same family. The
Quintii set an example for the emperors of the author's own time.
The threats presented by Fidenae and Veii were serious, as their
geographical nearness will confirm. When Rome first became
mistress of Italy, one severe military threat remained within the
peninsula itself: the Samnites.[18] After the Samnite Wars, the power
of Rome extended up to the hundred-and-thirtieth milestone. Even
temporary disasters such as the wars against Pyrrhus could not
overthrow her, even though the king advanced up to the eighteenth
milestone; immediately afterwards, 'terrore exercitus qui eum cum
consule sequebatur, in Campaniam se recepit'.[19] The war against

---

[18] See for these wars E.T. Salmon, *Samnium and the Samnites* (Cambridge
1967), which does not, however, discuss the treatment of the wars against
the Samnites in the later *breviaria* (cf. my review in *BIOR* 27 [1970], 396-397).
[19] II 12,2.

Hannibal ended almost as well. After Cannae, no distance from
Rome is mentioned until eight years later, ten years after the
beginning of the war.[20] By that time the danger had waned somewhat, as the following sentence shows: 'mox consulum cum exercitu
venientium metu Hannibal ad Campaniam se recepit'.[21]

References to the *miliaria* are a striking characteristic of Eutropius' *Breviarium* and not of others, such as that of Festus. There
are a number of reasons for this, for instance, the fact that Festus
had a more restricted task.[22] There is more to it than this, though.
Eutropius first mentions the *miliaria* when he wishes to indicate the
modest extent of Roman territory under the kings.[23] Here speaks
the proud Roman, who knows how powerful Rome eventually
became. Herein, too, lies the point of departure for the discussion
of those periods in which the existence of Rome was threatened.
A description of such dangerous times might arouse a sense of
danger in the mind of both writer and reader of the *Breviarium*.
Eutropius projects the tensions of his own time onto the earlier
history of Rome, and even onto the time of the kings. Topographical
indications by means of *miliaria* in historiography can not, of
course, have antedated the use of these stones in road construction.
The oldest surviving milestone dates from the first Punic War,[24]
while the first reference to such stones in historical literature is to
be found in Polybius (III, 39,8) in his account of the construction
of the via domitia by Cn. Domitius Ahenobarbus in 118 B.C.[25]
Nevertheless, this does not mean that Eutropius introduces an
anachronism in order to give an historially ignorant public a certain
impression of the past. After all, this, the presentation of a certain
point of view, became the objective of historians such as Livy, and
of Florus with Justin in his wake.[26] Increased activity in the field

----

[20] III 14,1. In fact, eight years. The year in question is 211 B.C., *P.
Sulpicio Cn. Fulvio consulibus*.

[21] Contradicted by the defeat of Cn. Fulvius, which the author does not
fail to mention; cf. Liv. 26, 9-11.

[22] See below, p. 173 ff.

[23] I 8,3: *adhuc ... usque ad quintum decimum miliarium possideret*.

[24] See Kroll, *s.v.* 'miliarium', *RE*, Suppl. VI, Col. 399. The stone was
erected by the aediles P. Claudius Pulcher and C. Furius Paulus, presumably
in 253 B.C. (see Broughton, *Magistrates* I, 211). *ILS* 5801.

[25] F. W. Walbank, *Commentary on Polybius* I (1957), *ad. loc.*; Kroll
(*loc. cit.*), Col. 400, line 46 ff.

[26] E.g. the anachronisms in Livy II 11,17; III 6,7; 69,8; V 4,12; Florus I
22,44; Justin XXII, 6,9.

of road construction probably stimulated their use, as did the erection of the *miliarium aureum* [27] by Augustus in 29 B.C. From Augustus onwards the use of *miliaria* became widespread, distances were usually indicated in 'miles', notably for the main roads running through the Empire. The custom thus developed of reckoning distances almost exclusively according to the number of milestones: *ad lapidem primum, secundum,* etc.[28]

This clear and useful retrospective method of indicating distances did not always have the same connotations. When Livy mentions distances from Rome, he usually has a straightforward piece of information to impart which very rarely directly concerns Rome herself. He merely wishes to give a relative indication of the distance between places A and B, which are so many *miliaria* apart. Eutropius, however, in discussing barbarians or rebellious citizens [29] threatening the city, almost always mentions their distance from Rome. Florus before him also did so with some emotion: 'Quid ergo miramur moventi castra a tertio lapide Hannibali iterum ipsos deos—deos inquam, nec fateri pudebit—restitisse?' Although this emotion also occurs in Livy, it is exceptional.[30]

We did Eutropius no injustice when we said that he projects the tensions of his own time (in 369 Valens defeated the Goths) onto an earlier period in the history of Rome, in this case the time of the kings. His contemporary, Aurelius Victor, is not free from such fears either. Their study of the history of the past century had taught these officials to recognize the dangers constantly threatening the Danubian and far Eastern borders of the Empire. Victor refers to a *commune Romani malum orbis*, a wide-spread evil, threatening the Roman world.[31] Their own career must also have awakened these two civil servants to the fear that a catastrophe might take place. Indeed, they did not have to wait for the battle at Adrianople, where Valens fell, for the temporary nature of apparently permanent

---

[27] *Miliarium aureum*, see *RE*, Suppl. IV, Col. 499.

[28] The only exceptions, which are not, however, of importance in this case, are VIII 8, 4 and IX 2,3.

[29] Useful information in D.S., *Dict. des ant., s.v.* 'Miliarium'. Cf. Varro, *RR.* III 2; Plin. *NH.* 23,159; Quintil. IV 5,22; Plin. *Epist.* X 24; Tac. *Ann.* XV, 60; *Hist.* II 24, 45; IV 11; Amm. Marc. XIX 8.5; XXXI 3,5; and elsewhere.

[30] E.g. V 4,12: *intra vicesimum lapidem in conspectu prope urbis nostrae . . .*

[31] *De Caes.* 33,33. In this connection see C. G. Starr, *art. cit.*, 585, on the third century: 'an era in which the Mediterranean world was rent by internal war and grounded by invasions from without'.

political and military institutions such as the Roman Empire to be brought home to them.

In discussing this matter I should like to present the question of *Quellenforschung* in an entirely new light. It must have been evident to writers in the third century, whose writings have not survived, that the very existence of Rome was, to say the least, assailable. Indeed, this must have become clear to many when Valerian was taken prisoner by the Persians. Now if writers like Eutropius were familiar with these older writings, as we may assume with some confidence, it is to be expected that something of the third-century mentality, of its insecurity, doubts and disquiet, coloured their own work. It is curious, to say the least, that for more than a century scholars have been diligent in attempting to trace verbal derivation from writings that are no longer extant, whereas derivation of moods, which is plausible enough where the events in question are sensational, is ignored. Then as now, man had the ingrained habit of comparing the present to the past. This common human tendency alone is enough to lead us to expect derivation of moods. In the second century A.D., Florus' history quotes distances that come very close to Eutropius' alarming reports.[32] This work, written two centuries earlier, had become a standard textbook in the course of time, which suggests yet another possible influence: the rhetorical stories taught at school. These had perhaps as important an effect as the authors' personal experiences in the imperial service, or comparisons with whatever dreadful events had taken place a century earlier. Reading, personal experience, and the desire to find a reflection of the past in the present are three of the factors that influenced Eutropius in writing as he did.[33]

CHRONOLOGY

The chronology in Eutropius' *Breviarum* is not entirely consistent, but it is practical. It is also entirely conventional.

To start with I shall give a list of the various dating methods used. (A): Triple datings, dates calculated from or for the time of the kings; (B): Double datings based on the consular years and a.u.c.; (C): A.u.c. datings (the relatively large number of datings

---

[32] Florus I 22,44.

[33] Only then can one proceed to ask whence he derived his topographical indications. Schanz' theory that they were taken from a 'handbook' seems acceptable. See above, note 16.

based exclusively on the years of consuls are not included); (E):
Three passages in (C), indicated by an asterisk, which will be discussed separately; (D): Datings according to the month calendar,
and one synchronism (with Alexander the Great); these will also
be discussed separately.

A.

I 1,2   Is (Romulus) cum inter pastores latrocinaretur, decem
          et octo annos natus urbem exiguam in Palatino monte
          constituit, XI Kal. Maias, Olympiadis sextae anno
          tertio, post Troiae excidium, ut qui plurimum mini-
          mumque tradunt, anno trecentesimo nonagesimo
          quarto.

IV 10,1   Tertium deinde bellum contra Carthaginem suscipitur,
          sexcentesimo et altero ab urbe condita anno, L. Manlio
          Censorino et M. Manilio consulibus, anno quinqua-
          gesimo primo postquam secundum Punicum trans-
          actum erat.

I 11,1   Secundo quoque anno iterum Tarquinius ut recipere-
          retur in regnum bellum Romanis intulit, auxilium ei
          ferente Porsenna, Tusciae rege, et Romam paene
          cepit. Verum tum quoque victus est.

I 11,2   Tertio anno post reges exactos Tarquinius cum suscipi
          non posset in regnum neque ei Porsenna, qui pacem
          cum Romanis fecerat, praestaret auxilium, Tusculum
          se contulit, quae civitas non longe ab urbe est, atque
          ibi per quattuordecim annos privatus cum uxore
          consenuit.

I 15,1   Octavo decimo anno postquam reges eiecti erant
          expulsus ex urbe Q. Marcius, dux Romanus, qui Co-
          riolos ceperat, Volscorum civitatem, ad ipsos Volscos
          contendit iratus et auxilia contra Romanos accepit.

B.

II 15   C. Fabio Licino C. Claudio Canina consulibus anno
          urbis conditae quadringentesimo sexagesimo primo
          legati Alexandrini a Ptolomaeo missi Romam venere
          et a Romanis amicitiam, quam petierant, obtinuerunt.

X 18,3   Is status erat Romanae rei Ioviano eodem et Var-

roniano consulibus anno urbis conditae millesimo centesimo et octavo decimo.

IV 22,1   Anno sexcentesimo vicesimo septimo ab urbe condita
C. Cassius Longinus et Sex. Domitius Calvinus consules Gallis transalpinis bellum intulerunt.

IV 23,1   M. Porcio Catone et Q. Marcio Rege consulibus sexcentesimo tricesimo et tertio anno ab urbe condita
Narbone in Gallia colonia deducta est.

VI 6,1   Anno urbis conditae sexcentesimo septuagesimo sexto
L. Licinio Lucullo et M. Aurelio Cotta consulibus
mortuus est Nicomedes, rex Bithyniae, et per testa-
mentum populum Romanum fecit heredem. Mithridates pace rupta Bithyniam et Asiam rursus voluit
invadere.

VI· 8,1   Sexcentesimo octogesimo primo anno urbis conditae,
P. Cornelio Lentulo et Cn. Aufidio Oreste consulibus
duo tantum gravia bella in imperio Romano erant,
Mithridaticum et Macedonicum.

VI 15   M. Tullio Cicerone oratore et C. Antonio consulibus,
anno ab urbe condita sexcentesimo octogesimo nono,
L. Sergius Catilina, nobilissimi generis vir, sed ingenii
pravissimi, ad delendam patriam coniuravit cum qui-
busdam claris quidem, sed audacibus viris.

VI 16   Sexcentesimo nonagesimo anno urbis conditae D. Iunio
Silano et L. Murena consulibus Metellus de Creta
triumphavit, Pompeius de bello piratico et Mithri-
datico. Nulla umquam pompa triumphi similis fuit.
Ducti sunt ante eius currum filii Mithridatis, filius
Tigranis et Aristobulus, rex Iudaeorum; praelata est
ingens pecunia et auri atque argenti infinitum. Hoc
tempore nullum per orbem terrarum grave bellum
erat.

VIII 1,1   Anno octingentesimo et quinquagesimo ab urbe
condita, Vetere et Valente consulibus res publica ad
prosperrimum statum rediit bonis principibus ingenti
felicitate commissa. Domitiano enim, exitiabili tyran-
no, Nerva successit.

C.

X 17,2   Annis mille centum et duobus de viginti fere, ex quo Romanum imperium conditum erat.

*   V 4   Anno urbis conditae sexcentesimo sexagesimo secundo primum Romae bellum civile commotum est, eodem anno etiam Mithridaticum.

* II 18,1   Anno quadringentesimo septuagesimo septimo, cum iam clarum urbis Romae nomen esset, arma tamen extra Italiam mota non fuerant ... census est habitus.

III 10,1   Quingentesimo et quadragesimo anno a condita urbe L. Aemilius Paulus P. Terentius Varro contra Hannibalem mittuntur.

* VI 7,1-2 Anno urbis Romae sexcentesimo septuagesimo octavo Macedoniam provinciam Marcus Licinius Lucullus accepit ... Et in Italia novum bellum subito commotum est. Septuaginta enim quattuor gladiatores ducibus Spartaco Crixo et Oenomao effracto Capuae ludo fugerunt, et per Italiam vagantes paene non levius in ea quam Hannibal moverat paraverunt.

VI 17,1   Anno urbis conditae sexcentesimo nonagesimo tertio Gaius Iulius Caesar qui postea imperavit cum Lucio Bibulo consul est factus.

VI 18,1   Anno urbis conditae sexcentesimo nonagesimo septimo M. Licinius Crassus ... contra Parthos missus est.

VII 1   Anno urbis septingentesimo fere ac nono interfecto Caesare civilia bella reparata sunt.

D.

II 27,1-2 Numquam in mari tantis copiis pugnatum est ... Contra Lilybaeum civitatem Siciliae pugnatum est ingenti virtute Romanorum ... Pugnatum est VI Idus Martias.

X 16,2   (Iulianus) hostili manu interfectus est VI. Kal. imperii anno septimo, aetatis altero et tricesimo.

X 18,2   (Iovianus) decessit imperii mense septimo, tertio decimo Kal. Mart., aetatis, ut qui plurimum vel minimum tradunt, tertio et tricesimo anno.

II 7,3   (Latini ... superati sunt; ac de his perdomitis trium-
           phatum est) Statuae consulibus ob meritum victoriae
           in Rostris positae sunt. Eo anno etiam Alexandria ab
           Alexandro Macedone condita est.

A

Very important dates are given in three forms (cf. Thucydides,
whose system of dating is to give the year of office of the Athenian
archons, Spartan ephors and of Hera's priestess in Argos).

The date of the foundation of Rome (I 1,2) is given as follows:

a. XI Kal. Maias. According to the monthly calendar, in keeping
   with tradition (21 April);
b. the third year of the sixth Olympiad, i.e. 753 B.C.;
c. 394 years after the fall of Troy (1148 B.C.), i.e. 754 B.C.

The point is that Varro's reckoning of 753 is retained here.
Eutropius or his source was aware that there were various systems
of time-reckoning in use (*ut qui plurimum minimumque tradunt*),[34]
and that these yielded different dates. Those best known for the
fall of Troy are 1184/83 or 1148/47. The latter is that used by
Eutropius. If we count from the fall of Troy up to (and excluding)
the foundation of Rome, then we arrive at the date 754. It was the
vivid Greek imagination, shared by historians, that insisted on
bridging the gap of four centuries between Aeneas (whose dates
are known from the date of the conquest of Troy) and the year of
the foundation of the city. However, if we base our calculations on
the history of Alba Longa with its thirteen kings, at a rate of three
kings per century (Herodotus similarly counted in generations) we
arrive at a total of 430 years, which means that Troy fell in 1184
and not in 1148.

For the Third Punic War (IV 10,1) he also gives three dates, but
these are not established in the same way as the dates for the
foundation of Rome:

a. ab urbe condita;
b. consular year;
c. number of years between the Second and Third Punic Wars.

He has learned from experience. Method c. is most suitable for a
breviarium, and, indeed, a quite obvious one to use. His relative

---

[34] For an explanation of these words, see below, p. 135.

dating from the Second War, is emotive in effect: 'Thus long did our forefathers tolerate Carthage!' In terms of formal calendars, however, one might say that only two systems, that of the *fasti consulares* and that which reckoned a.u.c., were employed.

Up to I 15 he follows a different, equally practical, system: the dates traditionally assigned to the kings. He continues to use this method for the eight years following their expulsion. From I 16 onwards, he uses the consular years. Throughout the history of the republic, this method of dating was, of course, generally followed, but it was still used in imperial times. In adhering to it, Eutropius follows the example of such illustrious predecessors as Tacitus.

B

We often find the use of consular years and dates a.u.c. combined. The beginnings of overseas relations: the first embassy to Rome from Ptolemy II, and the request for a treaty. Rome, represented as the mightier power, complies (II 15) (273 B.C.).

The end of the *Breviarium* is also marked by a double dating (X 18,3) and these two examples would seem to indicate that other double datings may have a particular significance.

The beginning of the conquest of Gallia Transalpina (IV 22,1) and the foundation there of Narbo as a colony six years later (IV 23,1). In the first case he gives, though not as part of his dating method (perhaps an irrelevant distinction) the names of the consuls in office (124 and 118 B.C.). This civilian colony is mentioned with remarkable emphasis.[35] Eutropius might have spoken in the words of Cicero, 'specula populi Romani ac propugnaculum istis ipsis nationibus oppositum et obiectum'[36] and he must have remembered Postumus' Gallic Empire and others who had saved the Imperium Romanum (in spite of their rebellion).[37]

Another year of sufficient importance to merit double dating is that marking expansion in the East: the year 74 B.C., when Bithynia fell to Rome (after the death of the Bithynian king) and the last Mithridatic War began (VI 6,1); this was to last much longer

---

[35] Cf. for instance Vell. I 15; II 7,8 and Cic. *Brut.* 43, 160.

[36] Cic. *pro Font.* V 13.

[37] IX 9; 11. For Postumus, see N. Jankowski, 'Das gallische Gegenreich (259-274 n. Chr.) und seine soziale Basis im Spiegel der *Historia Augusta*', *Helikon* 7 (1967), 125-194.

owing to the events that took place three years later (VI, 8,1).[38]
The degree of interest aroused by Mithridates is shown a third time
in VI 16, which in a way rounds off the account of Roman overseas expansion: 'Hoc tempore (62 B.C.) nullum per orbem terrarum
grave bellum erat'.

Events within the country had meanwhile taken a less favourable
turn. To Eutropius, the conspiracy of Catilina was of sufficient
significance to merit double dating (VI 15). One should not, however, infer that the single dating method is reserved for minor
events. Rather, the writer applies more than one method of dating
when he introduces a break in the composition of the narrative or
for particular emphasis.[39]

C

It is apparent from those places where the author uses only dates
a.u.c. that events which are given no more than a single date can
be of historical importance, even though they receive no particular
emphasis within the framework of the *Breviarum*:
X 17: It was necessary, though humiliating, for Jovian to abandon
his plans for further expansion. The year of this decision deserved
to be remembered as a warning, and is here expressed, most fittingly,
a.u.c.: 'pacem cum Sapore, necessariam quidem, sed ignobilem,
fecit multatus finibus ac nonnulla imperii Romani parte tradita.
Quod ante eum annis mille centum et duobus de viginti fere, ex quo
Romanum imperium conditum erat, numquam accidit';

V   4   the civil war between Marius and Sulla;[40]
VI 7   the war against Spartacus, a *novum bellum*;
VI 17 Caesar's consulship;[41]
VI 18 Second consulship of Crassus and Pompey (55 B.C.).

The inclusion of the latter two circumstances is important, for,
after mentioning Carrhae, Eutropius says, 'Hinc iam bellum civile
successit exsecrandum et lacrimabile, quo praeter calamitates, quae

---

[38] For the *bellum Macedonicum* and M. Lucullus' activities there between
72 and 70 B.C., see Cic. *Verr.* II 23 ff., Plut.*Caes*, 4,1. Besides Eutr. VI 7; 8,10,
see also Fest. 9,3-4; Amm. Marc. 27,4,11.

[39] E.g. VIII 1,1, Nerva.

[40] This war and the *bellum sociale* are described as *bella funestissima*
(V 9,2).

[41] VI 17 is indirectly a double time indication, for besides the date a.u.c.
Eutropius has written 'C. Iulius Caesar, qui postea imperavit, cum L.
Bibulo consul est factus'.

in proeliis acciderunt, etiam populi Romani fortuna mutata est'
(VI 19). This ominous date is in perfect accord with the civil war
that broke out after the death of Caesar, counting from the foundation of the city; but how long would she continue to exist? The
date of the civil war is indicated a.u.c., as was the year of disasters,
216 B.C. (III 10,1). In one other instance does an a.u.c. dating mark
the conclusion of a period of war within Italy (dated fairly arbitrarily
as 477 a.u.c.): this was the first war outside Italy (II 18).[42]

It is a notorious fact that not all historians have given the date
of the foundation of Rome the same place in their chronological
systems. We find, for instance, 751/0 (Cato-Polybius), 753 (Varro),
752 (*Fasti Capitolini*).[43] Judging by the frequency of correspondence,
we may assume that Eutropius' source, or sources, follows the *Fasti*.

D

Now and then he dates an event according to the month calendar,
but these instances are largely, to my mind, a matter of chance.
For instance, the battle of Lilybaeum, VI Idus Martias (II 27,1-2),
and the death of Julian and Jovian which were, perhaps, still fresh
in people's memories (X 16,2 and 18,2). Furthermore, the latter
date marks the conclusion of the *Breviarum*, as XI Kal. Maias, the
foundation of Rome, marked its beginning (I 1,2).

There are seventeen dates for which Eutropius used the fasti
consulares, naturally for the history of the Republic. In doing so
he followed the example set by the old histories, and presumably
also oral tradition.[44] He proves himself a worthy heir of a tradition
of writing senators, in that he does not refer to the regnal years of
the emperors [45] except in connection with their death, and not even

---

[42] If the year of foundation is taken to be 752 B.C. here, as it is often
elsewhere, the year meant in II 18 is 275, and the census referred to is that
of that year. Nevertheless, we may not take Eutropius too literally in this
matter since the years a.u.c. do not always tally. (However, 275 B.C. remains
the most likely date for this census, see p. 133). For the various dates for the
foundation of Rome to be reconstructed from Eutropius' text, see the
list on p. 137.

[43] See *Lexikon der alten Welt* (1965, *s.v.* 'Zeitrechnung', col. 3321 [H.
Kaletsch]). E. J. Bickerman, *Chronology of the Ancient World* (London 1968),
77.

[44] Odd as it may seem, until far into the present century classics students
at one of the Dutch universities were expected to know the names of the
consuls for the period 200 B.C. to 200 A.D.!

[45] Cf. R. Syme, *Tacitus* (1958), 390 ff.: 'The Roman senator could not
bear to use the regnal years of emperors.'

always then. He never indicates an event as having taken place during a particular regnal year. It is typical of him that when he does wish to date an event occurring during the reign of Augustus, he does so with reference to his consulship (VII, 8,1: 'duodecimo anno quam consul fuerat').

Synchronisms, i.e. dating by events occurring other than in Rome, play a very minor part. Eutropius gives only one (II, 7,3): the Latins were defeated in the same year as that in which Alexander the Great founded Egyptian Alexandria. For the sake of completeness, it should be observed that, in recounting a series of events, he sometimes dates subsequent occurrences from the beginning of Hannibal's invasion (III 14,1; 23).

The following conclusion may be drawn from the chronological data. The practice of double dating, of dating according to the persons in consular office, and the use of dates a.u.c., point to a system (introduced either by Eutropius himself or by his source) which he followed quite deliberately. This method is conventional in its adherence to the Fasti Capitolini and is not influenced by the custom of placing events according to regnal years. Eutropius was a conventional historian, but he was, first and foremost, a senator. As regards the accuracy of his dates, considering that this concise *Breviarium* covered more than 1000 years of Roman history, one can only agree with what has been said of a historian much greater than he: 'Exact chronology was often impracticable—and often superfluous.'[46] The division into periods is comparatively easy to follow. Only one point marking such a period remains ambiguous (II 18,1), unless one assumes that the words *arma ... extra Italiam mota non fuerant* contain an allusion to a fact considered of such importance as to be regarded as a turning point in the history of Rome.

E

There are a number of dates that are difficult to place within the chronological framework. For instance, the year 477 a.u.c. (II 18,1), in which a census was held. The only explanation that will fit the latter piece of information is that Eutropius held the date of the foundation of Rome to be 752 B.C.; we then arrive at 275 B.C., a census year.[47] Subsequently, in 18,3, he mentions the opening of

---

[46] Syme, *op. cit.*, 390.
[47] Broughton, *op. cit.*, gives 479 a.u.c.

hostilities against the Carthaginians: *Ap. Claudio Q.* (this should be *M.*) *Fulvio consulibus*. Again, if the year 752 is taken to mark the beginning of the Roman era, then the census presents no problems, but we do find ourselves in difficulties as regards the end of the wars that were previously restricted to Italy. Now Eutropius does not in so many words connect these two facts, but the words *arma ... extra Italiam mota non fuerunt* suggest that the Romans were soon after waging war outside Italy. The passage continues, *et contra Afros bellum susceptum est* (§ 3), which could point to activities outside Italy before 264 B.C.[48] Hence the idea that the census in question is that of 265/4 B.C. It must be admitted that this year would be satisfactory for two reasons. Firstly, because it would meet the requirement that, as Eutropius' text implies, this census took place just before the beginning of the First Punic War, and secondly because in this year C. Marcius Rutilus enjoyed the unique honour of a second term of office as censor. Nevertheless, this unprecedented honour is not mentioned in the *breviaria*, and if it had been a reason for mentioning this census, then surely Eutropius would at least have hinted at it.[49]

The census of 275 B.C., however, would seem the most likely in the light of other events given special attention in the *breviaria*. If in the entire book only one census is mentioned at all, there must be a special reason why it was remembered. For the year 275 B.C. such a reason is not hard to find. It was noted for the actions of the plebeian censor C. Fabricius Luscinus. He it was who had proved incorruptible in the struggle against Pyrrhus; consul in 282, wounded at the battle of Asculum, consul again in 278, twice *triumphator*, he was eminently suitable for the office of censor. He it was who expelled the patrician P. Cornelius Rufinus from the senate—although opinions differ as to his motives. In any case he was considered the censor *par excellence*.[50] As early as the second century A.D. he was being mentioned in the *breviaria*.[51]

---

[48] We do not know whether Paianios deliberately took a different line from Eutropius; he has 470 a.u.c. instead of 477 a.u.c. In any event, the year 282 B.C. is unlikely to be historically correct as a date marking the beginning of expansion beyond Italy.

[49] For C. Marcius Rutilus, see Broughton, *op. cit.*, 179 and 202.

[50] J. Suolahti, *The Roman Censors. A Study on Social Structure* (Helsinki 1963), 256 ff., esp. 258-9: 'The mythical glow which formed about him later was such that he was held up as the ideal and model of Roman qualities. He was thus well adapted to become the ideal of censor.'

[51] Florus I 13,22; Liv. *Per.* 14.

V 4: the year 662 a.u.c. was remarkable for a number of events:

a. the outbreak of the first Civil War;
b. the outbreak of the Mithridatic Wars;
c. Marius' sixth consulship.

If we take the foundation of Rome to have occurred in 752 B.C., which dating is given in Eutropius' chronology somewhat more frequently than any other, 662 years a.u.c. would correspond to the year 90 B.C. Yet this date cannot be regarded as the year of outbreak of the Civil War, or of the Mithridatic Wars, or indeed of Marius' sixth consulship, which we know him to have held in 100 B.C. Nor would it help to consider the years 663 or 664 a.u.c. If we are to make any sense of the information given (though it should always be borne in mind that the minor historian did not necessarily select his material with due care, so that any attempt at coordination is to overrate him) then we should read, 'Anno urbis conditae sexcentesimo sexagesimo *sexto*', instead of *secundo* and '... C. Marius *septiens*', instead of *sexiens*. For 666 years a.u.c. is in our terms 86 B.C., the year of Marius' seventh consulship, and a year to which both the *bellum civile* and the *bellum Mithridaticum* may plausibly be dated.[52] The events in question are already sufficiently involved, and, to add to the confusion, the readings are inconclusive, to say the least, the word *sexagesimo* being lacking in FGLO, only occurring in PD. Presumably his failure to find this word prompted Paianios to conduct his own research. Unfortunately, his conclusion was incorrect. His calculations resulted in a dating of 672 a.u.c., i.e. 80 B.C., which is impossible.

VI 7 taken together with VI 8 and 10 contains information about M. Licinius Lucullus, known after his adoption as M. Terentius Varro Lucullus. He was the younger brother of L. Licinius Lucullus, who is here erroneously referred to as his *consobrinus*. M. Lucullus was consul in 73 and proconsul of Macedonia in 72 and 71. In 71 he was ordered to help Crassus in the war against Spartacus.

VI 7 gives 678 a.u.c. as the date of the beginning of his proconsulship. This would place it in the year 74, which is two years too early, unless we accept a chronology starting from 750 B.C.—which is unlikely in view of VI 8.

---

[52] In general, it is impossible to correct all Eutropius' errors, but I have made an exception in the case of his chronology, for which the systems used are normally readily traced.

VI 8 gives 681 a.u.c. which, if we take 752 as the year of foundation, tallies with 71 B.C. and the consuls mentioned, P. Cornelius Lentulus and Cn. Aufidius Orestes.

The most likely explanation of the discrepancies in these chapters is that Eutropius' account of the Luculli as military commanders places their generalship between the years 74 and 70 B.C., and that no further chronological specification within that period was considered necessary.

Ut qui plurimum minimumque tradunt

The expression 'ut qui plurimum minimumque tradunt' occurs twice, in I 1,2 and X 18,1. We can find the former, but not the latter, in Paianios' Greek translation: κατὰ τοὺς τὸ πλεῖστόν τε καὶ ἐλάχιστον παραδεδωκότες. This rendering, 'as those historians (say, who) recount the longest and shortest time', needs an explanation. Is it the author's intention to indicate a mean? Or should the sentence be understood as follows: ut (eos praeteream) qui ... tradunt? [53] A third possibility is that Eutropius is saying that both parties, those who assign the earliest and those who assign the latest possible date to the fall of Troy, agree that a period of 394 years elapsed between the fall of Troy and the foundation of Rome. If the latter interpretation, which comes closest to the text, is correct, then Eutropius was guilty of a very serious blunder, for in that case there must have been a tradition stating that Rome was founded in 790 (1184 — 394 = 790). In fact, he probably subscribed to the view that Troy fell in 1148 and Rome was founded (394 years later) in 754. The third interpretation could then be paraphrased as follows: 'as regards the time from the destruction of Troy to the foundation of Rome, I am inclined to compromise, and to find a position between the two extremes'. But this still does not help us to find the correct translation of the above phrase.

One could try to find a parallel for the words *plurimum minimumque* in Greek usage, though this is not a very profitable line of approach, either. Nevertheless, I noted Herodotus I 202, 1: ὁ δὲ Ἀράξας λέγεται καὶ μέζων καὶ ἐλάσσων εἶναι τοῦ Ἴστρου. This must be a case of two groups of people holding different opinions: one

---

[53] This interpretation was first suggested by seventeenth-century editors, and was included, for instance, in the Leiden edition of Henricus Verheyk in 1793, and even in 1935, in Q. O. Polenta's edition: 'per non parlare di quelli che di più e di quelli che di meno tramandano'.

considers the Araxes to be larger, the other thinks it is smaller than the Istros. The explanation given by Ed. Meyer, that this indicates a 'median', is unsatisfactory.[54]

Ps.-Xenophon has 'Aθπ. II 1: τῶν μὲν πολεμίων ἥττους τε σφᾶς αὐτοὺς ἡγοῦνται καὶ μείζους (Wil. ὀλείζους). If we follow the text as it has survived rather than Wil.'s reconstruction, 'both less and more' means 'able to cope with'. According to Meyer this is 'eine durchaus unanstössige, dem fünften Jahrhundert geläufige Redensart'. This is undoubtedly putting it too strongly, for he cannot name a single parallel.

However interesting such speculations may be, common Greek usage of the fifth century B.C. still proves nothing for common Latin usage of the fourth century A.D. I could not find a single Greek parallel for Eutropius' words. Comparing them with the expression *uno mense aut altero*, 'hardly (or 'at most') two months' in A.V. *de Caes.* 37,10, merely confuses the issue. Perhaps, however, A.V. *de Caes.* 41,22 can be of use: *Statimque triennium post minimum fatali bello Constantinus cadit.* This can only mean '*about* three years later'.

X 18,2 concerns the age at which Jovian died. Eutropius says that he was 33 years of age, but we know that there was at least one other account according to which he died at the age of 40: *annos gerens proxime quadraginta* (*Epit.* 44,4). It does not seem likely that Eutropius went to such lengths to establish a median from among varying accounts of Jovian's age at his death to arrive at the age of 33, even in speaking of contemporary history.[55] It is much more probable that he wrote down his own estimate of the emperor's age. Six or seven years' difference between the emperor's actual age (if the Epitomist is right) and Eutropius' estimate of his age is still, after all, a possible margin of error. Thirty-three as a median age means that some people thought that he died at 26 years of age, and others at 40. A difference of as much as fourteen

---

[54] B. G. Niebuhr, *Kl. Schr.* I 154; Ed. Meyer, *Forsch.*, II 404.

[55] This opinion was held by many early commentators; it is summed up as follows by Verheyk in his 1793 edition: 'Sunt enim qui plures annos Joviano tribuant. Velut ipse Victor in Epitome. *Interiit*, inquit, *annos gerens proxime quadraginta*. Sunt etiam qui pauciores: mediam inter utrosque viam insistit Eutropius.' Not surprisingly, however, Verheyk fails to specify the sources which refer to Jovian as having been still younger, for no such source has ever existed. Amm. Marc. 25,10,13; Eutr. *loc. cit.*, and Socrat. 3, 26.5, all give his age as 33 years, whereas only *Epit.* 44,4 gives it as 40 years.

years, if the emperor was never considered to have lived past forty, is a very curious margin even for a fragmentary traditional history to leave.

It would therefore seem most likely that the words *ut qui plurimum minimumque tradunt* in both cases indicate no calculated median but an estimate.

NOTE

On p. 131, note 42, I noted that Eutropius' a.u.c. dates are not reliable. Apparently he cannot make up his mind when Rome was founded. A list of the dates he uses, converted into dates B.C., follows below.

Year of the foundation of Rome

750 B.C.: VI 6,1.[56]
751 B.C.: IV 22,1; 23,2.
752 B.C.; VI 7; 8,1; 15; 16; 17,1; 18; VII 1.
      V 4 probably also belongs in this group.[57]
753 B.C.: I 1,2
754 B.C.: X 17,2; 1118 years a.u.c. corresponds to 364 A.D. I.e., the date of the foundation of Rome is here 754 B.C.
756 B.C.: III 10,1.

PERSONAL EXPERIENCE

References to contemporary events are to be found in various places. The best known is that in which Eutropius recounts that he took part in Julian's expedition in the East (X 16,1): 'hinc Iulianus rerum potitus est ingentique apparatu Parthis intulit bellum, cui expeditioni ego quoque interfui.' However, he seldom mentions himself even when he refers to his own time. IX 13,2: 'Zenobia autem posteros, qui adhuc manent, Romae reliquit.' The term used has become stereotyped, e.g. for the reconstruction of Carthage: 'quae nunc manet' (IV 21). The general knowledge of his audience was apparently such that they knew Mogontiacum,

---

[56] For the dating of L. Licinius Lucullus' activities, see Broughton, *op. cit.*, 106 ff., to whose conclusions I have nothing to add. Cf. also Broughton's *Supplement to the Magistrates of the Roman Republic* (1960), 34-35.

[57] See above, p. 134.

but had difficulty in distinguishing the various Drusi of the Julio-Claudian dynasty. He therefore mentions that Claudius was the son of Drusus, *qui apud Mogontiacum monumentum habet*. This is no *flosculus* culled from Suetonius, but a helpful reference to a monument that was apparently still extant.[58]

Inevitably he addresses the emperor in the introduction. He addresses him on one other occasion, and it is no coincidence that he does so in comparing emperorship and dictatorship. Moreover, this is the only point (I, 12,2) at which he interrupts his own narrative: 'Neque quicquam similius potest dici quam dictatura antiqua huic imperii potestati, quam nunc tranquillitas vestra habet, maxime cum Augustus quoque Octavianus, de quo postea dicemus, et ante cum C. Caesar sub dictaturae nomine atque honore regnaverint.' It seems a curious way of explaining this republican office. Is this 'aside' evidence of abysmal ignorance or didactic ingenuity? Perhaps both: the ignorance is then mainly the readers' or the listeners', the ingenuity Eutropius'. The divided emperorship was, in his own time and immediately before, a controversial military and political issue, to which he alludes in his discussion of Marcus Aurelius and Lucius Verus. XIII 9,2: 'Tumque primum Romana res publica duobus aequo iure imperium administrantibus paruit, cum usque ad eos singulos semper habuisset Augustos.' One can well imagine that the writer was longing to produce better work, though forced to mention these trivial details. The end of his *Breviarium* may be read as an expression of his desire to write a greater historical work, although perhaps too much importance has been attached to this statement.[59]

On a number of occasions Eutropius makes good use of his knowledge of contemporary military affairs. One of the best examples of this is his treatment of war-elephants, particularly as used by Pyrrhus and Hannibal.

Florus had already paved the way with an obviously rhetorical discursiveness quite different from, for instance, Appian's sober account. Although he knew and used Florus' work, Eutropius imposed certain limitations on his own work, which is perhaps why

---

[58] Erected by Tiberius after 9 B.C. See Suet. *Claud.* I; Cass. Dio LV 2,3. For its present state, see M. Besnier in *RE* 30 (1932), col. 2423.

[59] X 18,3 (See p. 189): 'Nam reliqua stilo maiore dicenda sunt. Quae nunc non tam praetermittimus, quam ad maiorem scribendi diligentiam reservamus.'

he does not refer to the greatest battles. In a way, he was fortunate in that his patron, the emperor himself, had no time to read extensive rhetorical accounts *à la* Florus. Eutropius thus avoids falling into the same pitfalls as his predecessor, who knew the elephant only as big game. In Florus' time the elephant was no longer used in battle; in Eutropius' age the Romans were once again confronted with these awe-inspiring animals in the wars against the Persians, so this subject was sure to be of general interest. Eutropius knew what was expected of him; the elephant had become part of the stock repertoire of history and Eutropius could not therefore leave him out. But his account is sober, as is that of Appian—with whom, incidentally, he has little else in common. The explanation for his matter-of-fact rendering is obvious. He could not afford to speak of a well-known phenomenon with high-flown rhetoric. He is restrained because he and his contemporaries, officers and civil servants alike, know all about battle elephants. Ammianus Marcellinus uses the same technique, and for the same reasons, in his exposé of Julian's expedition against the Persians.[60] On the other hand, if one compares the relevant passages in Florus and Eutropius, the differences are quite unmistakable.

Florus I 13,8-10.

Actum erat, nisi elephanti, converso in spectaculum bello, procucurrissent, quorum cum magnitudine tum deformitate et novo odore simul ac stridore consternati equi, cum incognitas sibi beluas amplius quam erant suspicarentur, fugam stragemque late dederunt. In Apulia deinde apud Asculum melius dimicatum est Curio Fabricioque consulibus. Iam quippe terror beluarum exoleverat, et Gaius Numicius quartae legionis hastatus unius proboscide abscisa mori posse beluas ostenderat. Itaque in ipsas pila congesta sunt, et in turres vibratae faces tota hostium agmina ardentibus ruinis operuerunt.

I 13,12

Nam provectis in primam aciem rursus elephantis, unum ex eis pullum adacti in caput teli gravis ictus avertit; qui cum per stragem suorum recurrens stridore quereretur, mater agnovit et quasi

---

[60] For Florus' account, see above, p. 16. See also *Mnem.* 18 (1965), 384; 21 (1968), 272. In addition to the classical evidence listed there, see also the more recent studies quoted in *RE* 5, Col. 2248/57 (Wellmann); *RAC* 4, Col. 1001 ff. (Opelt), esp. 1022-3.

vindicaret exiluit, tum omnia circa quasi hostilia gravi mole permiscuit. Ac sic eaedem ferae, quae primam victoriam abstulerunt, secundam parem fecerunt, tertiam sine controversia tradiderunt.

I 13,28

Sed nihil libentius populus Romanus aspexit quam illas, quas ita timuerat, cum turribus suis beluas, quae non sine sensu captivitatis summissis cervicibus victores equos sequebantur.

Eutr. II 11,3

Commissa mox pugna, cum iam Pyrrus fugeret, elephantorum auxilio vicit, quos incognitos Romani expaverunt. Sed nox proelio finem dedit; Laevinus tamen per noctem fugit, Pyrrus Romanos mille octingentos cepit et eos summo honore tractavit, occisos sepelivit. Quos cum adverso vulnere et truci vultu etiam mortuos iacere vidisset, tulisse ad caelum manus dicitur cum hac voce: se totius orbis dominum esse potuisse, si tales sibi milites contigissent.

II 14,3

Curius in consulatu triumphavit. Primus Romam elephantos quattuor duxit.

II 24

L. Caecilio Metello C. Furio Placido consulibus Metellus in Sicilia Afrorum ducem cum centum triginta elephantis et magnis copiis venientem superavit, viginti milia hostium cecidit, sex et viginti elephantos cepit, reliquos errantes per Numidas, quos in auxilium habebat, collegit et Romam deduxit ingenti pompa, cum (CXXX) elephantorum numerus omnia itinera compleret.

IV 27,3

(Q. Caecilius Metellus) Iugurtham variis proeliis vicit, elephantes eius occidit vel cepit ...

As we said, Ammianus Marcellinus does not need many words to weave the war-elephants into his story. Nevertheless, there are lingering echoes in his words of the fear this awesome weapon inspired: 'Post hos elephanti gradientium collium specie, motuque immanium corporum, proprinquantibus exitium intentabant, documentis praeteritis formidati' (24,6,8).

Appian's account of the battle at Thapsus is entirely different.[61] Scipio took the field against Caesar with sixty elephants, provided by King Juba. The news of the presence of these animals made a great impression on Caesar's soldiers, even before the battle: ὅ τε τῶν ἐλεφάντων πόλεμος ἀήθης σφίσιν ὢν ἐξέπλησσεν. When Juba subsequently withdrew, leaving only half his elephants with Scipio, 'Caesar's men plucked up courage to such a degree that the fifth legion begged to be drawn up opposite the elephants, and it overcame them valiantly. From that day to the present this legion has borne the figure of an elephant on its standards'.[62] Is is easy to understand why, after this historic event, elephants held no more terrors for the Roman legions for several centuries.

ROME AND THE BARBARIANS [63]

The writers of *breviaria* write about foreign policy under the republic with intense national pride, as when Egypt actually requests an alliance (II 15). Eutropius refuses to be intimidated by the past glory of famous adversaries; the way in which Athens is referred to as a *civitas Achaiae* (V 6) is simply insulting to this glorious city: *ab Aristone Atheniensi Mithridati tradita est.* Jerusalem, though also conquered, fares better: *quae fuit urbs nobilissima Palaestinae* (VII 19,3). It goes without saying that this official favoured the city of Rome, but it must have made many people bitter (though probably not Eutropius) to think that the eternal city, like other cities, had become dependent on the whims of the emperor: *Alexander Severus Romae quoque favorabilis fuit* (VIII 23). Athens, Jerusalem, even Rome, whatever their past fame, had ceased to present any political or military problems.

The foremost contemporary problem was Rome's relationship to

---

[61] *B.C.* II 96.

[62] The translation is that of H. White in the Loeb edition of Appian, III, 405. Cf. *b. Afr.* 83-85.

[63] Even before the battle of Adrianople, Rome's relationship with the barbarians betrayed traces of a type of patriotism that was to contribute to developments ensuing immediately after Eutropius. This patriotism has been brilliantly described by F. Paschoud, *Roma Aeterna, études sur le patriotisme romain dans l'occident à l'époque des grandes invasions.* Inst. suisse de Rome, 1967, 20. Paschoud discusses high-ranking pagans and Christians, but the seeds of their feelings about Rome had already been sown in the widely-read *epitomes*, and particularly in Eutropius. M. Fuhrmann's brilliant study, 'Die Romidee der Spätantike' (with its excellent bibliography), *HZ*, 207 (1968), 529-561, continues Paschoud's work in a discussion on the veneration accorded Rome at a later period.

the 'barbarians'. Eutropius, as a typical member of the senatorial class, combines humanity with a profound conviction of the rightness of Roman domination. He was apparently, or preferred to seem, oblivious of the fact that this situation gave rise to tension among the subjected peoples. His manner of taking Rome's power for granted sometimes strikes us as cynical, although it probably springs rather from a naive consciousness of superiority. He is entirely unaffected by the doubts that plagued Tacitus, as the following two passages show.

Samnites (II 9,1-3):

Postea Samnites Romanos T. Veturio et Sp. Postumio consulibus ingenti dedecore vicerunt et sub iugum miserunt. Pax tamen a senatu et populo soluta est, quae cum ipsis propter necessitatem facta fuerat ... Neque ullus hostis fuit intra Italiam, qui Romanam virtutem magis fatigaverit.

Corinth (IV 14,1):

Corinthiis quoque bellum indictum est, nobilissimae Graeciae civitati, propter iniuriam legatorum Romanorum.[64]

Moreover, criticism of the murder of the enemy commander Viriathus is implied rather than stated: 'Et cum interfectores eius (sc. Viriathi) praemium a Caepione consule[65] peterent, responsum est numquam Romanis placuisse imperatores a suis militibus interfici' (IV 16,3).

The behaviour of Q. Servilius Caepio certainly did not live up to this hypocritical assurance.[66] One can scarcely imagine that Eutropius did not know the true story of how Caepio bribed Viriathus' men to betray him. The writer of De viris illustribus certainly did know what happened, which shows that the perfidious part played by the Roman commander must have been familiar to many, indeed that the popular history books had helped to make the facts common knowledge.[67] Livy's periocha also exposes the betrayal and its instigator, and devotes some words of praise to the brave opponent, for whom Eutropius feels nothing but contempt ('pastor primo fuit,

---

[64] Cf. Liv. Perioch. 52. Florus I 32: 'facinus indignum'. See above, p. 7.
[65] Caepio, consul in 140, proconsul in 139 B.C. See Broughton, Magistrates, 477 ff.
[66] Esp. App. Ib. 70, 74-75.
[67] De vir. ill. 71,3.

mox latronum dux').[68] Valerius Maximus termed the deed a
perfidia on both sides, the Spanish traitors and Caepio.[69] Even
Velleius Paterculus could not pass over it in silence, and wrote that
Viriathus was killed *fraude magis quam virtute Servili Caepionis.*[70]

It would seem that Eutropius is alone in his opinion. Yet the
Christian authors also remain unmoved by the perfidity of the
Roman commander. Orosius has only a glancing reference to the
murder of Viriathus,[71] and, like Eutropius, creates the impression
that the Romans had dissociated themselves from the murder.
Nevertheless, it would oversimplify the case to assume that the two
versions arise from different sources. Eutropius despises the
latrones.[72] His attitude can be traced back to that of Florus, which
need not necessarily entail direct derivation: 'vir calliditatis
acerrimae, qui ex venatore latro, ex latrone subito dux et imperator'.[73] And here lies the reason for the Romans' lack of chivalry
and implacable hatred: Viriathus had indeed constituted a serious
threat, and might well have become the Romulus of Spain. As
always, magnanimity towards the enemy petered out as soon as
this enemy became, or seemed to have become, a serious threat to
the safety of Rome. Eutropius' humaneness, like Florus', is severely
limited.

The author took great pleasue in detailing the numbers of soldiers
mobilized and the booty amassed in the wars of conquest. Sometimes, as in the case of the size of the fleet in the First Punic War,
such information is fairly reliable; compared to Polybius' numbers,
those given by Eutropius are 'slight variants due to careless transmission'.[74] Sometimes, too, the information supplied by Eutropius

---

[68] *Perioch.* 54: 'Viriathus a proditoribus consilio Servili Caepionis interfectus est ab exercitu suo multum comploratus ac nobiliter sepultus; vir
duxque magnus et per quattuordecim annos, quibus Romanis gessit, fre-
quentius superior'.

[69] 'Viriathi etiam caedes duplicem perfidiae accusationem recepit, in
amicis, quod eorum manu interemptus est, in Q. Servilio Caepione consule,
quia in sceleris huius auctor inpunitate promissa fuit victoriamque non
meruit, sed emit.'

[70] See Vell. 2, 1,3 and the commentary by F. Portalupi (Turin 1967).

[71] V 22,15: 'percussores Sertorii praemium ne petendum quidem a Romanis esse duxerunt, quippe qui meminissent antea Viriati percussoribus
denegatum.'

[72] *Latrones* are well described in R. MacMullen, *Enemies of the Roman
Order* (1956), 255 ff., 351, note 4; id., *Historia* 14 (1965), 102, n. 33.

[73] Florus I 33,15. Cf. *Mnem.* 18 (1965), 377 note 1. The facts are also
given in P. Jal's edition of Florus I, 1967, p. 138.

[74] Walbank, *Commentary on Polybius* I 28,6 on Eutropius II 21,1.

(and Florus, for that matter) is more or less fictitious.[75] One may well ask to what purpose, then, these figures are included in a *breviarium*. Eutropius tells us, I think, in his introduction. He sees his task as a *per ordinem temporum brevis narratio*. The story is told, recited, in order to please the emperor ('ut ... possit ... laetari'). He has no intention of providing the emperor with a piece of scholarship that he would have to read attentively ('cognoscerat lectione').

Every time major decisions are mentioned, numbers serve to illustrate the *narratio*. When Rome goes to Africa during the First Punic War, when she subsequently wages war with Hannibal, when the Empire is torn by the civil war between Caesar and Pompey, the numbers of troops and details of the losses bring home the gravity of the situation.[76]

Plunder is taken completely for granted, as it was at the time the wars of conquest were conducted,[77] but it is only after the Third Macedonian and the Third Punic Wars that booty is mentioned frequently. The emphasis placed on the honesty of the Romans after the latter war is most significant (IV 12,2): 'Spolia ibi inventa, quae variarum civitatum excidiis Carthago collegerat, et ornamenta urbium civitatibus Siciliae, Italiae, Africae reddidit, quae sua recognoscebant.'

The richest booty of all was that gained by Aemilius Paullus after Pydna,[78] but Eutropius shifts the emphasis to accentuate the magnanimity of the conqueror towards King Perseus: 'nam et volentem ad pedes sibi cadere non permisit et iuxta se in sella conlocavit.'[79]

The benevolence of the conqueror had two main aspects. On the one hand he liberates the oppressed (IV 7,3): 'Macedonibus et Illyriis hae leges a Romanis datae: ut liberi essent et dimidium eorum tributorum praestarent, quae regibus praestitissent, ut appareret, populum Romanum pro aequitate magis quam avaritia dimicare.' It is no coincidence that Eutropius adduces this partic-

---

[75] See for instance Florus I 18,7. Cf. W. W. Tarn in *JHS* 27 (1907), 50, note 17.

[76] II 22; III 8; 9; 10; 11,4-5; VI 20.

[77] A complete list of the conquests mentioned, numerous as they are for a *breviarium*, is not necessary. II 21,2-3 and 22,2 discuss the First Punic War. The conditions of the peace with Antiochus III are given in IV 4,3.

[78] Cf. J. H. Collins, *Propaganda, Ethics, and Psychological Assumptions in Caesar's Writings*, thesis, Frankfurt a.M. 1956, 43.

[79] See Liv. 45,34,5 for the booty (cf. Eutr. IV, 8). Eutr. IV 7,2 on the magnanimity of Aemilius Paullus.

ular task of the Romans whilst placing Macedonia and Illyria, which had gained prominence by his own time, in historical perspective. The *breviarium* thus disseminates propaganda to discourage desertion to the barbarian side, and the imperial conquests in Pannonia were represented as having liberated the inhabitants from slavery.[80]

On the other hand, the Romans acted in a humane manner towards those they had conquered, as the example of Perseus was supposed to prove. Rome's mildness was all the more remarkable seeing that Perseus' activities could be construed as a rebellion.[81] Nor, after the First Punic War, did the Carthaginians have any cause to complain of the harshness of their Roman conquerors (II 27,2): 'Etiam Carthaginienses petiverunt, ut redimi eos captivos liceret, quos ex Afris Romani tenebant. Senatus iussit sine pretio eos dari, qui in publica custodia essent; qui autem a privatis tenerentur, ut pretio dominis reddito Carthaginem redirent atque id pretium ex fisco magis quam a Carthaginiensibus solveretur.'

The Second Punic War is used to illustrate the high standard of Roman military honour and the difference between the morality of the Romans and that of the Carthaginians (III 11,1): 'Hannibal Romanis obtulit, ut captivos redimerent, reponsumque est a senatu eos cives non esse necessarios, qui cum armati essent, capi potuissent.' The difference between the Romans, who refused to recognize their countrymen as citizens once they had been taken prisoner by the enemy, and the Carthaginians, who were glad to take back their men after the first war, is characteristic. The Roman's humaneness is limited, particularly towards his own fellow soldiers; he knows no greater bitterness than when confronted with what he considers cowardice. Yet this attitude is not consistent, as we see when Hannibal takes the proud Romans at their word, and feels at liberty to treat his prisoners accordingly (III, 11,2): 'ille omnes postea variis suppliciis interfecit et tres modios anulorum aureorum Carthaginem misit, quos ex manibus equitum Romanorum, senatorum et militum detraxerat.' This reaction of Hannibal's was always severely condemned by the Romans even though, according

---

[80] Defection to the enemy: see MacMullen, *op. cit.*, 362, note 29, which gives the relevant passages (cf. *ibid.*, 351, note 5). Pavel Oliva, *Pannonia and the Onset of Crisis in the Roman Empire* (Prague 1962) 287. For the Roman emperors as liberators, see Eutr. VIII 13,1 (under Marcus Aurelius); *vita Marci* 19,3; Oliva, *op. cit.*, 47,287.

[81] *Rebellavit* should be interpreted as a mutiny (IV 6,1); Florus' expression *se erexit* is somewhat clearer (I 28,1). Cf. *Mnem.* 1965, 375.

to the Roman code of honour, soldiers who surrendered were disgraced. Now, however, the Roman code of honour was conveniently ignored—naturally. The fact that the Romans had certain standards of permissible military behaviour did not mean that they would overlook the offence if another party, and the enemy at that, put the dishonoured soldiers to death.

We shall not discuss the accuracy of Eutropius' account, although it was probably not far from the truth. But if we try to analyse the personality of the historian as revealed in his work, we are struck by the curious combination of the stern morality (which is much praised) of the Roman republican leaders on the one hand, and its Carthaginian repercussions, which can only be seen as wanton cruelty, on the other.[82] Both the story and the dual attitude are characteristic of Eutropius, and perhaps also of his time. The solidarity of imperial subjects had to be perfect, in the fourth century A.D. as in other times; anyone who did not live up to these standards was condemned to be cut off from society. Nevertheless, the enemy who took this to mean that he could with impunity kill those who were no longer welcome in Rome, was the cruel barbarian and always would be, in harsh contrast to Rome's humane attitude in Spain (III 17): 'regem Hispaniarum magno proelio victum in amicitiam accepit et primus omnium a victo obsides non poposcit'.

In III 21-22, Eutropius makes it quite clear what he means by Carthage's *perfidia*. The actual terms of the peace are immaterial here.[83] The estimated cost of a war often increases as protracted negotiations drag on, to the irritation of the victor. In this case, the length of the negotiations is interpreted as a *nova perfidia*, for which the Carthaginians were made to pay.[84] Here again our investigation is not concerned with the accuracy of the account, but with the information considered relevant for his *breviarium* by an official who likes to see quick results. Eutropius must have known what

---

[82] For the distinction between runaway slaves and deserters, see Walbank's *Commentary on Polybius* XV 18,3 (p. 468).

[83] In any case, Polybius XV 18 differs in certain details from Liv. 30,37 and App. *Lib.* 54. Cf. Walbank, *Comm.*, *loc. cit.*

[84] III 21,3: 'ut quingenta milia pondo argenti darent.' III 22,2: 'additis quingentis milibus pondo argenti centum milibus librarum propter novam perfidiam.' The surviving texts do not agree, which has led to desperate attempts to make the figures correspond to those given by Livy and Pliny the Elder (33,51); commentators in classical times also went to great lengths to try to solve this infinitely complex problem. See the edition of Verheyk, *loc. cit.*

wars cost, but in his time no barbarian nation was as rich in spoil as were the wealthy Carthaginians centuries before. He was well aware of the fact that, in his own time, wars were an expensive business, and he deplores the civil war waged against Magnentius ten years earlier (X 12,1): 'ingentes Romani imperii vires ea dimicatione consumptae sunt, ad quaelibet bella externa idoneae, quae multum triumphorum possent securitatisque conferre.'

Time and again we see that what he admires in the terms for peace set by previous generations of Romans is the self-restraint which governed their treatment of a conquered enemy. He notes this attitude in discussing the conditions of the peace set Antiochus III, *quamquam victo* (IV, 4,3). His accounts of conquests of barbarians are therefore seldom if ever provocative. The enemies of old, now members of the Imperium Romanum, cannot have taken exception to this textbook, which perhaps partly explains its popularity. Moreover, the retailing of honours accorded generals in the past must have gratified the upper classes. Here again, Eutropius knew what would interest his public: military distinctions, and the triumph as ultimate ideal. Indeed, triumphs are described in disproportionate detail. In the case of the Syrian war, Scipio's triumph (*Scipio Romam rediit, ingenti gloria triumphavit*) had long lost its sting, even for Syrian Roman readers.

As we have seen, there are limits to mildness when the interests of the state are at stake. The historian decides for himself if *clementia*, which he believes should be the rule, is rightly abandoned. It is likewise his personal opinion if he says that the behaviour of individual Roman citizens is not consonant with the interests of the state. Indeed, it is with surprising severity that he condemns the Civil War, thus also censuring C. Julius Caesar [85] (IV 19,1): 'hinc iam bellum civile successit exsecrandum et lacrimabile, quo praeter calamitates, quae in proeliis acciderunt, etiam populi Romani fortuna mutata est.' The tears that Caesar later wept at the news of Pompey's death (V 21,3) do not, however, absolve him from his grave responsibility. Eutropius' attitude towards Caesar is nevertheless ambiguous. He refers to Caesar's return from Gaul, yet without taking sides in the conflict between the general and the senate (VI 19,2): 'Caesar enim rediens ex Gallia victor coepit poscere alterum consulatum atque ita, ut sine dubietate aliqua ei

---

[85] See also p. 15.

deferretur.' At the same time, the opposition of Marcellus and others is termed *iniuria*; this is in connection with the senate's demand that Caesar disband his troops, which Eutropius, consciously or unconsciously following the lead of his source, apparently considers an 'injustice'. Yet Eutropius makes no attempt to exonerate the man who *adversum patriam cum exercitu venit*. He also criticizes Caesar's last years: 'agere insolentius coepit et contra consuetudinem Romanae libertatis' (VI 35).

Of all kinds of wars, he considers civil war the most reprehensible. Eutropius was the first fourth-century writer to blame Constantius II for causing such a war. Later, Ammianus, Orosius and the Epitomist were to agree with him.[86]

The Romans themselves had realized this early on, and their historians followed a fairly general mode of thought. Therefore, even if a war had started inside the country, it had to look as if it were waged outside. The struggle against Sertorius had to be a foreign war, which it was certainly not. Nevertheless, it would be incorrect to attribute this attitude to the war in Spain to moral disapproval of civil war. It had to be camouflaged as a hostile encounter with Spaniards, no doubt because the Roman conqueror could celebrate a triumph only if he were the victor in a foreign war.[87]

The writings of Florus and Eutropius have one element in common. They have no illusions, either about the republican senators during the civil war, or about the enormous significance of the battle of Actium,[88] though Florus surpasses Eutropius by far in that he sometimes tries to trace the causes of a war, a refinement which one need not expect of Eutropius.[89]

The views of Eutropius and of his contemporaries on the limits of imperial tolerance are perhaps best summed up in the paragraph on the actions of Titus, which he describes with apparent approval. Rebellions by conquered nations are effectively and severely countered, but he turns a blind eye to criticism of the emperor in high places in Rome itself, which was likewise a form of rebellion

---

[86] Eutr. X 15,2; Amm. Marc. 21,1,2; *Epit.* 42,18; Oros. 7,29,18. Cf. P. Jal, *La guerre civile à Rome* (Paris 1963), 460.

[87] Florus II 9,6; Eutr. VI 5,2. Jal, *op. cit.*, 440.

[88] Eutr. V. 7,4; Jal, *op. cit.*, 157 (senators). Actium: Florus II 21,11; Eutr. VII 7.

[89] Causes of war: Florus II 9,6. Jal, *op. cit.*, 361.

(VII 21,2): 'in oppugnatione Hierosolymorum sub patre militans duodecim propugnatores duodecim sagittarum confixit ictibus. Romae tantae civilitatis in imperio fuit, ut nullum omnino punierit, convictor adversum se coniurationis dimiserit vel in eadem familiaritate, qua antea, habuerit.'

It was the tolerant emperors, especially Augustus and Trajan, who enjoyed the highest esteem. Their conquests are listed, their failures practically ignored. Augustus' good fortune (VII 9-10) is not so highly praised as Trajan's goodness. This has often been overlooked, because the best-known expression in the *breviarium*, *felicior Augusto, melior Traiano* (VIII 5,3), has stuck in people's memories and given the impression that the emperors were equally appreciated. This impression, however, is incorrect. Trajan is the favourite. The four chapters in his praise (VII 2-5) are unique in Eutropius' work.

This is what he had in mind when he promised Valens that he would tell his tale plainly and concisely, but 'additis etiam his, quae in principum vita egregia extiterunt'. It has been said,[90] in my opinion erroneously, that he writes in greater detail of these, his two favourite emperors, in order to explain and justify the expression 'more fortunate than Augustus, better than Trajan'—a phrase with which the senate later greeted emperors at their investiture. If such had been his intention, he would not have created so obvious a distinction in his account of their periods of rule. There is no doubt that Eutropius preferred Trajan even to Augustus. Moreover, the policy of conquest adhered to by the former was of greater relevance than ever in the fourth century.

The *breviarium* is a book about people. Names are given, but issues are seldom explained; as he promised the emperor, his inspiration was to be the *inlustrium virorum facta*. He rarely describes battles, except those of the Second Punic War, and even then he omits all reference to Zama, to name but one. Marius and Metellus, and later Sulla (*ingentem virum*) are mentioned in connection with the war against Jugurtha. The causes of the conflict, or the course of the military undertakings, enter the picture very briefly, if at all. It may well be true that, to us, Roman history is *sine nominibus*, but the fourth-century senator at any rate went to some

---

[90] Pichon, *Histoire de la littérature latine*, 788.

trouble to avoid this situation. Unfortunately his efforts were not crowned with success. His work was too short—indeed, it had to be, after all, its chief objective was brevity. Meanwhile, the imperial biographies (including, surely, the *Historia Augusta*), which are roughly contemporary with the *breviaria*, were eagerly read. They provided the reading public with material which was not to be found in the *breviaria*.

The biographies were also better qualified than any *breviarium* to satisfy the public demand for exciting anecdotal detail. However, this is not to say that such anecdotes are lacking in Eutropius' work.

For instance:

II 5,1: How L. Manlius acquired the cognomen Torquatus; and

II 6,2-3: How Valerius acquired the cognomen Corvinus. The account of the wars against Pyrrhus is enlivened by much circumstantial detail:

II 11,3: Pyrrhus' well-known comment on the courage of the Romans;

II 12,3 and 14,1: C. Fabricius Luscinus;

II 13,3: Cineas, Pyrrhus' envoy, and his opinion of the Romans;

II 21-25: The customary account of the heroism of M. Atilius Regulus in 256 B.C. brightens the discussion of the First Punic War;[91] and

IV 8,1: Perseus' ship.

It has been wrongly suggested that Eutropius adopted the fashion of including anecdotes in his narrative specifically for his account of imperial times,[92] i.e., in only five instances: VII 18,3: Vitellius' banquet; VII 21: Titus; IX 13,1: Aurelian and Tetricus IX 18,2: the removal of the body of Numerian, a detail that is also to be found elsewhere; X 18,1: particulars about Jovian's death. The above list, however, disproves this suggestion.

Senate and Emperor [93]

Eutropius was a conscientious, restrained writer, who was by no means indifferent to the problems of his time. One burning political issue was that of the influence of the senate, to which he

---

[91] References, s.v. 'Atilius' (51) in *RE* (v. Rohden) and Broughton, *Magistrates* I, p. 209.

[92] Schanz, *Geschichte der römischen Litteratur*, IV[2], 78.

[93] A summary of the following arguments was given by the present author in 'Rome à travers trois auteurs du quatrième siècle', *Mnem.* 21 (1968), 273 ff.

himself belonged. In his preoccupation with this matter, he is at one with Aurelius Victor. Both quote the year 235 as marking the end of the collaboration between emperor and senate. They describe Maximinus Thrax in almost identical terms: [94] the military proclaim him emperor 'cum nulla senatus intercessisset auctoritas'. Eutropius, a prouder man than Victor, keeps silent on the pusillanimity of the senate; nor does he refer to the humble origins of this emperor, although he often does so in other cases. To my mind, there is no doubt that the extreme brevity with which Eutropius writes of Maximinus is inspired by contempt. His ideal of co-operation between senate and emperor is that achieved by Trajan: 'In my position as emperor, I treat the common citizen as I should wish to be treated by an emperor if I were a common citizen.'[95] What he admired in Trajan was the fact that he respected the prerogatives of the senate, the most important of which was the *consecratio* of the deceased emperor. It is of great interest to note that Eutropius is alone in recording the *consecratio* (or its omission) of nearly all the emperors.

The passages in which he mentions the *consecratio* of deceased emperors may be placed in five categories. The first category (A) contains straightforward statements of the usual course of events. The second is an isolated case; in C, as we shall see, the wording has been varied intentionally. In the fourth group, it was not, if Eutropius' phrase is taken literally, the senate who carried out the consecration. The last group (E) lists the names of emperors who were not thus honoured.

Once again, the accuracy of Eutropius' statement whether an emperor was or was not consecrated is not here at issue.[96] The point is to see what he says about the events in question.

---

[94] *De Caes.* 25; Eutr. IX 1. I do not share the negative opinion of Syme, *Emperors and Biography*, (Oxford 1971), 189. The passage that to my mind best illustrates the importance Eutropius attaches to a thorough cultural grounding is X 10,2, where he judges Vetranio favourably, although he cannot refrain from mentioning his lack of cultural background: 'quem grandaevum iam et cunctis amabilem diuturnitate et felicitate militiae ad tuendum Illyricum principem creaverunt, virum probum et morum veterum ac iucundae civilitatis, sed omnium liberalium artium expertem adeo, ut ne elementa quidem prima litterarum nisi grandaevus et iam imperator acceperit.'

[95] VIII 5; see J. H. Thiel, 'Trajanus', *Kon. Akad. v. Wetenschappen, Akademiedagen* no. 8 (1955), 20.

[96] It is difficult, even for modern historians, to be sure about this. In *L'Imperatore Probo* (Rome 1952), G. Vitucci, for instance, on the basis

CONSECRATIO

A

VII 10,5 Augustus:	moriens Divus appellatus est
VII 13,5 Claudius:	Post mortem consecratus est Divusque appellatus.
VII 20,2 Vespasianus:	inter Divos relatus est
VII 22,2 Titus:	inter Divos relatus est
VIII 1,2 Nerva:	inter Divos relatus est
VIII 5,2 Traianus:	inter Divos relatus est solusque omnium intra urbem sepultus est
VIII 7,3 Hadrianus:	Senatus ei tribuere noluit divinos honores, tamen cum successor ipsius T. Aurelius Antoninus Fulvius hoc vehementer exigeret, etsi universi senatores palam resisterent, tandem obtinuit.
VIII 8,4 Antoninus:	atque inter Divos relatus est et merito consecratus.
VIII 10,4 Verus:	inter deos relatus est.
VIII 14,2 Marcus:	omnibus certatim adnitentibus inter Divos relatus est.
VIII 19,2 Sept. Severus:	Divus appellatus est
VIII 20,2 Caracalla:	funere publico elatus est.
IX 3 Philippi:	inter Divos tamen relati sunt.
IX 11,2 Claudius II:	Divus appellatus est. Senatus eum ingenti honore decoravit, scilicet ut in curia clipeus ipsi aureus, item in Capitolio statua aurea poneretur.

---

of the knowledge available at that time, rightly assumed that Probus was not consecrated. An inscription in honour of L. Caesonius Ovinius Manlius Rufianus Bassus, which was found not long ago, tells us that he was 'electo a *divo Probo* ad pre(side)ndum iud(icio) mag(no)'. See G. Barbieri in the *Acta des IV. Intern. Kongresses für griechische und lateinische Epigraphik* (1962) (Vienna 1964). However, it would exaggerate the reliability of the epigraphical material to draw the conclusion that this definitely confirms Probus' deification. Eutropius, after eulogizing the emperor, states (IX 17,3) 'interfectus tamen est Sirmi tumultu militari in turri ferrata'. Cf. Victor 37,4; *Epit.* 37,4; *vita Probi* 21,4. I cannot subscribe to Syme's conclusion (*op. cit.*, 225): 'Clearly drawing on KG'.

X 1,3 Constantius I: inter Divos relatus est.

X 16,2 Julianus: inter Divos relatus est.

B

IX 28 Diocletianus: Contigit igitur ei, quod nulli post natos homines, ut cum privatus obisset, inter Divos tamen referretur.

C

IX 4 Decius senior: meruit inter Divos referri

IX 15,2 Aurelianus: meruit quoque inter Divos referri.

X 8,2 Constantinus Magnus: atque inter Divos meruit referri.

X 15,2 Constantius II: meruitque inter Divos referri.

D

IX 2,3 Gordianus: Miles ... ipsum Divum appellavit

X 18,2 Iovianus: benignitate principum, qui ei successerunt, inter Divos relatus est.

E

VII 11,3 Tiberius: ingenti omnium gaudio murtuus est.

VII 12,4 Caligula: cum adversum cunctos ingenti avaritia, libidine, crudelitate saeviret, interfectus in Palatio est.

VII 15,1 Nero: ... execrabilis ab omnibus simul destitutus est et a senatu hostis iudicatus.

VII 23,1 Domitianus: Neroni aut Caligulae aut Tiberio similior quam patri vel fratri suo.

VII 23,6 Domitianus: Funus eius cum ingenti dedecore per vespillones exportatum et ignobiliter est sepultum.

VIII 15   Commodus: Obiit morte subita ... tanta
                                       execratione omnium, ut hostis
                                       humani generis etiam mortuus
                                       iudicaretur.
VIII 19,2 Geta: hostis publicus iudicatus con-
                                       festim periit.

The terminology used in this context is most revealing, and has
never, to my knowledge, been studied thoroughly.[97] There is a large
group of emperors whom the senate deified as a matter of course.
The terms customarily employed by Eutropius are 'Divus apellatus
est' or 'inter Divos relatus est'.[98] He goes on to give a meticulous
account of deviations from the usual ritual of deification. Trajan,
whom he admired so much, was accorded the honour of having his
remains buried within the city; Diocletian was consecrated even
though, having abdicated, he was no longer emperor at his death;
Claudius II was further honoured with the erection of a golden
statue and shield.[99] Where Eutropius himself was particularly
strongly in favour of the honour conferred, for instance, in the
cases of Antoninus Pius and Marcus Aurelius, he says so.[100] He
also tells us if there were any difficulties attendant upon the consecration, as in the case of Hadrian, Gordian I and Jovian.[101] The
well-known instances in which this honour was withheld are also
mentioned: Tiberius, Caligula, Nero and Domitian;[102] Eutropius
further states that Commodus and Geta were not consecrated
either. His statement about Commodus is in conflict with Victor,
who recounts that this emperor was finally consecrated thanks to
the efforts of Septimius Severus, and on account of his father's
merits.[103] Here again Eutropius (if, that is, he agreed with Victor)

---

[97] The best summary of Eutropius' treatment of consecration, even though
it does not point out the differences in terminology, is that of F. Taeger,
Charisma II (1960), 633.

[98] See the list given above.

[99] VIII 5,2 (Trajan), cf. VIII 4: 'ob haec per orbem terrarum deo proximus
nihil non venerationis meruit et vivus et mortuus'; IX 28 (Diocletian);
IX 11,2 (Claudius II).

[100] VIII 8,4 (Antoninus Pius); VIII 14,2 (Marcus Aurelius).

[101] VIII 7,3 (Hadrian); IX 2,3 (Gordian); cf. S. J. Oost, 'The Death of
the Emperor Gordian III' in *C. Ph.* 53 (1958), 106-7; X 18,2 (Jovian).

[102] VII 11,3 (Tiberius); VII 12,4 (Caligula); VII 15,1 (Nero); VII 23,1
and 6 (Domitian).

[103] Victor *De Caes.* 20,30. Cf. Cassius Dio 75,7; Herodian 2,10,3. For
further information see J. A. Straub art. 'Commodus' in *RAC* III, col. 255.

proves rather uncommunicative: he makes no reference to this occasion on which the senate was overruled. Geta never was consecrated; his *damnatio memoriae* was never repealed, despite his brother and murderer Caracalla's witticism, 'sit divus, dum non sit vivus': let them deify him, as long as they do not revive him.[104] Eutropius is equally reticent about the deification of Gallienus. The earliest surviving version of this event, which was most humiliating for the senate, is Victor's: Claudius II compelled the senators to consecrate his predecessor: *subacti a Claudio*.[105] Eutropius suppresses the event altogether; coming from this emperor it was too profound a mortification to be borne. He does, however, mention the fact that Antoninus Pius also demanded his predecessor's *consecratio*.[106] Another notable omission in Eutropius' account is a story of Victor's to the effect that, towards the end of his life, Hadrian had a number of senators imprisoned in order to have them put to death. This rumour was proved false after the emperor's death. And the senators were so happy about their return that they were swayed by the request of the new emperor.[107]

Eutropius is incapable of demeaning himself by providing history with a happy ending.[108] Perhaps the fact that he does not subscribe to Victor's oblique praise of Caesar underlies his bluntness, which sometimes makes him appear implacable. Like the anonymous author of *De viris illustribus*, Victor is filled with admiration for Octavian's 'magnus avunculus'.[109] Eutropius' tone is different—he speaks of Caesar's 'shameless conduct, that contravened the traditional Roman idea of freedom'.[110] Brutus the assassin was in his eyes a hero inspired by his great ancestor, L. Iunius Brutus, who drove out Tarquinius Superbus.[111]

---

[104] *Vita Getae* 2,9.
[105] *De Caes.* 33,27; 30.
[106] Eutr. VIII 7,3: 'Cum . . . vehementer exigeret'.
[107] *De Caes.* 14,13-14.
[108] This attitude is reflected, later, in the *H.A.*: *vita Hadriani* 25,8; *vita Antonini Pii* 6,3. It has been convincingly demonstrated that Eutropius precedes the SHA, e.g. by W. Schmid, 'Eutropspuren in der Historia Augusta', *Bonner Historia-Augusta Colloquium* 1963 (1964), 123-133. For Hadrian's *consecratio* see F. Vittinghoff, 'Der Staatsfeind in der römischen Kaiserzeit', *Neue deutsche Forschungen*, Bd. 84 (Berlin 1936), 87-89; more recently G. W. Clarke, 'The Date of the Consecratio of Vespasian', *Historia* 15 (1966), 318-327, esp. 320 ff.
[109] *De viris illustribus* 78; Aurelius Victor, *De Caes.* 1,1.
[110] Eutr. VI 25 (cf. p. 15, above).
[111] *Ibid.*

Both Bruti, ancestor and descendant, were laid to rest in a mausoleum of harmless rhetorical verbiage. There was no question of republican, let alone revolutionary, aspirations among officials like Eutropius. He was a loyal servant of his emperor. Yet it is significant that in the decade in which Victor and Eutropius were writing, it was possible for the central figure of the Roman revolution, Gaius Julius Caesar, to inspire two interpretations as different as theirs. A study of the sources that equates these two abbreviators and assumes their dependency on a single source, as is so often done, defeats its own purposes. *Quellenforschung* is useless in this connection, and what is more, it obstructs our view of two personalities—both admittedly 'minor' historians, but nevertheless entirely dissimilar in all other respects. Their personality is revealed, more than anywhere else, in their attitude to Caesar. Caesar's consecration, described in many surviving sources, is omitted by Eutropius. Once again, his silence is significant.

The most interesting cases are those in which Eutropius is in favour of the consecration, but where the ritual of apotheosis could not be observed because, for instance, the body could not be found. This happened in the case of Decius. Aurelian managed to arrange his consecration, but there are indications that his name was often erased from inscriptions. The Christian emperors, such as Constantine the Great and Constantius II, also presented difficulties, in that the pagan rites could not be performed in their entirety. It is quite clear why the *consecratio* of both Constantine and his son were incomplete according to pagan beliefs: the body had not been burned, and the apotheosis was thus not carried out in accordance with the prescribed ritual.[112] It is understandable that a pagan senator, who respected tradition, cannot in such cases say that an emperor *inter Divos relatus est*.

It is thus no coincidence that Eutropius uses a different terminology for each of these four emperors, preferring to say *meruit inter Divos referri*. I am inclined to feel that this is an unusually subtle instance of senatorial theology; *mereo* means to deserve; it also means to be rewarded, to be given a claim to, to be promised.[113]

---

[112] Cf. the excellent summary by L. Koepp, 'Die Konsekrationsmünzen Kaiser Konstantins und ihre religionspolitische Bedeutung', *Jahrb. f.A.u. Chr.* 1 (1958), 94-104, esp. 95.

[113] For *mereo* in the sense of 'to show oneself to be worthy of something' and hence 'to lay a claim to something', see VIII 4 and IV 12,4. This meaning of course occurs frequently on funerary inscriptions: b.m.f. = *bene merenti*

This ambiguous term was most convenient for the senate. I think it probable, although it is not capable of proof, that the terminology is not Eutropius' own, but that it originated in senatorial practice. The subtlety of the phrasing employed in connection with precisely these four emperors, all of whom should have been consecrated, but for some circumstance that made regular deification impossible in each case, can be no accident. Such subtlety of expression occurs nowhere else in Eutropius.

These nuances escaped his Byzantine translators. They cannot be blamed for this, since the *consecratio* was a pre-Byzantine and pre-Christian custom.[114] Eutropius did not restrict the use of the second phrase, 'meruit inter Divos referri', to the Christian emperors, he also uses this expression for Decius and Aurelian. As a rule, he handles the controversy between paganism and Christianity with the utmost restraint. Many scholars have been surprised to note that he does not even mention Constantine's conversion to Christianity. His only reference to Christianity is when he condemns Julian for his persecution of Christians, even though the persecution was bloodless.[115] Generally speaking, this may be a diplomatic silence; on the other hand, his repugnance to bloody persecution bears out the humanity characteristic of Eutropius, though very Roman in type.[116]

Before imperial times, apotheosis was an exceptional distinction. Tradition has it that Romulus was honoured in this manner (I 2,2): 'ad deos transisse creditus est et consecratus'. Camillus, who had saved the city from the Gauls, was regarded as a second Romulus

---

fecit (e.g. C.I.L., VI, 7778, 16450). It is not inconceivable that Eutropius derived his use of *mereo* from the terminology used on tomb inscriptions.

[114] IX 4 (Decius); IX 15,2 (Aurelius); X 8,2 (Constantine the Great); X 15,2 (Constantius II). Unfortunately Paianios, the translator, says nothing about the consecration of Constantius II. About Decius and his son he says: καὶ τῆς θεῶν ἔτυχον ἀμφότεροι τιμῆς For Aurelian and for Constantine he gives the same stereotyped translation: καὶ αὐτὸς συνηριθμήθη τοῖς θεοῖς See also 'Consecration' *RAC* III, col. 284 (L. Koepp—A. Herrmann). G. Herzog-Hauser, 'Kaiserkult' in *RE* Suppl. IV, 806-853 gives the history of the *consecratio* of each emperor. The best study of the ritual is by E. Bickermann, 'Die römische Kaiserapotheose', *ARW* 27 (1929), 1-31. For the Christian emperors, especially Constantine the Great, see A. Kaniuth, *Die Beisetzung Konstantins des Grossen. Unters. zur religiösen Haltung des Kaisers* (1941).

[115] X 16,3; cf. Ammianus Marcellinus 22,10,7; 25,4,20. Aurelius Victor does mention Christianity (but only in passing) in connection with Constantine (41,12). For Festus see below, p. 178.

[116] For other expressions of this sentiment, see: II 27,4; III 17; IV 16,3.

'quasi et ipse patriae conditor' (I 20,3), and was consequently deemed worthy of the same honour as Romulus (II 4): 'honor ei post Romulum secundus delatus est'. But these were the only two to be consecrated, for such honours accorded ill with the spirit of the Republic. In imperial times, however, *consecratio* was a matter to be handled by the senate, and thus constituted a problem with which Eutropius was also confronted.

THE EMPEROR DURING HIS LIFETIME

There was a connection between the living, reigning emperor and his successor, which sometimes led the successor to insist on deification against the will of the senate. This is said even of Antoninus Pius (VIII 7,3), and Victor says the same of Claudius II with respect to Gallienus (*De Caes.* 33,27). Although the senators must have resented imperial interference as undermining their own authority, it did not affect the general principle that Victor expressed as follows (33,30): 'adeo principes atque optimi mortalium vitae decore quam quaesitis nominibus atque compositis, quantum coniciatur, caelum adeunt seu fama hominum dei celebrantur modo.'

The policies of the living nearly always affected the honours accorded the dead. This need not surprise us. The form of worship granted after his death was a continuation of the homage the living emperor enjoyed in Eutropius' time; and it is an established fact that the living emperor was worshipped as a god. The historian proclaims this worship, in a sense, in his dedication to Valens: 'tranquillitatis tuae ... mens divina'. Scipio Africanus was another who was already considered a privileged being who spoke with the gods during his lifetime (III 20,2): 'cui viro divinum quiddam inesse existimabatur, adeo ut putaretur etiam cum numinibus habere sermonem'. Augustus was considered almost divine, even before his death (VII 8,4): 'vir, qui non inmerito ex maxima parte deo similis est putatus'. Trajan, too, was granted near-divine status before he died (VIII 4): 'per orbem terrarum deo proximus ... et vivus et mortuus'.

The honours showered on the emperor did not, however, mean that the historian did not feel at liberty to pass value judgements on many emperors, based on their deeds. If we compare Eutropius' approach with the usual historical view, determinded chiefly by Tacitus, of the Julio-Claudian dynasty, we see that his attitude is only in part conformist. Tiberius (VII 11,1), Caligula (VII 12) and

Nero (VII 14 and especially 15) are treated unfavourably. It would seem as if subtlety were out of the question: the 'simple' listener did not want subtlety. All the more surprising, then, the chapter on Claudius (VII 13). Admittedly, Eutropius does not conceal *quaedam crudeliter et insulse*, but it is abundantly clear that he admired the emperor's moderation as a ruler. The question inevitably arises, where this view originated, for it is completely opposed to the traditional view of the despot dominated by his wives and freedmen. The answer is not hard to find. In spite of Tacitus, there was a flourishing senatorial tradition that remembered past honours bestowed on its class. Eutropius draws on this when he says, 'tam civilis autem circa quosdam amicos extitit, ut etiam Plautium, nobilem virum, qui expeditione Brittanica multa egregie fecerat, triumphantem ipse prosequeretur et conscendenti Capitolium laevus incederet' (§ 4). The importance Eutropius attached to this imperial honour emerges from the fact that he had just (§ 2) called Cn. Sentius and A. Plautius *illustres ac nobiles viros*. The two references to Plautius as a *vir nobilis* (repetition is unusual in a *breviarium*) underline both his importance and that of Claudius' gesture. It is the senator who speaks here.

The same senatorial sense of honour determines the historian's valuation of many emperors in yet another way. Finance and territorial expansion are tasks of the greatest importance in which Vespasian excelled and for these he is highly praised; but he is also praised for his restraint—which should always be interpreted to mean being on good terms with the senate (cf. VII 19,12).

Those who transgress the code of values set forth by Eutropius come to a bad end. This happened to Domitian, who committed the major sins of *libido, iracundia, crudelitas, avaritia* and *superbia*, besides the murder of senators, arrogation of divine honours, financial excesses (a golden statue), and almost consistently unsuccessful attempts at territorial expansion. No other fate was possible for an emperor who thus became the exact opposite of his father and brother than to be murdered by his own servants and be buried like a dead cur or beggar. He has gone down in history as a prime example of the *exitiabilis tyrannus* (VII 23; VIII 1).[117] Con-

---

[117] Not even Commodus is so thoroughly despised (VIII 5), probably because he also had a number of military successes to his credit, notably against the Germans. In modern works he is also sometimes more favourably judged than formerly, e.g. Oliva, *op. cit.*, 299-300.

versely, the example of liberality is Titus whose life, described in
two chapters (VII 21-22), is in sharp contrast with that of his
younger brother. The words used to characterize his rule are
familiaritas, facilitas and *liberalitas*—terms that reflect the emperor's relationships with highly-placed men in his direct surround-
ings. Eutropius probably stresses this particular case quite
deliberately, having learned, during his term of office, how important was a satisfactory relationship between the emperor and
his government officials. The very fact that neither Vespasian nor
Titus allowed themselves to listen to *delatores* restored the atmosphere of co-operation between the emperor and the upper *ordines*.

The events of the year 68/69 are also discussed in unexpected
detail, perhaps in view of later usurpations, such as those in the
third century. He is particularly interested in the origins of the
emperors. For Galba, *antiquissimae nobilitatis senator* suffices.
Otho's background requires more extensive treatment, in itself no
good sign.[118] Vitellius needs still more space—and all this serves
as a prelude for Vespasian, *obscure quidem natus sed optimis com-
parandus*.[119] His interest in the emperors' origins, lively though it
is, is not as intense as that of Aurelius Victor.[120] Not for nothing
were the emperors who succeeded the Julio-Claudian dynasty often
scrutinized as to their background, and frequently judged on that
basis. The emperors of 68/69 are no exception. Nerva: *nobilitatis
moderatae*; Trajan: *familia antiqua magis quam clara*, with a
description which also serves to 'place' Hadrian, *consobrinus suae
filius*; Antoninus: *genere claro sed non admodum vetere*; Marcus
Aurelius is the first about whose background he has no reservations:
*haud dubie nobilissimus, quippe cum eius origo paterna a Numa
Pompilio, materna a Solentino rege penderet*.[121] The next interesting
case, much later, is Septimius Severus, whose humble origins we
have seen pointed out by Victor. The fact that he was a self-made

---

[118] For Otho, whose ancestry was in fact most distinguished, see F.
Klingner, 'Die Geschichte des Kaisers Otho bei Tacitus', *Sächsische Akad.
der Wiss.*, 92 (1940), 3-27 (= Wege der Forschung 97 (1969), 388-412).

[119] The year of the three emperors: Otho: 'materno genere nobilior quam
paterno, neutro tamen obscuro' (VII 17,1). Vitellius: 'familia honorata
magis quam nobili. Nam pater eius non admodum clare natus tres tamen
ordinarios gesserat consulatus' (VII 18,1). For the actual ties of the emperors
with their social environment, see Syme, *Tacitus* (1958), 150 ff. (Galba),
205 (Otho), 386 (Vitellius).

[120] See above, p. 21, note 7.

[121] VIII 1,1; 2,1; 6,1; 9,1.

man also emerges clearly enough from Eutropius' account: he tells us that the emperor came from Africa and gives details of his career, but he does not mention the humble social position of the family. The military anarchy produced a long series of family trees notable chiefly for their obscurity: *obscurissimo genere* (Maximinus Thrax), *obscurissime natus obscurius imperavit* (Aemilius), *obscurissime natus* (Postumus), *vilissimus opifex* (Marius), *obscurissime natus* (Diocletian), *villissime natus* (Carausius).[122] Eutropius does not allow such considerations to cloud his judgement of their rule. Postumus and Diocletian come off particularly well, as does Carausius.

The closer a historian gets to his own time, the more cautiously must he proceed. Yet even Constantine the Great's origins are weighed in the balance when Eutropius says that he succeeded his father, *ex obscuriore matrimonia eius filius* (X 2,2).

The emperor's *acclamatio* by the senate was an important occasion. If it did not take place, the author does not fail to say so (IX 1: Maximinus, IX 7: Valerian, IX 11,1: Claudius II). The senate was deprived of this 'right' by the soldiers. Of Pertinax the author says, 'ex senatus consulto imperare iussus' (VIII 16), nor is the fact omitted that Tetricus was a senator, and had to put up with many mutinies on the part of the soldiers who elected him (IX 10). The hostility between soldiers and senate largely determined Eutropius' view of the past, and particularly of the previous century. He must have agreed with Victor (37,5): 'abhinc militaris potentia convaluit ac senatui imperium creandique ius principis ereptum ad nostram memoriam, incertum, an ipso cupiente per desidiam an metu seu dissensionum odio'.

According to the Suda, Eutropius was an Italian.[123] His origin did not, however, preclude Eutropius' acceptance of emperors from elsewhere. Sometimes he even gives the impression that he regards the non-Italic origins of many leaders as a symbol of the universality of the Empire. He displays not a trace of dissatisfaction with Trajan's background, although he does stress the fact that the

---

[122] IX 2,1; 6,1; 9,1; 9,2; 19,2; 21,1. Sometimes these comments are notoriously erroneous. For Septimius Severus see T. D. Barnes, 'The family and career of Septimius Severus', *Historia* 16 (1967), 87 ff. I should like to stress once more that Eutropius' blunders have been pointed out time and again. My present concern, however, is with his personality and his enormous success.

[123] See p. 115.

emperor's father was the first of his line to achieve the heights of consular dignity (VIII 2,1). No more is Severus' African origin held against him. Nevertheless, the author likes to include information of this nature: *Decius, e Pannonia inferiore*; *Aurelianus Dacia Ripensi oriundus*; *Carus Narbone natus in Gallia*; *Maximianus Galerius in Dacia haud longe a Serdica natus*; *Licinius Dacia oriundus*.[124] These little details must have been important to Eutropius. We can understand him better if we assume, and there are ample grounds for such an assumption, that his readers and listeners liked to read about a fellow-countryman who succeeded in becoming the leader of the empire. It must be admitted that a painful contrast is thus created between the insignificant details supplied and the important facts he sometimes omits. Constantine may serve as an example. His rule is praised, but our pagan author makes no reference whatsoever to the emperor's conversion to Christianity.

Eutropius' high opinion of the emperor deserves further analysis. He points out that Constantine was very popular in the provinces, mainly because of his military successes; the author refers more particularly to the conquests in Gaul, where Constantine defeated the Alamanni and the Franks. Chapters X 4-8 are decidedly unequal in their appreciation of the emperor and his deeds. Good deeds and bad are placed side by side, with no attempt at unification. The emperor's origins, of interest to Eutropius, are also pointed out here.[125] There are evil deeds, committed for political reasons: the death of Licinius was *contra religionem sacramenti*; Crispus' name is avoided, the murders neither concealed nor condoned (X 6,3): 'verum insolentia rerum secundarum aliquantum Constantinus ex illa favorabili animi docilitate mutavit. primum necessitudines persecutus egregium virum filium et sororis filium, commodae indolis iuvenem, interfecit, mox uxorem, post numerosos amicos'. However, the following chapter appears to have been designed to eliminate the unfavourable impression: it is a continuous flow of praise.

---

[124] IX 4 (cf. *RE* 29, col. 1250); 13,1 (cf. *RE* 9, col. 1351); 18,1 (cf. *RE* 4, col. 2456: including the emperor's wish to have been born a Roman); 22,1 (cf. *RE* 28, col. 2517); X 4,1.

[125] Constantine, *obscurus* on his mother's side, was nevertheless the son of an Augustus, as was Maxentius, and hence of better lineage than Licinius and Maximinus Daia, who were *homines novi* (X 4,2).

Constantine's reign most clearly shows the degree to which an abbreviator's working methods were influenced by politics. As we have seen, Eutropius did not succeed in shaping the relevant chapters into a coherent whole, a failing to be attributed, not to his sources, but to the delicate nature of the subject. Christian tradition had rendered this emperor's position unimpeachable, and had become a force which the pagan had to take into account. Nevertheless, he was quite at liberty to criticize the emperor's conduct in matters upon which he, an experienced civil servant, was an expert: the emperor's legislation (X 8,1) included unnecessary details and severe decrees for which Eutropius could apparently muster no admiration, though we do not know exactly at which measures his criticism was directed.[126] The struggles for the succession, both before and after Constantine, are discussed in greater detail than we would expect from a *breviarium*. His discursiveness is understandable if we remember the importance the senator-historian attaches to legitimacy. The *acclamatio* had always, after all, been essentially a matter for the senate. It would be foolish to attack Eutropius on the score of his diplomatic treatment of the greatest of Christian emperors. His analysis is more than capable of standing comparison with the efforts of others. Victor also refers to the death of Crispus, but he also glosses over the fact that he was murdered with the words *incertum qua causa* (*de Caes.* 41,11). Although this smacks of servility, we should not underestimate Victor. Having mentioned the execution of Crispus and the punishment of a vulgar rebel on Cyprus, he goes on to say: 'quo excruciato, ut fas erat, servili aut latronum more, condenda urbe formandisque religionibus ingentem animum avocavit, simul novando militiae ordine'. Eutropius was incapable of such masterly irony, which casually mentions the transfer of the capital, conversion to Christianity and military reforms all in one breath.

In this summary of Roman history women are virtually ignored. Of course, the Sabine virgins, Lucretia and Virginia, are part of the stock repertoire, even for those who do no more than summarize the earliest history of Rome (I 7,8-10, 18); no historian writing

---

[126] Some scholars feel that the words *plerasque superfluas* apply to his religious reforms as described in Sozomen. I 8-9 (Verheyk). *Nonnullas severas* (*leges*) implies an evaluation presumably of financial measures, cf. *De Caes.* 41,20. Praise of his military policy is differentiated by means of the words 'fortuna in bellis prospera fuit, verum ita, ut non superaret industriam' (X 7,1).

about Hadrian's accession could ignore Plotina's influence (VIII 6);
no more could Cleopatra (VI 22, VII 6,7) or Zenobia (IX 13) be
disregarded. But this is the sum of the abbreviator's interest in the
subject. Those who stress Suetonius' influence on Eutropius will not
find a trace of it here, at any rate.[127] No Livia, no Aggripinas, no
Julias. The *magister memoriae* had no time for frivolous matters.

One thread that runs throughout the book, whether the author
is discussing the time of the Kings, the Republic or the Empire,
is the dignity of war. War was always better than peace without
honour. Hence the open criticism of Jovian (X 17,1): a necessary
but dishonourable peace. So much, at least, he could afford to say
soon after the emperor's death—it goes without saying that it
would have been impossible while the emperor was still alive.[128]

Economic Problems

Eutropius barely touches upon economic problems. Slaves are
mentioned only on the occasion when they were used for the defence
of Rome during the Second Punic War (III 10). Roman politicians
often argued that the conquests in the provinces enabled the Roman
legions to 'liberate' the people from slavery to their previous
masters. Eutropius interprets the facts in this manner only once
(VIII 13,1): '[Marcus Aurelius] Pannoniis servitio liberatis ...
triumphavit'.[129]

One particular passage (IX 14) is always quoted in connection
with the debasement of the coinage which took place in Imperial
times: 'hoc (Aureliano) imperante etiam in urbe monetarii rebel-
laverunt vitiatis pecuniis[130] et Felicissimo rationali interfecto'.
Victor also mentions this event (35,6): 'neque secus intra urbem
monetae opifices deleti, qui, cum auctore Felicissimo rationali num-
mariam notam corrosissent, poenae metu bellum fecerant'. Its
gravity illustrates the independence and power attained by the
monetarii; it also shows the extent to which the process of devaluation, which had been going on for a long time, was aggravated by

---

[127] E.g. J. Wight Duff, *A Literary History of Rome in the Silver Age*
(London 1927), 643.

[128] This makes X 17,1 a *terminus post quem* for publication.

[129] An ideological controversy has developed around this subject. For
instance, Oliva, *op. cit.*, 286, reproaches Alföldi for adopting the point of
view of the emperor's biographer (sc. *vita Marci* 17,3).

[130] Paianios has τὴν περὶ τὸ νόμισμα ῥᾳδουργίαν.

these officials.[131] The full-scale war that it precipitated claimed seven thousand victims among the imperial troops. To be sure, the abbreviators did not mention events such as these for their economic interest, but because of their serious military repercussions. Their interest in the provinces was likewise determined by other than economic considerations.

The fact alone that an emperor came from the Danubian territories was enough to stimulate an interest in that province. Eutropius caters to this interest, but in moderation.[132] We are told no more about specific measures in the Danube region (except, of course, for military exploits) until Probus, who repealed Domitian's prohibition of viticulture in Gaul and Pannonia. [133] In comparing Eutropius and Victor, we find that the latter sometimes takes slightly more interest in economic matters, such as the reclamation of virgin soil in Pannonia, in which connection he refers to Galerius (*de Caes.* 40.9). Eutropius does not mention this project, but he does tell us of the dangers that threatened the area in the form of marauding bands of Sarmatians and Quadi (IX 8,2).

Abridged histories have always been spiced with particularly picturesque details. Here we see Marcus Aurelius faced with the realization of the gravity of the rebellions at the Danube front. In order to combat these difficulties he made a personal sacrifice: the sale of his most precious possessions (VIII 13,2). Such incidents look well in a textbook. Nevertheless, it would be unfair to think that the author is quite oblivious of economic considerations. Aurelian's reform of the coinage (IX 14) was certainly no picturesque detail, but an extremely serious undertaking. However, one would not expect the hasty reader of a *breviarium* to go to the trouble of gathering all the relevant information. Besides, it is doubtful whether Eutropius himself had access to these particulars.[134]

[131] See *RE* 9, col. 1373-4. L. Homo, *Essai sur le règne de l'empereur Aurélien* (Paris 1904), esp. 79, 155 ff., for Eutropius 164; K. Gross in *RAC* I (1950), col. 1006. R. Tuncan, 'Le délit des monétaires rebellés contre Aurélien', *Latomus* 28 (1969), 948-959.

[132] Oliva's book is most enlightening on this point. See also 'Illyricum in the Epitomators', in R. Syme, *Emperors and Biography*, 221-236; also 'Emperors from Illyricum', *ibid*. 194-207.

[133] Already referred to in Victor *de Caes.* 37,3. Eutr. IX 17,2, later in *vita Probi*, 18,8 Cf. Oliva *op. cit.*, 171, 315-6, with references to modern studies. T. D. Barnes' 'Three notes on the *vita Probi*', *CQ* 20 (1970), 198 ff. represents an attempt to indicate sources for Probus as the promotor of vineyards; cf. Syme, *op. cit.*, 224.

[134] Even though modern research is full of gaps, the general lines are

Economics were not his strongest point, nor of other classical historians. This is linked with the fact that economic history has little popular appeal; the few economic measures that did catch the fancy of the public, such as Probus' measures for the advancement of viticulture in Gaul and Pannonia, are infallibly recorded (IX 17,2). Of the details of Aurelian's monetary reforms, little is known; at any rate, they met with scant enthusiasm in Gaul and Britain. There are indications that Eutropius was told of the matter by Gallic informants who were more than likely to contrast Aurelian's attempted reforms with Julian's successful financial measures. These had been all the more welcome after the devastation and complete exhaustion left in the wake of Magnentius' insurrection (X 10,2), in which Gaul, too, had been deeply involved.[135] Julian is praised for his provincial policies on account of his deeds in Gaul—his economic reforms as well as his military exploits (X 16,3). It even looks as if Eutropius is rather vague about the difference between *aerarium* and *fiscus* (X 16,3; 1,2). He does not mention the Gracchi; their socio-economic importance did not interest him. No more, it seems, was he interested in the political and constitutional significance of their activities, even though it is precisely in these matters that he sometimes wishes to educate his readers.[136]

A study of his comments on provincial administration shows that Gaul, Africa and Asia are referred to most frequently; his information about Gaul is in general of greater importance than that given for the two other provinces. However, this need have no connection

---

relatively clear. See A. H. M. Jones, *Ec. Hist. Rev.*, Second Series, vol. 5 (1952-53), 297-8; C. H. V. Sutherland, *JRS* 51 (1961), 94-5; Jones, *Later Roman Empire* (Oxford, 1964), 26.

[135] Ammianus Marcellinus 16,5 14-15; *Epit.* 48, 4-8. Ammianus describes the campaign against Magnentius as an 'insuperabilis expeditio' (14,1,1). See Jones, *op. cit.*, I, 120. For the significance of Magnentius' rebellion (X 9,3) see S. Mazzarino, *Aspetti sociali del quarto secolo* (Rome 1951), 121.

[136] The position of Egypt in the Empire as a whole is discussed in VII 7: 'Aegyptus per Octavianum Augustum imperio Romano adiecta est praepositusque ei C. Cornelius Gallus. Hunc primum Aegyptus Romanum *iudicem* habuit'. In his own way, he explains the office of dictator in Republican times in I 12, 1-2 (his phrasing is extremely cautious), the people's tribune in I 13, and the military tribune in II 1 and 3; the joint emperorship of Marcus and Verus clearly means something new in his work (VIII 9,2). He appears to have heard vaguely of the struggle to get a plebeian elected consul, but places it in the wrong context (II 7,1) and finally refers twice to censorship without offering any explanation of the office of censor (I 16 and II 6,1).

with Eutropius' alleged Gallic origin,[137] but rather with the dramatic course of events in Gaul in the third and fourth centuries.

There is little point in searching for written sources of his information on provincial affairs. Schanz,[138] though apt to be somewhat dogmatic, is right in assuming that this modest work owed little to extensive study of the available sources. Every conquest had its legend, and scraps of the story, correct or otherwise, were passed on, usually by word of mouth, in official circles.

CHRISTIANITY

Eutropius does not mention Constantine's conversion. A possible reason for this omission is that he did not wish to sow or to aggravate religious dissension, an explanation that accords well with his disapproval of Julian's handling of religious matters (X 16,3): 'religionis Christianae nimius insectator, perinde tamen, ut cruore abstineret'. These words may be interpreted as a denunciation only of Julian, but they certainly also contain an indirect criticism of all Christian rulers who stooped to violence. Nevertheless this passage (and, indeed, his treatment of Constantine generally), in spite of its somewhat haphazard composition, bears the stamp of a considered opinion, which has allowed the emperor's many excellent qualities to outweigh other consideration. The passage in question is directly followed by the remark that Julian modelled himself on Marcus Aurelius, a choice which must have satisfied Eutropius, who greatly admired this emperor (VIII 11).

It is no coincidence, I feel, that many people were dissatisfied with the end of the *breviarium*. Nor does it seem hazardous to venture the hypothesis that the Anonymus Valesiani was among them, and that he himself supplied an ending which in his opinion placed the facts in a more accurate historical perspective than did Eutropius' account. Julian's words (6,33, ed. Moreau) reveal the *Anonymus* to be a Christian, indeed a fanatic, whose severe criticism is elsewhere derived from Orosius. It is worth investigating the differences between Eutropius and the Anonymus.

(1)   An. Val. is hostile to barbarians. He credits Constantine with an heroic action which Eutropius would never have recognized

---

[137] See above, p. 115.
[138] *Geschichte der römischen Literatur*, IV², 77: 'Für die Abfassung des Schriftchens konnte natürlich ein ausgewähltes Quellenstudium nicht in Frage kommen'.

as such and indeed does not even consider worth mentioning
(1,3): 'ferocem barbarum capillis tentis raptum ante pedes
Galerii imperatoris adduxerat'.

(2) As a corollary, their description of Constantine's character is
based on different material. Both, indeed, represent him as
ambitious, but the striking particulars adduced by An. Val.
are lacking in Eutropius (X 5; 7). The killing of the post horses
in order to avoid capture by Severus (2,4) is one example;
Victor also mentions this incident (40,2).

(3) The tradition that Philippus Arabs was a Christian (6,33) may
throw some light on An. Val.'s sources. Orosius (7,28) also
refers to Philippus Arabs as a Christian, which is not to say
that An. Val. based his writings on Orosius, though this is
likely. The tradition itself owes its existence to primitive
retrospective wishful thinking: Would it not be wonderful if
Rome's thousandth anniversary had been celebrated under a
Christian emperor? No doubt this pipe dream gave rise to the
crude historical fabrication. Be this as it may, and though no
direct dependence of the one on the other can be proved, An.
Val. and Orosius must have had a common source. That there
is at least a link between the two is confirmed by the following.

(4) An. Val. and Orosius condemn Licinius in the same terms[139]
for expelling the Christians from court—another incident not
mentioned by Eutropius, who prefers to avoid referring to the
persecutions as much as possible.

(5) Eutropius actually condones Licinius' action. The agressor was
Constantine (X 5): 'Licinio bellum intulit, quamquam necessi-
tudo et adfinitas cum eo esset; nam soror Constantia nupta
Licinio erat' and again (X 6): 'postremo Licinius victus apud
Nicomediam se dedidit et contra religionem sacramenti
occisus est'. The feeble excuse given by An. Val., 'ne iterum
depositam purpuram in pernicie rei publicae sumeret', is unsatisfactory. Hence his reiteration of the arguments set forth
in 5,20; this persecutor was another who deserved no better:
'quamvis omnibus iam ministris nefariae persecutionis extinctis,
hunc quoque in quantum exercere potuit persecutorem digna
punitio flagitaret'. In this character, and similarly denounced

---

[139] An. Val. 5,20, 'repentina rabie suscitatus'. Cf. Oros. 7,28,18. For
further similarities between An. Val. and Orosius, see Moreau's *Excerpta
Valesiana* (Teubner 1968²), 5,29 and 5,33-35.

by Orosius, Licinius went down in Christian history. Understandably, since passions ran so high, Eutropius' moderate opinion lost its effect. He did not take sides clearly enough, it was thought, and it was tempting to exaggerate matters even more. 'Licinius scelere avaritia libidine saeviebat, occisis ob divitias pluribus, uxoribus eorum corruptis' (5, 22).

(6) It is not surprising that Galerius (3,8) was also unpopular with An. Val., and that the dreadful suffering accompanying his sickness is interpreted as a divine punishment.[140] Eutropius takes a very different view, 'vir et probe moratus et egregius re militari', and also speaks of his humiliation at the hands of Diocletian. An. Val. passes over this matter in silence, and has nothing to add to the *breviarium* in this respect.[141]

(7) An. Val. also has the professed aim of presenting edifying information, albeit for a different section of the public—the Christians. They were no doubt most satisfied with what he said of Constantine: 'iusto ordine et pio vicem vertit. edicto si quidem statuit citra ullam caedem hominum paganorum templa claudi'.

(8) Thus the reign of Constantine can be made to look as if it had known no bloodshed. But this it is only possible to do if one suppresses the fact of Crispus' death, as does An. Val. He is nevertheless obliged to mention the military successes of Constantine's discredited son. Eutropius cuts a good figure in the face of this hypocrisy: although he does not mention Crispus by name, he does tell us that he was murdered by his own relatives. Furthermore, his previously quoted favourable opinion of this unfortunate prince implies condemnation of Constantine (X 5,3): 'primum necessitudines persecutus egregium virum filium et sororis filium, commodae indolis iuvenem, interfecit, mox uxorem, post numerosos amicos.'

We need not go into further, less striking, differences, for these are not matters of principle. The chief divergences are based on the Christian and pagan points of view. Victor and the *Epit. de Caes.* are on the side of Eutropius. The eight points mentioned above exemplify an essential disparity. A world of difference lies between the pagan and the Christian idea of what was relevant and necessary

---

[140] Cf. Lact. *de mort.* 33 and Eus. *HE* 8, 16,3 ff. See p. 101 ff.
[141] Eutr. X 2,1; IX 24 (cf. Amm. Marc. 14,11,10). See p. 117.

for the edification of an historically ignorant public. An. Val. did not, however, succeed in ousting Eutropius. Perhaps, after all, he was too common, whereas Eutropius maintains his dignity as a senator throughout. His observations about Constantine's legislative labours are extremely suggestive: some laws were good, others severe, but very many were superfluous. He immediately proceeds to refer to the foundation of Constantinople, 'ut Romae aemulam faceret' (X 8,1). It remains uncertain whether the author considered this a good or a superfluous move. An. Val. (6,30) is more effusive.[142]

'Miserable epitomes', says one modern author.[143] Perhaps so, but there are degrees of 'miserableness', and there is integrity besides, which has survived, for once, to become an historical exception. Eutropius' summary became the textbook of the Middle Ages, of the Byzantine world, and of the humanists.

Appendix

The whole work is very logical in composition and lacks the artificial links created by Victor. Now and then, the connection between three passages is somewhat tenuous, but even then the reader is scarcely ever led astray. For instance, VI 18 has been interpolated between 17 and 19, and 'hinc' (19,1) should, strictly speaking, follow the fighting in Gaul (17, especially the end of § 3). Nevertheless, these passages do not present any problems; indeed, the work as a whole is remarkably straightforward.

Renewed study of the text does not add much to our knowledge of historical events. Of the various editions, that of H. Droysen (1879) is the most valuable in its treatment of the philological aspects.

---

[142] Zosimus' attitude is quite different: 1I1,2, Julian as the great bene-factor of Constantinople; cf. Amm. Marc. 22,9,2; *Paneg. Lat.* XI 24. The question is whether pagan *breviaria* could be as readily transformed into Christian as some modern historians think. I feel that there is a world of difference between An. Val. and Eutropius, but in point of fact we know next to nothing about this anonymous Christian writer. Cf. Momigliano, *Conflict*, 87. However, it is doubtful whether we may say that the Christian passages are interpolations derived from Orosius and leave it at that. There is more than an interpretation at stake. For further differences to the pagan *breviaria* see An. Val. 2,4; 3,7; 4,10; 4,12; 6,30; 6,33.

[143] Syme, *op. cit.*, 144 and 105 (on Victor, Eutropius and Festus): 'poor and scrappy productions, all three' '... the three epitomators betray the low standard still prevalent in the days of Julian and Valentinian (and an abysmal ignorance about the past history of imperial Rome). Otherwise, who would have made the effort of writing, who would have read these meagre compilations?' Cf. A. Cameron, *Hermes* 92 (1964), 375-6.

The editions of C. Wagener (1884) and F. Ruehl (1887) are decidedly
less satisfactory: of the two the latter, though not as good as the
other, is the more widely used.[144] In places where the text is incomplete, the Greek translation can occasionally be used to provide
complementary or alternative readings.[145] Unfortunately, though,
Paianios is not always equally helpful, as we see in IV 27. Here the
Greek is a literal translation of the Latin text as we have it, and
thus of little use. The text cries out for improvement, most editors
preferring *corruptum* to *correctum*.[146]

Various passages could be cited which Ruehl's edition approaches
with exaggerated caution. One passage in particular merits individual attention, since it had historical consequences of some
significance.

In IX 8,1 Ruehl gives the following text: 'Nam iuvenis in Gallia
et Illyrico multa strenue fecit occiso apud Mursam Ingenuo, qui
purpuram sumpserat et † Trebelliano'. Victor (*de Caes.* 33,1) refers
to Regalianus besides Ingebus (= Ingenuus[147]). The credit for
amending Eutropius' text belongs to that 'illustre savante', Anne
le Fèvre.[148] A certain amount of significant evidence (including
numismatic material) pertaining to the rebellions of Ingenuus and
Regalianus has also been preserved.[149]

Ruehl's caution in refusing to substitute 'Regaliano' for 'Trebelliano' is undoubtedly (although he does not say so in so many words)
inspired by *Tyr. trig.* 26,2: '[Gallienus acted ruthlessly] in Trebel-
lianum factum in Isauria principem, ipsis Isauris sibi ducem
quaerentibus.' Ruehl probably thought that the author of this *vita*
might well have influenced Eutropius in this respect. However, once

---

[144] See the review of these three editions by M. Petschenig in *Bursian*,
72 (1892).
[145] III 7 (end); cf. K. Duncker, *De Paianio Eutropii interprete*, Progr.
Greiffenberg 1880.
[146] Petschenig, however, considers this change 'viel zu gewaltsam'
(*op. cit.*, 27). I noted excessive caution in V 9; furthermore in IX 7, where
the asterisk after *Norico* is unnecessary, and where one should not assume
a *lacuna* of two words, as Ruehl suggests. In XI 34, it is unnecessary to add
the word *civitatem*.
[147] See W. Schmid, 'Eutropspuren in der Historia Augusta', *Bonner
Historia-Augusta Colloquium* 1963 (Bonn 1964), note 10.
[148] See especially the important article by Schmid (esp. 126), who demonstrates that it is Salmasius who suggested this change.
[149] J. Fitz, *Ingenuus et Régalien*, Collection Latomus, 81 (1966),
49 ff., tacitly assumes, without discussing the text, that IX 8,1 is about
Regalianus.

we know that Eutropius did not come after the *Historia Augusta* but preceded it, this view is rendered untenable.

In order to explain 'Trebelliano' in Eutropius' text, scholars early adduced the fact that the author of the *vita* calls himself 'Trebellius Pollio', and assumed that Eutropius' use of the name derives from him. As we have seen, this is chronologically impossible. It is more satisfactory to assume that the *Historia Augusta* got his name from Eutropius,[150] but that does not solve all our problems. For it is not certain whether this error originated with Eutropius, or whether it dates back to an earlier stage of textual tradition. W. Schmid has put forward a strong case for the latter possibility. As we see, these minor historians were often unjustly criticized for errors for which they themselves were not even responsible. There will always be captious critics who refuse to be convinced and who accuse those who rectify Eutropius' text of tampering with it.[151] However, since there is no other passage in Eutropius where a fictitious ruler is introduced into the history of Rome, there is every reason to acquit Eutropius of this charge. The *Historia Augusta*, on the other hand, has a habit of introducing imaginary rulers. Eutropius certainly deserves the benefit of the doubt.

---

[150] Syme, *Ammianus*, 48.

[151] E. Hohl, most recently in *Klio* 27 (1934), 157 ff; cf. (against Hohl) Schmid, *art. cit.*, 127. The matter was taken up once more, using Hohl's arguments, by J. Rougé, 'L'Histoire Auguste et l'Isaurie au IVᵉ siècle, *REA* 88 (1966), 282, esp. 288 ff., 315.

CHAPTER FIVE

FESTUS

The Breviarium[1]

Festus' *breviarium*, like that by Eutropius, is dedicated to Valens; the beginning of the Bambergensis tells us why it was written. *Breviarium . . . de breviario rerum gestarum populi Romani.* It is a summary of a (or *the*) summary which Eutropius had presented to the emperor shortly before. Apparently the emperor considered Eutropius' work too lengthy, despite its conciseness.[2] Festus was to fulfil this demand for even greater brevity. How he approached his object will appear in due course.

We should first, however, point out that the obvious interpretation of the words *breviarium de breviario*, namely, that they refer to Eutropius' work, is not accepted unanimously. Wölfflin[3] contended, in an article which has since become famous, that these words should be seen as an expression of rivalry between this and other *breviaria*; Festus, according to Wölfflin, asserted that he had written the definitive *breviarium* of Roman history, an exemplar of its kind. In support of his contention, Wölfflin adduces parallel constructions such as βασιλεὺς βασιλέων and *dux ducum* (Seneca, *Med.* 233), which in later Latin gave rise to expressions such as

---

[1] Copies of the last edition (C. Wagener, 1886), having become scarce, the new edition of J. W. Eadie, *The Breviarium of Festus, a Critical Edition with Historical Commentary*, (London 1967) was most welcome. There is a good short review of the text as given by Eadie by Sc. Mariotti in *RFIC* 95 (1967), 503. For a further fragment found in the Royal Library in Copenhagen, see J. W. Eadie, 'The Breviarium of Festus: a Fragment in Copenhagen', *Bull. Inst. Cl. Stud.* (London), 14 (1967), 93-95. An extensive review of the edition itself is given by T. D. Barnes, *JRS* 58 (1968), 263-5. See also A. Cameron in *CR*, n.s., 19 (1969), 305-307.

[2] A. Momigliano in *The Conflict between Paganism and Christianity in the Fourth Century* (Oxford 1963), esp. 'Pagan and Christian Historiography in the Fourth Century A.D.', 85-86.

[3] E. Wölfflin, 'Das Breviarium des Festus', *ALL* 13 (1904), 69 ff., 173 ff. Cameron (*art. cit.*, 305) says that Momigliano 'mischievously suggested that Valens found Eutropius too long'. He continues, 'The true answer is that Festus wrote with a view to Valens' projected war with Persia in 370' (306). These two views are not necessarily mutually exclusive. In any case, Momigliano can certainly not be considered 'mischievous', since his interpretation suggests an entirely credible explanation of the words 'breviarium de breviario'.

saecula saeculorum, disciplina disciplinarum (Macrob. *Sat.* 1,24,21).
The decisive objection to these examples is that, since these expressions all involve a plural concept they are not, strictly speaking,
comparable with *breviarium de breviario* (or its genitive, *breviarii*).
In any case, it was presumptuous enough for Festus to undertake
to write a *breviarium* of the *breviarium* (commissioned by the
emperor), by Eutropius, a civil servant with an excellent reputation.
Indeed, Festus' style throughout bespeaks his presumption.[4]

There are two passages, at the beginning and at the end of the
work, which require some explanation.[5] Firstly, in chapter 1: 'Your
Grace ordered me to be brief. I shall obey your command with
pleasure, because I lack the faculty of discoursing upon my subject
at length. In accordance with the example set by mathematicians,
who reduce large sums of small change to smaller totals, I shall
only record achievements and dispense with detail. Accept, therefore, what amounts to a mere enumeration, shorter even than a
brief survey of the facts. Allow me to present, most glorious ruler,
the years and dates of the Commonwealth, so that you may be
enabled to appreciate the facts of the past, and not merely to
read them.'[6]

The words *breviter dictis* (abl. comp.) *brevius conputetur* clearly
mean the same as the expression *breviarium de breviario* in the
Incipit. Our comparison of the chronological data given by Festus
and Eutropius will presently demonstrate that his analogy of the
calculones is entirely appropriate. Instead of Eutropius' detailed
information on the reigns of the kings and magistrates' terms of
office, Festus gives the totals.[7] This method is so marked as to
strike the reader comparing the two *breviaria* immediately. It should,
moreover, be stressed at the outset in order not to mislead the
unwary into thinking that no mediaeval scribe could have possessed
the knowledge required to add the *Incipit* to an existing manuscript.
Mediaeval scribes, however ignorant of many historical matters,

---

[4] Momigliano *op. cit.*, 86: 'He was not modest, but literal'.

[5] Oddly enough, Eadie did not comment on either.

[6] Chapter 1: 'Brevem fieri clementia tua praecepit. Parebo libens praecepto, quippe cui desit facultas latius eloquendi; ac morem secutus calculonum, qui ingentes summas aeris brevioribus exprimunt, res gestas signabo,
non eloquar. Accipe ergo, quod breviter dictis brevius conputetur: ut
annos et aetatem rei publicae ac praeteriti facta temporis non tam legere
tibi, gloriosissime princeps, quam numerare videaris'.

[7] See p. 124 ff., (Eutropius' chronology).

were often extremely well trained in one field, that of chronology.

Secondly chapter 30: 'How eloquent must be the man who is to
describe your deeds. For these I shall prepare myself, even though
I am not equal to the task of telling them and though I am too old.
Long last the happiness that was granted to you by the will of my
god and by the friendly god whom you trust and to whom you are
entrusted, in order that the palm of peace which formerly extended
over Persia may crown this victory over the Goths.' [8]

These last words of the *breviarium* constitute an indication of the
date of writing. Valens' victory over the Goths took place in 369;
the book must therefore have been written soon after.

The emperor himself wanted the author to be brief. It is therefore unfair to hold the author's brevity against him; as a civil servant,
he had to obey. He again stresses the necessity of being brief at the
beginning of chapter 3: *breviter intimabo*.[9]

In chapter 1, Festus tells how he intends to set about being brief.
In any summary, the main thing is to decide what is essential and
what is of lesser importance. Festus' technique is that of *enumeratio*
rather than *elocutio*; *signare, non eloqui*; *conputare*, as do the
calculones.[10] This will enable the emperor to *numerare* the facts of

---

[8] Chapter 30: 'Quam magno deinceps ore tua, princeps invicte, facta
sunt personanda! Quibus me licet inparem dicendi nisu et aevo graviorem
parabo. Maneat modo concessa dei nutu et ab amico, cui credis et creditus
es, numine indulta felicitas, ut ad hanc ingentem de Gothis etiam Babyloniae
tibi palma pacis accedat'.

[9] The use of this verb in prose goes back to Apuleius and Tertullian. It
is also used by Ammianus Marcellinus. Its original connotations, 'confiden-
tially speaking', were eventually lost and it became an ordinary *verbum
dicendi* (Wölfflin, *art. cit.*, 177).

[10] The image of the *calculo* probably originated in the schools. *TLL* gives
'calculo: elementorum magister'. Cf. Aug. *ord*. 2,12,35: 'litteris et numeris
repeitis nata est ... librariorum et calculonum professio'. In addition to
'calculo', there is also the form 'cauculo': *Anth*. 96,1: 'indictus teneram
succepit cauculo pubem'. 'Calculare' is synonymous with 'computare'.
Although his parallels are not quite convincing, Sperber's hypothesis, viz.
that the *calculo* was a treasury official engaged in the calculation of taxes, is
worth mentioning for its plausibility. D. Sperber, 'Calculo - logistes - ḥashban',
CQ n.s., 19 (1969), 374-378. It seems to me, however, that the 'market
inspector', the ḥashban or λογιστής, was a different official, as is demonstrated
in the texts adduced by Sperber himself. The situation in which a *calculo*
was required is vividly depicted in his illuminating suggestions (*art. cit.*,
376): 'Throughout the whole of the fourth century the relationship between
the debased denarius and (first the aureus and then) the solidus was very
fluid, changing almost continuously year by year, and also having regional

the past, and to avoid *legere* the historical stories usually woven around the facts. The choice, as so often, is that between writing a list of dates and a book of stories. The emperor needed the former. Faced with the necessity of an expedition to the East, he wished to know certain facts: how often and at what times Rome had been in contact with the East. This subject could not be discussed without due consideration of the entire development of the Imperium Romanum, however simplified. To us, treatment of the expansion in the East as a separate subject would be quite natural; to a civil servant, breathing the tradition of the Imperium, it would be unthinkable to isolate the part from the whole.[11]

Festus gives his *enumeratio*, a mere list of dates and lengths of reigns in chapter 2. It is the shortest possible survey of the dates of the kings, of the republican consuls and of the emperors.

Chapter 3 thus represents a fresh start: 'sub his tribus imperandi generibus, hoc est regio, consulari, imperatorio quantum Roma profecerit, breviter intimabo'. Chapter 4 continues: 'quo ordine autem singulas provincias Romana respublica adsecuta sit, infra ostenditur'. With these words, Festus introduces his discussion of the expansion of the Imperium Romanum, comprising six short chapters.

THE AUTHOR'S TASK DEFINED

In chapters 10 and 15 he arrives at his true object. First he deals with the East in general (10-14), and then he reaches the *raison*

---

variations ... In this fluid and everchanging situation, officials of the treasury and those concerned with taxation must have been faced with much the same problem, namely the translation of (popular) reckoning in terms of vast sums of debased *aes* currency into more compact and manageable accounts, in terms of gold. This would have been of especial concern to the tax officials, since, as we have mentioned above, all taxes (after 366) were collected in pure gold. There must surely have been some kind of official accountants (*calculones*) whose task it was to calculate these mathematical translations "qui ingentes summas aeris brevioribus exprimunt".'

[11] The parallel of the Atthidographers seems appropriate here. These regarded πάτριος πολιτεία as an indivisible entity and, however different their political views, could discuss the political problems of their own time only within the framework of constitutional history as a whole. In his review of Jacoby's *Atthis*, *CR*, n.s., 1 (1951), 84, A. W. Gomme touches upon this attitude, and says, 'Androtion could have reached his goal by better means than writing another book beginning with Cecrops and repeating what his predecessors had said about the kings and the life-archons and the rest'. His reasoning, however, is based on a modern attitude, which allows us to isolate certain periods in constitutional history. Androtion was incapable of doing so, as indeed were the abbreviators in dealing with Roman expansion.

d'être of his commission—Persia, which occupies almost half of the *breviarium* (15-29). The remarks prefacing these two parts are sufficiently eloquent.[12] Chapters 1 to 9 were necessary, but not specifically geared to the emperor's new expedition. The florid introductions in 10 and 15 are, as it were, windowdressing: the writer makes use of old words, fraught with meaning. Persia is called Babylonia; the weapons of the Persians are those of the barbarians of old—*sagittae*. The Romans, of course, used *pila*.

The use of the word *breviarium* is no different from that of the word *epitome*, as Wölffin has already established.[13] If ever 'epitome' was originally used to denote a summary or abridgement of one particular work (for instance the Epitome of Livy's history) whereas 'breviarium' was used for a short survey of the entire historical corpus, by the fourth century this distinction had long been forgotten. Eutropius' *brevis narratio* (see his *praef.*) was given the title 'Breviarium ab urbe condita'; nevertheless, should any further proof be needed, after Wölfflin, to demonstrate the fact that the two words are used interchangeably, it is provided by the Suda *s.v.* Εὐτρόπιος: τὴν ῥωμαϊκὴν ἱστορίαν ἐπιτομικῶς ... ἔγραψε. Paianios cannot, unfortunately, be adduced in support, since he did not translate the word *breviarium* in the dedication of Eutropius' book.

His work clearly places Festus as an heir to the tradition of Florus and Eutropius, being a late offshoot of those practical summaries that were required reading in the schools, and for statesmen and the military. The development of the genre was determined by ever-changing needs. A further explanation of the position of Festus' *Breviarium* beside and in contrast to that of Eutropius, is given in Momigliano's brilliant exposé.[14]

---

[12] Chapter 10,1: 'Nunc Eoas partes totumque Orientem ac positas sub vicino sole provincias, qui auctores sceptris tuis paraverint, explicabo, quo studium clementiae tuae, quod in isdem propagandis habes, amplius incitetur'. Chapter 15,1: 'Scio nunc, inclyte princeps, quo tua pergat intentio. Requiris profecto, quotiens Babyloniae ac Romanorum arma conlata sint et quibus vicibus sagittis pila contenderint'. Another promise of brevity is in chapter 15: 'breviter eventus enumerabo bellorum'.

[13] E. Wölfflin, 'Epitome', *ALL* 12 (1902), 342. Eadie's grounds for disagreeing with Wölfflin (p. 1 ff.) are not convincing. 'He is over-concerned with the word breviarium', as T. D. Barnes rightly says in his review of Eadie's edition, *JRS* 58 (1968), 264.

[14] A. Momigliano, *Conflict*, 85-86: 'After the social and political earthquakes of the third century a new leading class had emerged which clearly had some difficulty in remembering the simple facts of Roman history. This explains why Eutropius and (Rufius?) Festus were both commissioned

Festus the man

Festus was a pagan, as he makes clear in chapter 30: 'maneat modo concessa dei nutu et ab amico, cui credis et creditus es, numine indulta felicitas'. The words *dei nutu* apply to his own, pagan, god; he describes the Christian god as an *amicum numen, cui credis et creditus es*. He could hardly have been more subtle. Great tact was expected of a pagan civil servant employed by a Christian emperor, but Festus was obviously able to meet this challenge.[15]

The dedication of the Bambergensis calls him *magister memoriae*. Many attempts have been made to identify the historian with contemporary namesakes, the most promising line of research being that identifying him with Festinus of Tridentum. The latter, like our Festus, also held the post of *magister memoriae* in the course of his career, under both Valens and Valentinian. The main facts about him are to be found in Ammianus and Eunapius;[16] they merit separate discussion though, since this identification is not, in my view, satisfactory.

Ammianus calls Festinus of Tridentum 'a man of the most humble and obscure parentage',[17] and informs us that he was also an intimate childhood friend of Maximinus, whose reign of terror as *praefectus annonae* and *vicarius urbis Romae* is described elsewhere.[18] Of Festinus' career we hear that he was *consularis* in Syria and later *magister memoriae*, thus far with a good record of service. He subsequently became governor of Asia. Under the influence of Maximinus, Ammianus continues, he became a cruel persecutor of

---

by the Emperor Valens to prepare a brief summary of Roman history. Eutropius was the first to obey the royal command. But his seventy-seven pages (in the Teubner edition) must have proved too many for Valens. Festus, who followed, restricted himself to about twenty pages. He was not modest, but literal, when he commended his work to the 'gloriossisimus princeps' as being even shorter than a summary—a mere enumeration of facts. The new men who, coming from the provincial armies or from Germany, acquired power and wealth, wanted some knowledge of the Roman past. They had to mix with the surviving members of the senatorial aristocracy in which knowledge of Roman history and antiquities was *de rigueur*. The establishment of a new senate in Constantinople, by adding another privileged class, complicated this educational problem.'

[15] See *Mnem.* 21 (1968), 278-9.

[16] Amm. Marc. 29,2,22; Eunapius 7,6,6-13 (ed. Giangrande). *FHG* IV 39 contains all that is known about him from classical sources.

[17] Amm. Marc. 29,2,22; 'ultimi sanguinis et ignoti'.

[18] Amm. Marc. 28, 1, 5 ff; Ensslin in *RE*, Suppl. V (1931), *s.v.* 'Maximinus (6)', Cf. A. Chastagnol, *La préfecture urbaine à Rome* (1960), 95.

the innocent, speculating on the emperor's fear of the slightest suspicion of rebellion. Astrological consultation and witchcraft were severely punished. The most horrible example is the case of the woman who used incantations to cure feverish patients; even though Festinus had made use of her services when his own daughter was ill, he had the woman put to death.[19]

We have some reason for assuming that this Festinus was a Christian. In the first place, the Christians were against astrology and 'black magic'. A Christian was therefore 'by nature' zealous in suppressing these 'malefactors'. Eusebius (*Chron. ad* 371) observes: 'Maximinus praefectus annonae maleficos ab imperatore investigare iussus, plurimos Romae nobilium occidit'. This was not to criticize Maximinus,[20] it was left to the pagans to do so. In 376 Ausonius' ascendancy over the mind of the young Gratian at last bore fruit in his hostility to Maximinus. Ausonius himself became prefect of Gaul in 378, thereby uniting the prefecture of Italy. The Christian poet, now high in imperial favour, allowed the pagan senators to be revenged on Maximinus. An embassy sent to Trèves charged him, and succeeded in having him executed.[21] The animosity of high-ranking pagans makes it seem almost certain that Maximinus was a Christian.[22] This places Festinus in a fresh light. Their intimate friendship would suggest that they held similar religious views. These grounds alone are, of course, insufficient to provide conclusive evidence of their religious convictions. But there is more. When he was governor of Asia, Festinus had the philosopher Maximus executed in Ephesus; the Egyptian philosopher Coiranos met with the same fate.[23] Seeck, with whose conclusion I am inclined to agree, connects the persecution of philosophers and astrologers with Christian sympathies on the part of Festinus.[24] The great enemy of the Christians, Zosimus, is especially vehement in his disapproval of Festus, the flames of which were possibly fanned by his dislike of the religious fanaticism expressed in

---

[19] For this and other examples of cruelty and witch-hunting, see A. A. Barb, 'The Survival of Magic Arts', *Conflict*, 100-125.

[20] Possibly no criticism was expressed because Maximinus was a Christian.

[21] Symm. *or*. IV 12, *epist*. X 2; Amm. Marc. 28, 1,7 and 57.

[22] Symm. *or*. IV 11, Cf. Seeck, *Geschichte des Untergangs der antiken Welt* V, 42 and 442.

[23] Amm. Marc. 29,2, 23-28; Suda *s.v.* Φῆστος; Zosim. IV 15,2.

[24] Seeck says. '(er) verfolgte *als eifriger Christ* alle, die heidnischer Zauberei verdächtig waren, mit grösster Härte', *RE* XII, *s.v.* 'Festus (10)', col. 2257.

the trials. In this, he followed the rhetor Libanius, whose autobiography unfortunately throws no light on Festus' religion. It
seems likely however, that the dangers that beset the celebrated
pagan teacher under Festus' governorship of Asia were of Christian
origin.[25]

Our most important source of information on Festus' mentality
is Eunapius, who describes him as 'a man of a murderous disposition
with the soul of a butcher'. He goes on to relate that, in 379, Festus
wished to justify himself to Theodosius on the score of certain
accusations that had been made against him. This journey was
successful: he 'escaped from all charges'. In order to celebrate his
success, Eunapius continues, 'he announced that he would give a
magnificent banquet to those who held the most distinguished
offices or were of the highest nobility. Now it was the third day
after the January Calends,[26] as the Romans call them, and they
all saluted him and promised to come to the banquet. Then Festus
entered the temple of the godesses Nemesis, though he had never
professed any reverence for the gods, nay it was for their worship
of the gods that he punished all his victims with death'.[27] The
goddesses, however, avenged themselves. He had come to their
temple because he was in great torment over a dream. He dreamed
that his victim, the philosopher Maximus, dragged him down to
the underworld. Festus was advised to invoke the aid of the
goddesses of the underworld, the Erinyes. In desperation he did so,
but to no avail. On leaving the temple, he 'slipped, fell and died'.[28]
Our point is contained in the words καὶ τοί γε οὐδέποτε φήσας
θεραπεύειν θεούς, ἀλλ' οὓς ἐκόλασε ἅπαντας διὰ τοῦτο ἀνῃρηκώς, which
in no way characterize Festus as an unbeliever. Θεραπεύειν θεούς
means to worship gods, i.e. to adhere, in some way, to a pagan
religion. According to Eunapius' account, Festus professed mono-
theism.[29] In short, the persecutor of the philosophers was a Christian;
the historian however, was evidently a pagan.

---

[25] Libanius I 156 ff. As A. F. Norman, in his excellent book *Libanius'
Autobiography (Oration I)* (Oxford 1965), 194, rightly says in connection
with ch. 157: 'An example of the disability suffered by a rhetor who lacks
the support of the administration. Libanius' position was vulnerable at this
time'.

[26] According to Seeck, December 30th, *loc. cit.*

[27] Translation by W. C. Wright in the Loeb series, 1952.

[28] Probably of a stroke.

[29] Eunapius VII 6,12; cf. *Mnem.* 21 (1968) 278, n. 4. Cf. also Momigliano,
Conflict, 95, 98.

Identification of the historian with Festinus or Festus of Tridentum is far from new, although early supporters of this theory were not as sure of their case as are their modern counterparts.[30] Garroni published a strong defence of this view in 1915.[31] We may fully endorse his negative conclusion: the identification of Festus the historian, defended by Mommsen and others, with Rufus Festus Avienus the nobleman from Volsinii and author of a poem to the goddess Nortia (*ILS* 2944) is incorrect. The mere fact that the poet was a nobleman shows that he cannot have been the same man as Festinus of Tridentum, simply because the latter, as Ammianus states explicitly, was of humble origin.

Garroni's positive conclusion, the identification of the historian as Festinus of Tridentum, is untenable. Garroni is well aware of the difficulties. He, too, believes that the historian is a pagan. In order to be able to maintain the identification in the face of all objections, he postulates that Festus' life may be divided into three periods. In the first, pagan, period he wrote the *breviarium*, subsequently he was converted to Christianity and persecuted philosophers and astrologers, and finally, frightened by a bad dream, he reverted to paganism at the end of his life. All this is decidedly speculative and is, moreover, in conflict with the words of Eunapius, according to whom Festus the persecutor (of Tridentum) said that he had never (οὐδέποτε) worshipped 'the gods'. This can only mean that he had never been a polytheist, and hence that there can never have been any pagan periods in his life.

Other arguments, in themselves less convincing, can only weaken Garroni's position without necessarily refuting it. For instance, Zonaras' statement (XIII 16) that Valens was tolerant towards the pagan religions suggests that a career such as the historian's was possible under Valens, but throws no light on the identification proposed by Garroni.

To recapitulate, all that we know for certain up to now is that

---

[30] Boissonade (*ad* p. 63, p. 329 of his 1822 edition) does not commit himself, but states 'Huetus putat quod jam putaverat Valesius, hunc Rufum [i.e. in Eunapius] auctorem esse Breviarii quod adhuc habemus'.

[31] A. Garroni, 'L'iscrizione di Rufio Festo Avieno e l'autore del "Breviarium Historiae Romanae"', *Bull. Comm.*, 43 (1915), 133. Modern scholars tend to support him, e.g. J. Matthews, *Historia* 16 (1967), 486, n. 8 and 494-5; R. Syme, *Ammianus*, 105; T. D. Barnes, *JRS* 58 (1968), 264. Cf. also A. Cameron, *CQ*, n.s., 17 (1967), 392, esp. n. 4; *CR*, n.s. 19 (1969), 305-307.

one of Valens' civil servants was commissioned to write a very short history of Rome for the emperor; this was occasioned by the Persian expedition, which was to start in 370/1.

The work itself is the chief proof of the fact that the man wished to be more concise than Eutropius. In support of this is the argument that he is indicated as *magister memoriae*; he may even have succeeded Eutropius in that office. This second argument, however, is weaker than the first, which every reader comparing the two works can see for himself, besides which, it is based exclusively on an *incipit* found in only one manuscript. The question may, of course, be raised as to whether some later scribe was shrewd enough to notice the parallel between the two works, and to draw the conclusion that the latter was in many respects a summary of the former. If so, nothing could be easier than the assumption that the careers of Eutropius and Festus must also have run a similar course and that both must therefore have occupied the office of *magister memoriae*.[32]

I have no intention of adding to all the existing uncertainties by defending this suggestion, but it should be borne in mind by those who support the identification of the historian Festus with Fest(in)us of Tridentum, simply because both were *magister memoriae*. After all, we can only be sure that this was so in the case of Fest(in)us.

Personally, I am willing to accept the coincidence that there were two civil servants who held the same post in quick succession. As we have seen, according to Ammianus Festinus of Tridentum first held the position of *consularis Syriae* (*c.* 365), subsequently became *magister memoriae*, and finally became *proconsul Asiae* (from 372 to 378). He would have been *magister memoriae* between 365 and 372.[33] It is by no means impossible for two men, one named Festus and another named Fest(in)us, to have held the post of *magister memoriae* within these seven years. The reasoning of those who consider the similarity of their names suspiciously coincidental is very weak indeed.[34] And yet, in the last analysis, this is the only

---

[32] Eadie, *op. cit.*, 6, is being rather naive when he says that 'it seems unlikely that the official title *magister memoriae*, which does not appear in any other MS, could have been inserted by a scribe'.

[33] Thus Eadie, rightly, *loc. cit.*

[34] Eadie says, *loc. cit.*, 'That two Festi occupied the same position, under the same Emperor, within a few years of one another seems rather improbable'. One cannot overemphasize the unreliability of such arguments. I

evidence on which those who persist in considering the two men as one must rest their case. So weak, in fact, is this argument as to constitute additional grounds for rejecting the theory of their identity. The chief argument militating against this theory, however, is the fact that Festinus of Tridentum was a Christian, whereas Festus the historian was a pagan.[35]

Festinus of Tridentum is known to have lodged a complaint with Valens against a certain Eutropius.[36] No trace of hostility or rivalry between the two writers is to be found in the work of either Eutropius or Festus. Admittedly, it is not certain whether this Eutropius is the historian, but, since both *breviaria* antedate the lawsuit, it is not surprising that we can find no trace of this legal quarrel in the two works. On the whole, it is best to follow Eadie's example, and not allow ourselves to be diverted from the point at issue, i.e. the problem of identifying Festus.[37]

THE ENUMERATIO

The chronological pattern of chapter 2 is the same as Eutropius', as the following will show.

Eutropius:	Festus:
X 18,3 Is status erat Romanae rei Ioviano eodem et Varroniano consulibus anno urbis conditae millesimo centesimo et octovo decimo.	Ab urbe condita in ortum perennitatis vestrae ... anni numerantur MCXVII

---

myself know of at least one case parallel to that of Festus and Festinus, that of a Rev. Blaauw and a Rev. Blaauwendraad, who were each vicar to the same parish within a short time of each other. People are all too readily inclined to reduce similar occurrences or similar names to a single event or to a single man. This process has been convincingly illustrated by Sir William Tarn in *Alexander the Great* II, 1948, 346 n. 2: 'In the sixteenth month after the publication of my first book (*Antigonos Gonatas*) Britain declared war on Germany. In the sixteenth month after the publication of my last book (*The Greeks in Bactria and India*) Britain declared war on Germany. Two thousand years hence, some scholar, were this coincidence known, would certainly command general assent if he said that the two books were one'.

[35] Eadie, *op. cit.*, 9, also believes that the historian was a pagan. Cameron, however, has his doubts. *CR* 1969, 306.

[36] Amm. Marc. 29, 1, 36; Lib. *or.* 1,159, see Norman's commentary, *op. cit.*

[37] Eadie, *op. cit.*, 16-17, esp. n. 2.

I 2,2 (Romulus) anno regni tricesimo septimo ad deos transisse creditus est et consecratus

Romulus regnavit annos XXXVIII

I 2,3 Deinde Romae per quinos dies senatores imperavunt et his regnantibus annus unus completus est

senatores per quinos dies annum unum (regnarunt)

I 3 (Numa) morbo decessit quadragesimo et tertio imperii anno

Numa Pompilius regnavit annos XLIII

I 4 (Tullus Hostilius) Cum triginta et duos annos regnasset, fulmine ictus cum domo sua arsit.

Tullus Hostilius regnavit annos XXXII.

I 5 (Ancus Marcius) vicesimo et quarto anno imperii morbo periit

Ancus Marcius regnavit annos XXIIII

I 6 (Tarquinius Priscus) tricesimo octavo imperii anno ... occisus est

Priscus Tarquinius regnavit annos XXXVIII.

I 7 (Servius Tullius) *number of years obtained by deduction*; *see* I 8,3

Servius Tullius regnavit annos XLIII.

I 8,3 (Tarquinius Superbus) cumque imperasset annos quattuor et viginti cum uxore et liberis suis fugit.

L. Tarquinius Superbus expulsus regno est, anno XXIIII.

Ita Romae regnatum est per septem reges annis ducentis quadraginta tribus

Sic sub regibus numerantur CCXLIII.

VII 1 Anno urbis septingentesimo fere ac nono interfecto Caesare civilia bella reparata sunt (44 B.C.)

Consules fuerunt a Bruto et Publicola in Pansam et Hirtium ... per annos CCCCLXVII.

Missi ad eum (Antonium) persequendum duo consules, Pansa et Hirtius (43 B.C.)

Novem enim annis Romae consules defuerunt, ita sub decemviris annis duobus, sub tribunis militaribus annis tribus, sine magistratibus Roma fuit annis quattuor.[38]

VII 8,1 Ita bellis toto orbe confectis Octavianus Augustus Romam rediit, duodecimo anno, quam consul fuerat ... 3. Ita ab initio principatus eius usque ad finem quinquaginta et sex anni fuerunt.

X 18,3 Is status erat Romani rei Ioviano eodem et Varroniano consulibus anno urbis conditae millesimo centesimo et octavo decimo

Imperatores ab Octaviano Caesare Augusto in Iovianum fuerunt numero XLIII per annos CCCCVII

The period of the Kings   243 years

stated explicitly by both authors

The Republic   467 years

stated explicitly by Festus, in Eutropius the number of years has to be deduced from the dates a.u.c. (VII 1): a.u.c. 710 (up to and including 43 B.C.) *minus* 243 = 467 years.

The *Imperium*   407 years

stated explicitly by Festus; in Eutropius the number of years has to be deduced from the dates a.u.c. (X 18,3): 1117 — (243 + 467) = 407.

The comparison with the *calculones* (chapter 1) now falls into place. By giving the totals 467 and 407, and not listing the consuls

[38] These nine years are included in the 467 years of the Republic. They are to be found in Eutr. 1,18 and II,3.

for every year or the length of the reign of each emperor, he reduced the entire complex of numerical data to the sum of its parts.

Notwithstanding its terseness, the author took some pains to avoid oversimplification. As a concession to past glories, each of the kings is mentioned separately, but the consular years, frequently mentioned by Eutropius, have been omitted.[39] Apart from the data given for the early kings, though, the simplification is indeed rather drastic. The traditional dates of the Decemviri, 451-0 B.C. (two years), of the 'anarchy' (four years), and of the military tribunes (three years), are to be found in Eutropius and were taken over by Festus;[40] it is impossible to state with any certainty whence this pattern of chronology ultimately derives. As for Festus, it is clear by now that his work is indeed a *breviarium de breviario*. Anyone with Eutropius' book within reach, and there must have been many in view of its popularity, might easily have drawn this conclusion.

The enumeration of chronological data in the *breviaria* was of considerable importance in the fourth century. In those times of war and upheaval it was good to remember that there was continuity in all things.[41] The emperor Valens was thus included in a series of legitimate rulers. Moreover—and this was Eutropius' idea—it was a pleasing thought for both author and reader to reflect that Rome had started almost from scratch: 'non amplius quam usque Portum atque Ostiam intra octavum (Eutropius is more accurate, quintum) decimum miliarium a portis urbis Romae'. The picture evoked by Festus was familiar to all from Virgil: that of the palace of Evander, 'Romae parvae et a pastoribus conditae'.[42] Thus the Empire came into being and then grew 'quum finitimae circum civitates premerent'. In Festus' time, the same forces were pressing in on her frontiers; it was comforting to think how Rome, at an early, humble, stage in her existence, had survived their pressure.

---

[39] This reminds me of the reduced number of facts given in Dutch school textbooks about the history of the country. In the nineteenth century every child had to know the names of all the Dutch counts (vassals of the German emperors) in the Middle Ages, as well as their regnal years; at present a summary suffices. Cf. the drastic reduction in the knowledge of Roman history required by the Dutch universities, see above, p. 131, n. 44.

[40] Eutr. II, 3; cf. the list given by Eadie, *op. cit.*, 100; for a bibliography of modern *Quellenforschung*, *ibid.*, 70.

[41] This cannot help but remind one of Florus' concept of history as an organic whole, see above, p. 3.

[42] Cf. *Aen.* VIII 97 ff.

Sources

The question whether, in the above chapter and elsewhere, Festus worked independently, or whether his errors were his own or derived from other authors, has been widely discussed. Suffice it to refer my readers to the bibliography compiled by Eadie.[43] So much, at any rate, is clear, that he relied on Florus and Eutropius to a considerable degree. It is equally certain that Aurelius Victor, his contemporary, was of little use to him. Not only in the material sense, but Victor's way of thinking was completely different; his pessimism, his complicated style, his incessant moralizing in laborious terms—all this was quite foreign to Festus.

There is yet another reason why it is more prudent to leave the problem of sources for what it is. We know next to nothing of the manner of education in the schools, of the stories told in army camps, or of the stock anecdotes perennially current in imperial offices. To refer almost everything back to a single source is to simplify the problem all too crudely. As I have remarked before,[44] this error has been perpetrated in modern historiography by the introduction of the anonymous author known after his discoverer as 'Enmann's historian', supposedly an imperial historian. Far be it from me to deny that such a historian may have lived at some time; on the other hand, one should remember that, throughout history, all cultures have handed down a traditional corpus of knowledge, part history and part legend, the common heritage of a people, a generation, or a social group. It would be all too facile to solve the problem by assuming that the writers of school textbooks relied on one written source on which they based their frequently inferior scribblings. What is worse, this assumption clouds our perception of the character of the scribblers, some of whom are surprisingly original.

The following two passages from Livy's *Periochae* are most suggestive when compared to the corresponding passages in Festus.

Periocha 127:

Parthi Labieno, quo Pompeianarum partium fuerat, duce in Syriam inruperunt ... totam eam provinciam occupaverent

Festus 18:

Parthi Labieno, qui Pompeianarum partium fuerat ac victus ad Persas refugerat, duce in Syriam inruperunt ac totam provinciam occuparunt

---

[43] Eadie, *op. cit.*, 70-98: 'The Sources of the Breviarium'.
[44] See above, p. 20 f. and the passages referred to there (n. 6).

Periocha 130:	Festus 18:
M. Antonius ... Mediam ingressus bellum ... Parthis intulit ... et cum duabus legionibus amissis ...	M. Antonius Mediam ingressus ... bellum Parthis intulit, et primis eos proeliis vicit. Post duabus legionibus amissis ...

Even though Festus did indeed sometimes draw his information from written sources, this should not lead us to think that Festus depended directly on the *Periochae*. Such a conclusion, readily supported by the striking similarity with the corresponding passages in Festus' work, is not, of course, the only possibility. Eadie thinks that the information Festus imparts in these passages derives from a History, now lost, on which the *Periochae* may also have been based.[45] He does not give any valid reasons for his contention— indeed they must be hard to find, and impossible to justify. T. D. Barnes' review of Eadie's book, an intelligent listing of desperate attempts,[46] shows how little *Quellenforschung* can in fact contribute to our knowledge of the matter. Whether we like it or no, the only art to employ is the *difficillima ars nesciendi*.

HISTORIANS AND THEIR AMBITIONS

The difficulty of tracking down one single source for similar statements made by different authors is best illustrated by comparing the daring plans for the future unfolded by even the most insignificant historians. Festus says in chapter 30: 'Quibus (sc. tuis factis) me licet imparem dicendi nisu[47] et aevo graviorem parabo'. The author hopes that he will one day be able to describe the deeds of Valens, *magno ore personanda*.

This is comparable to the sentiments expressed by Jerome and Eutropius:

---

[45] Eadie, *op. cit.*, 83.

[46] *JRS* 58 (1968), 264, *sub* 3.

[47] One would expect 'impar' to be followed by the dative. 'Nisu' may also, however, be a dative. For datives ending in -*u* (in the *u*-stems), see Leumann-Hofmann in Stolz-Schmalz, *Lateinische Grammatik*[5], 1926, 271. Perhaps Festus is vaguely reminded of some fragment of poetry; the same goes for 'aevo graviorem', (cf. *Aen.* II 435). For the dative ending in -*u* in the *sermo dactylicus*, see E. Bednara, *ALL* 14 (1906), 344. However, it is impossible to be sure about this, particularly since it may also be interpreted as an ablative, for instance, an *abl. respect.*: 'imparem (aliis) dicendi nisu'. For numerous examples of the *abl. respect.* with 'impar', see *TLL*.

Hieron. *Chron.* praef.:

reliquum tempus Gratiani et
Theodosii latioris historiae stilo
reservavi, non quo de viventibus
timuerim libere et vere scribere—
timor enim dei hominum timo-
rem expellit—, sed quoniam de-
bacchantibus adhuc in terra nostra barbaris incerta sunt omnia.

Eutr. X 18,3:

nam reliqua stilo maiore dicenda
sunt. Quae nunc non tam praetermittimus, quam ad maiorem
scribendi diligentiam reservamus.

The promise of a future, generally more ambitious, work which
the author hopes to write some day is also to be found elsewhere.[48]
Vell. Paterc. II 99,3: 'iusto servemus operi'; Tac. *Hist.* I 1: 'princi-
patum divi Nervae et imperium Traiani, uberiorem securioremque
materiam senectuti seposui'; Amm. Marc. 31,16,9; 'scribant reliqua
potiores ... quos id (si libuerit) adgressuros procudere linguas ad
maiores moneo stilos'; *SHA, Firmus* etc., 15,10: 'nam Diocletianus
et qui secuntur stilo maiore dicendi sunt'.

   There are thus no grounds for assuming that any one of these
authors was dependent on any of the others.[49] It is extremely misleading and by no means convincing to conduct a study of the
sources based only on these indications, and then conclude that
the authors were mutually dependent.[50] The entire passage in
chapter 30 belongs to the usual *topos* of modesty, as indeed do the
previously quoted words from chapter 1, 'quippe cui desit facultas
eloquendi... res gestas signabo, non eloquar'. A well-tried formula,
this, to commend the work in question in modest terms, leaving a
more ambitious work for the future. The *vita Probi* (1, 6) says, 'neque
ego nunc facultatem eloquentiamque polliceor, sed res gestas', and
Barnes, who quotes these words, wonders: 'Is this parody of Festus

---

[48] The relevant passages have been comprehensively listed by R. Helm
in his illuminating article, 'Hieronymus und Eutrop', *RhM*, N.F., 76 (1927),
138-170, 254-306, esp. 305 ff. In poetry, cf. Stat. *Theb.* I 32; Hor. c. IV
2,33; Nemes. *Cyn.* 63.

[49] Helm, too, wants to disregard these passages in discussing Eutropius'
influence on Jerome: 'Die Ähnlichkeit im Wortlaut hat also bei diesem aus
der Topik entlehnten Satze etwas durchaus Natürliches und Selbstverständ-
liches' (*art. cit.*, 306).

[50] O. Seeck goes even further in his conclusions (Symm., *praef.* CXXXII).
On the basis of Eutr. X 18,3 (see above) and Symm. *Epist.* III 47, 'sed haec
stilo exequenda tibi arte alios, cui pollet Minerva, concedemus', he identifies
the historian Eutropius as Symmachus' correspondent in *Epist.* III 46-53.

or of a long line of epitomators?'[51] The answer is, neither; there is no question of parody but of a long line of historians using a similar *captatio benevolentiae*. Of his contemporaries, we may mention Eutropius and Ammianus; the former writes in his *praef.*: 'Res Romanas ... per ordinem temporum *brevi* narratione collegi *strictim* additis etiam his, quae in principum vita egregia extiterunt, ut tranquillitatis tuae possit mens divina laetari prius se inlustrium virorum facta in administrando imperio secutam, quam cognosceret lectione'.

However, brevity is not necessarily the soul of wit, as Ammianus himself suggests, probably in order to dissociate himself from a current whim of fashion (15,1,1): 'tunc enim laudanda est brevitas, cum moras rumpens intempestivas, nihil subtrahit cognitioni gestorum'.

FESTUS AND AMMIANUS MARCELLINUS

It is with some hesitation that I oppose part of Mommsen's famous study 'Ammians Geographica',[52] in which he traces Festus' influence on Ammianus.[53] The following passages illustrate their supposed interrelatedness:

A. *Cyprus*

Festus 13:

Eam (Cyprum) *rex foederatus* regebat, sed tanta fuit *penuria aerarii* ... ut ... Cyprus confiscari iuberetur. Quo accepto rex Cyprius nuntio *venenum sumpsit* ... *Cato* Cyprias opes Romam navibus advexit. Ita ius eius insulae *avarius magis quam iustius* sumus adsecuti.

Ammianus 14,3,15:

Nec piget dicere *avide magis* hanc insulam populum Romanum invasisse *quam iuste*. Ptolmaeo enim *rege foederato* nobis et socio, *ob aerarii nostri angustias* iusso sine ulla culpa proscribi, ideoque *hausto veneno*, voluntaria morte deleto, et tributaria facta est, et velut hostiles eius exuviae classi impositae, in urbem advectae sunt per *Catonem*.

Mommsen comments, 'Jede Redewendung bei Ammian lässt sich in der Weise auf Festus zurückführen, dass überall bei dem Aus-

---

[51] *JRS* 58 (1968), 264, *sub* 2.

[52] *Hermes* 16 (1881), 602-636 (= *Ges. Schr.* VII [1909], 393-425).

[53] A view adopted by R. Syme, *op. cit.*, 105: 'and he certainly took details of geography from Festus. The confrontation proves it.'

schreiber das Bestreben hervortritt zu steigern und zu coloriren'.[54] May the reader judge for himself: the corresponding words have been italicized. I cannot bring myself to share Mommsen's assurance. It would be possible to find examples of similarity of presentation in many abridged historical compilations. After all, the order of presentation is generally determined by the course of events; in this case, the similarities of vocabulary are not remarkable, and the moral judgement placed at the beginning by one author and at the end by the other, may well be a stock expression of 'establishment' opinion of this conquest.

The persistence with which modern scholars who, like myself, do not regard the linguistic similarities as decisive, still try to defend the theory of mutual dependence is truly remarkable. They argue that it is merely a question of 'linguistic variations' which, even where writers do not slavishly copy one another, almost inevitably lead to incidental 'verbal correspondence'.[55] They reverse Mommsen's reasoning and abandon his basic premise. To him 'verbal correspondence' formed the cornerstone of his theory of the interdependence of two authors. This remains a good principle. Those who base their reasoning on 'linguistic variations', forfeit their right to claim interrelationship for any two authors: they have cut the ground from under their own feet.

According to Mommsen, the passages below can also be adduced to show that Ammianus follows Festus:

B. Notes on the history of Cilicia and Isauria (14,8,4)

C. Syria and Palestine (14,8,10 and 12)

D. Thrace (27,4,4; 10,12)

E. Egypt near Cyrene (22,16,24)

B. *Cilicia and Isauria*

Festus 12:

Cilices et Isauros, qui se piratis ac praedonibus maritimis iunxerant, Servilius pro consule ad praedo-

Ammianus 14,8,4:

Hae duae provinciae, bello quondam piratico catervis mixtae praedonum, a Servilio pro con-

---

[54] *Ges. Schr.* VII, 397.

[55] T. Damsholt, 'Zur Benutzung von dem *Breviarium* des Eutrop in der *Historia Augusta*', *Class. et Med.* 25 (1964), 138-150, esp. 150: 'Es ist nur von sprachlichen Variationen die Rede, die ... wo die Verfasser nicht einander sklavisch abschreiben, fast notwendigerweise dann und wann zufällige verbale Übereinstimmungen mit sich führen müssen.'

num bellum missus subegit et   sule missae sub iugum, factae
viam per Taurum montem primus   sunt vectigales.
instituit; isque de Cilicibus et
Isauris triumphavit atque Isauri-
cus est cognominatus.

C. *Syria and Palestine*

Festus 14:   Ammianus 14,8,10:
Postea per Pompeium eadem loca   Has autem provincias . . Gnaeus
armis obtenta sunt. Syriae et   Pompeius superato Tigrane, reg-
Phoenice bello a Tigrane, Arme-   nis Armeniorum abstractas, di-
niorum rege, receptae sunt. Ara- cioni Romanae coniunxit.
bes et Iudaei in Palaestina victi
sunt.

                                  Ammianus 14,8,12:
                                  Verum has quoque regiones pari
                                  sorte Pompeius Iudeis domitis et
                                  Hierosolymis captis, in provin-
                                  ciae speciem delata iuris dictione
                                  formavit.

Neither B[56] nor C shows any trace of verbal or informational
contextual similarity. We cannot, therefore, agree with Mommsen
when he says: 'An diesen (*sc.* Abriss des Festus) schliesst sich
Ammian . . . auf das engste an'.[57]

D. *Thrace*

At this point, it is advisable to include the relevant passages from
Florus and Eutropius in our comparison. The restrained tone of the
latter is a striking confirmation of his dignified objectivity, which
we have already had occasion to point out earlier.

Festus 9:   Florus I 39,3 and 2:
In Thraciae regionibus etiam Scor- Saevissimi omnium Thracum
disci habitarunt, pariter crudeles Scordisci fuere, sed calliditas
et callidi. Multa de saevitia prae- quoque ad robur accesserat . . .
dictorum fabulosa memorantur,   nihil interim per id omne tempus

---

[56] For Isauria and Cilicia as the centre of interest in fourth-century
sources, see J. Rougé, 'L'Histoire Auguste et l'Isaurie au IVe siècle', *REA*
68 (1966), 282-315; Syme, *Ammianus*, 43-52.
[57] Mommsen, *art. cit.*, 397.

quod hostiis captivorum diis suis aliquando litaverint, quod humanum sanguinem in ossibus capitum potare sint soliti.

residuum crudelitatis fuit in captivos saevientibus: litare dis sanguine humano, bibere in ossibus capitum.

Amm. Marc. 27,4,4:

Et partem earum habitavere Scordisci ... saevi quondam et truces, et (ut antiquitas docet) hostiis captivorum Bellonae litantes et Marti, humanumque sanguinem in ossibus capitum cavis bibentes avidius, quorum asperitate ... saepe res Romana vexata postremo omnem amisit exercitum, cum rectore.

Eutr. IV 24:

C. Cato consul Scordiscis intulit bellum ignominioseque pugnavit (cf. IV 27,5 and V 7,1).

Mommsen rightly points out certain idiosyncracies 'ausschmückender Art' in Ammianus' account—Bellona, Mars, *cavis*, *avidius, cum rectore* (Ammianus has in mind the defeat of C. Porcius Cato in 114 B.C., 'bei welcher aber der Feldherr keineswegs umkam'); furthermore, Mommsen regards 'longe nunc ab iisdem provinciis disparati', a reference to the removal of the Scordisci to Lower Pannonia (CIL III, p. 415), as an afterthought based on Ptolemy 2,15,2. It is not necessary, however, to search so far afield. Festus has an interpolation, 'pariter crudeles et callidi', lacking in Ammianus. Such details were freely incorporated by all authors handling the same material, with or without rhetorical embellishments. The facts had already been given by Florus.[58]

E. *Egypt near Cyrene*

Mommsen calls the following 'ganz entscheidend',[59] conclusive evidence of the use Ammianus made of information given by Festus:

Festus 13:

Cyrenas cum ceteris civitatibus Libyae Pentapolis Ptolomaei Antiquioris liberalitate suscepimus.

Ammianus 22,16,24:

Aridiorem Libyam supremo Apionis regis consecuti sumus arbitrio.

[58] The above passages are discussed by Mommsen, *art. cit.*, 397-398; see also Eadie, *op. cit.*, 117. Cameron gives an example of Florus' influence: Laevinus as consul in 211 B.C. instead of praetorius (*CR* 1969, 306). Whether this comes from Florus, however, is uncertain.

[59] Mommsen, *art. cit.*, 297.

| Libyam supremo Appionis regis arbitrio sumus adsecuti. | Cyrenas cum residuis civitatibus Libyae Pentapoleos Ptolemaei liberalitate suscepimus. |

The acquisition of Cyrene by the Romans was traditionally assigned to the year 96 or 75 B.C. The former date is that of the death of King Ptolemaeus Apion, in the latter the Romans occupied the country. The two events are linked by others besides Festus,[60] thus confusing the issue. Peculiar to Festus and Ammianus, however, is the distinction between the regions of Libya and Cyrene, and between two kings, Ptolemaeus and Apion. The error partly arose from the fact that Cyrenaica at that time consisted of two provinces: Libya *pentapolis* (or *superior*), whose capital was Cyrene, and Libya *sicca* (or *inferior*). It is likely, says Mommsen, that Festus had the latter in mind in referring to Libya, an interpretation which Ammianus explicitly states. Mommsen's impressive exposé ends with the words: 'Diese gleichmässige Falschbesserung einer unverstandenen Ueberlieferung führt mit zwingender Notwendigkeit zu der Annahme, dass der spätere Schriftsteller sie von dem früheren übernommen hat.'[61] Mommsen is most perceptive, his discovery is highly interesting, and yet my doubts as to whether this is an instance of direct borrowing are not allayed. The problem is of an organizational nature which later officials could not be expected to understand. Reduced to its simplest terms, the question is why the Roman authorities of the time waited for more than twenty years before exercising the right of occupation conferred by their inheritance. For the Romans officially stayed out of Libya from 96 to 75. Hence the explanation, possibly known to many members of the 'establishment', that Cyrene and Libya were in fact two kingdoms, ruled by two kings.[62] Ammianus' reference to a fact that was in all probability common knowledge need not necessarily be derived from any one particular author.[63]

---

[60] For instance, Eutr. VI 11.

[61] Mommsen, *art. cit.*, 399.

[62] Neither writer had the vaguest idea which Ptolemy. 'Ptolemaeus antiquior' means simply 'a former Ptolemy'. Ammianus' words 'Ptolemaei liberalitate' are best translated as the' magnanimity of a Ptolemy'.

[63] See *RE*, *s.v.* 'Ptolemaios VIII. Euergetes II', col. 1734, line 48. His bastard son Ptolemaios Apion (*RE*, no. 29, col. 1737 ff.) was the lawful heir to the independent kingdom of Cyrene. Cf. *RE* 23 (1959), col. 1738, line 40 ff. To my knowledge the most recent extensive discussion of the matter is that by E. Will, *Histoire politique du monde hellénistique* II (Nancy

The seeds of uncertainty were originally sown by the will of Ptolemy VIII Euergetes II,[64] usually dated 155 B.C., which named Rome as conditional legatee, provided that there was no other heir. An heir was born, however, and Rome therefore lost her claim to the inheritance. Nevertheless, one wonders, and this is no more than a suggestion on my part, whether 'Ptolemaeus Antiquior' is a reference to this particular king and the will of 155. I do not by any means wish to suggest that Festus was aware of the existence of this older will, but this hypothesis would help to explain the curious use of the epithet Antiquior.[65]

The problem of Cyrene has been discussed at considerable length in recent years. Modern historians, too, are intrigued by the fact that the senate waited for more than twenty years before—very hesitantly—exerting pressure on Cyrene. Today, we have better means at our disposal than the fourth-century historians for judging this matter, which plays a not inconsiderable part in the complex problem of Roman imperialism under the late Republic. As such, it is beyond the scope of our present subject. Nevertheless, we may agree with Badian when he remarks, after a short survey of the case of Cyrene: 'Cyrene in 96 was a wealthy, profitable and—under a Ptolemy—a well-organised country, where annexation would have been both lucrative and easy; yet it was allowed to slip into anarchy in preference; and, in a period of bitter political controversy in Rome, not a voice was raised in protest. This is a clear example of Roman attitude towards expansion and exploitation at this time, and indeed an outstanding one.'[66] It is not surprising that a civil servant like Festus, who was fairly familiar with provincial history (as is shown by the 'Provincial List', to be discussed presently), regarded the affair of Cyrene under Roman rule as a striking

---

1967), 371, 410. The bequeathal of Cyrene was widely discussed at the time, as we may see from the relatively large number of references; see Note p. 196.

[64] Nicknamed 'Physcon'. See *SEG* IX, no. 7; E. Badian, *Foreign Clientelae* (Oxford, 1958), 109 ff.; Will, *op. cit.*, II 305; *RE* 23, col. 1721 ff., esp. 1724.

[65] For 'Antiquior' in this sense, *TLL* cites, besides the passage in Festus, Cicero *Brut.* 61: 'nec . . . habeo quemquam antiquiorem, cuius scripta proferenda putem'; Aug. *civ.* 3,3: 'neque . . . minus . . . recentior Caesar . . . quam . . . antiquior Romulus'; Tert. *nat.* 2,12: 'omnem patrem filiis antiquiorem'.

[66] E. Badian, *Roman Imperialism in the late Republic* (Oxford 1968), 29 ff., esp. 36; Badian lists the most recent literature, the most important being S. I. Oost, 'Cyrene 96-74 B.C.', *C.Ph.* 58 (1963), 11-25.

example of neglect, and hence a warning to his own time. He was undoubtedly not alone in his opinion, so that, Mommsen notwithstanding, Ammianus need not necessarily have derived the aforementioned passage specifically from Festus.

NOTE

The Legacy of Cyrene

Our sources of information for this matter are as follows:

App. *Mithr.* 12,121: Κυρήνην γὰρ αὐτὴν Ἀπίων βασιλεὺς τοῦ Λαγιδῶν γένους νόθος ἐν διαθήκαις ἀπέλιπεν.

App. *Bell. civ.* 1,13,111: τοῦ δ᾽ ἐπιόντος ἔτους, ἕκτης ἑβδομηκοστῆς καὶ ἑκατοστῆς ὀλυμπιάδος οὔσης, δύο μὲν ἐκ διαθηκῶν ἔθνη Ῥωμαίοις προσεγίγνετο Βιθυνία τε Νικομήδους ἀπολιπόντος καὶ Κυρήνη Πτολεμαίου, τοῦ Λαγίδου βασιλέως, ὃς ἐπίκλησιν ἦν Ἀπίων [67]

The legacy dated from 96 B.C., and not from the 176th Olympiad, which started in 76 B.C. and therefore included the year 74. Already the year of the legacy was being confused with the year of occupation.

Plut. *Luc.* 2,7: καὶ Κυρηναίοις (Lucullus) καταλαβὼν ἐκ τυραννίδων συνεχῶν καὶ πολέμων ταραττομένους ἀνέλαβε καὶ κατεστήσατο τὴν πολιτείαν (86/85, see Will, *op. cit.*, 405, 410).

Livy, *Perioch.* 70: Ptolemaeus Cyrenarum rex, cui nomen Apionis fuit, mortuus heredem populum Romanum reliquit, et eius regni civitates senatus liberas esse iussit.

Obsequens 49 (for the year 96): Ptolomaeus, rex Aegypti, Cyrenis mortuus SPQ Romanum heredum reliquit.

Justin 39,5,2: frater eius (Apion, the brother of Ptolemy IX) ex pellice susceptus, cui pater (Ptolemy VIII) Curenarum regnum testamento reliquerat, herede populo Romano instituto, decedit.

Sallust, *Hist.* fr. 43 (M): Publiusque Lentulus Marcellinus eodem auctore quaestor in novam provinciam Curenas missus est, quod ex mortui regis Apionis testamento nobis data prudentiore quam illas per gentis et minus gloriae avidi imperio continenda fuit.[68]

---

[67] See the commentary by Gabba (1958), *ad. loc.*, which does not, however, mention either Ammianus or Festus.

[68] For the career of Cn. Cornelius Lentulus Marcellinus, see Broughton, *Magistrates* II, 103: cos. 56, pr. 60. Cf. id., Suppl. p. 19, promag. Syriae 59: 'His title is not attested'.

Sallust's phrasing admits of the interpretation that the occupation was spread out over two stages (96 and 74 B.C.).

THE PROVINCIAL LIST

The most remarkable feature of all in Festus' work is his comprehensive list of the provinces, the so-called 'Provincial List'. Various scholars have compared it with similar lists dating from the fourth and early fifth centuries all of which, however, were compiled later than that of Festus. In fact, I feel that we may justifiably regard it as an innovation originating with this humble servant of Klio.

The list in question occupies chapters 4-6, 8 and 9, and 10-14. It omits Italy, but this was to be expected, since it was not required of him. Italy, as even a 'barbarian' emperor knew, had been the cradle of the Empire. Festus' commission was not to give a list of all the lands of the Empire, but of the conquered territories. It is not surprising that his list sometimes appears to be 'only a haphazard register',[69] compared to the detailed lists drawn up for administrative purposes.

The past always contains valuable lessons for the future. Even Festus had to delve somewhat deeper into the past than he had perhaps intended and could not, as we have seen,[70] discuss the East without first devoting some space to the Empire as a whole. However, his discursiveness, as we consider it, set a trend in the technique of historiography: the inclusion and incorporation of a provincial list within the framework of an enumeration of the facts. From a later period and with a later content, we have the Notitia Dignitatum, which we may safely ignore in searching for Festus' sources. If he was a member of the civil service, he may have copied the list from the official data, or he may have noted it down from memory. Administrative bodies in every country have reliable and competent heads of departments, whom experience has taught the art of apparently effortless reproduction of the details of their dealings. Presumably Festus was one of these commendable public servants.[71] Of course, these men did not possess total recall, and

---

[69] Eadie, *op. cit.*, 155.

[70] See above, p. 176 and n. 11

[71] Cf. *Mnem.* 21 (1968), 279. Amm. Marc. (16,7,5) calls Eutherius, *praepositus cubiculi*, 'inmensum quanta memoria vigens'. Cf. R. Syme, *Ammianus*, 95. For memorization exercises see H.-I. Marrou, *Histoire de l'éducation dans l'Antiquité* (Paris 1948), 92. With reference to so-called primitive peoples,

omissions were inevitable. Valentia is not included in the list in the British provinces (chapter 6), and this fact is generally taken, together with Valens' Persian campaign, to set a *terminus ante quem* for the book. Theodosius the Elder, sent to Britain by Valentinian, had retaken an area that was subsequently known as Valentia, after Valentinian.[72] One may assume that news of Theodosius' success did not reach the imperial capitals until the summer of 370. If, it is argued, the *breviarium* was written after that date, then it would have mentioned Valentia. Since it does not, the work must have been completed before the summer of 370.

The argument, which we owe to Mommsen's perspicacity, would seem to be tenable. Nevertheless I still have my doubts. Festus was no Mommsen. If it is correct to assume, as we did, that Festus spent a long life in the imperial civil service, then it is equally possible that he presented his knowledge of the past without taking much notice of the most recent changes. Moreover, since his work was commissioned by Valens, and not by Valentinian, he was undoubtedly on the staff of the former, and thus had little contact with Valentinian's administration.[73]

The question is incapable of resolution here. As soon as one takes account of the oral tradition and the influence on the author of personal knowledge acquired in the course of his career, as one must in dealing with historical reality, then the study of the sources is a much more complex matter than previous generations of scholars would have us believe. The Provincial List was, as far as we know, originally compiled by Festus himself. He probably relied heavily on his memory. Memories, however, being notoriously fallible, Valentia cannot be used as a clinching argument in establishing the date of writing.

As we see, one detail in the work of one of the least important writers on Rome's history is enough to confront us with a fundamental problem in historical research. *Quellenforschung* has too often regarded historians as impersonal beings, whose slips, blunders and

---

A. D. Nock remarks: 'Polynesian genealogies . . . had a special importance in the social structure and their memorizing and transmission was an integral part of the education', *CPh* 49 (1954), 130.

[72] Amm. Marc. 28,3,7.

[73] The reference to Valentinian, not Valens, as the emperor who commissioned Festus in the *Incipit* of some mss. must be a mistake (Cf. Schanz, *op. cit.*, IV², 83), and not a revised dedication of a second copy as contended by Eadie, *op. cit.*, 3.

major errors are to be registered and categorized by comparing written data. In many cases, though, this method is most unjust. Existing (un)certainties in the study of sources must first be swept away before the personality of the author may emerge from the mists of antiquity.[74]

CHARACTER AND CONTENT

In addition to the question of sources there is also that of the mentality and inclinations of the authors. In other words, Festus' writings teach us about Festus the man.[75]

The mentality of Festus, a civil servant, is that of the imperialist —patriotic and full of admiration for the past. He shares this admiration with Annaeus Florus, for instance, and has hence been called a 'minor Florus'.[76] This appellation is misleading. Florus occasionally condemns cruelty and certain conquests such as, for instance, the destruction of Corinth in 146 B.C. Festus, on the other hand, is full of praise, as is Livy's *Periocha*.[77]

Festus 7:

Periocha 52:

ad extremum legatis Romanorum apud Corinthum violatis, per L. Mummius proconsulem capta Corintho, Achaia omnis obtenta est.

quo omni Achaia in deditionem accepta Corinthon ex senatu consulto diruit, quia ibi legati Romani violati erant.

His heroes are the emperors Trajan, who conquered parts of the Parthian empire, and Aurelian, who restored Roman prestige in the East. His optimism strikes us as somewhat forced; but then, so does Ammianus' observation that (until Jovian) no Roman

---

[74] Differences in research methods in this field are comparable to those obtaining between Rohde and Wilamowitz: the latter formulates certain basic premises unacceptable to the former. Ulrich von Wilamowitz Moellendorff, *Zukunftphilologie! eine Erwiderung auf Friedrich Nietzsches 'Geburt der Tragödie'*, (Berlin 1872); Rohde reacted to this in a pamphlet entitled *Afterphilologie, zur Beleuchtung des von dem Dr. phil. U. v. W.M. herausgegebenen Pamphlets 'Zukunftphilologie', Sendschreiben eines Philologen an Richard Wagner*, (Leipzig 1872); the following year Wilamowitz returned to the attack in *Zukunftphilologie! zweites Stück*. He later repented of these 'juvenile' attacks, but his essential differences with his opponents in fact remained valid to a great extent. Cf. R. Pfeiffer, *Ausgewählte Schriften* (München 1960), 275-276.

[75] A summary of the following arguments is to be found in *Mnem.* 21 (1968), 279 ff.

[76] E. Wölfflin, *ALL* 13 (1904), 175. See below, n. 98.

[77] Cf. *Mnem.* 18 (1965), 374.

emperor had ever ceded conquered territory to the enemy: 'numquam enim ab urbis ortu inveniri potest annalibus replicatis (ut
arbitror), terrarum pars ulla nostrarum ab imperatore vel consule
hosti concessa'.[78]

A remarkable contrast, this, to Aurelius Victor's long list of
disasters culminating in the loss of Dacia under Gallienus.[79]
Aurelian's conduct in respect of this province made Eutropius in
particular feel bitter (*desperans eam posse retineri*). Festus appears
to have accepted it as a matter of course, provided only that no
Roman citizens were killed.

Festus 8,2:

Traianus Dacos sub rege Decibalo
vicit et Daciam trans Danubium
in solo barbariae provinciam fecit
... sed sub Gallieno imperatore
amissa est et per Aurelianum,
translatis exinde Romanis, duae
Daciae in regionibus Moesiae et
Dardaniae factae sunt.

Eutr. VIII 2,2 (Traianus):

Daciam Decibalo victo subegit
provincia trans Danubium facta
...

IX 8,2 (Gallienus):

Dacia, quae a Traiano ultra
Danubium fuerat adiecta, tum
amissa ...

IX 15,1 (Aurelianus):

Provinciam Daciam, quam Traianus ultra Danubium fecerat,
intermisit, vastato omni Illyrico
et Moesia desperans eam posse
retineri, abductosque Romanos
ex urbibus et agris Daciae in
media Moesia collocavit appella-
vitque eam Daciam, quae nunc
duas Moesias dividit et est in
dextra Danubio in mare fluenti,
cum antea fuerit in laeva.

The difference between Festus and Aurelius Victor is even more
striking. The latter lists disasters that had befallen the Roman
Empire under Gallienus, including the loss of Dacia. This was the

---

[78] 25,9,9. This opinion is shared by Festus, who describes Jovian as
cupidor regni quam gloriae (ch. 29). As to losses, he knew better. He would
not have agreed with Ammianus' 'never'.

[79] For this emperor, see above, p. 75 ff..

end of the matter. He does not mention the evacuation of the
population under Aurelian, a measure which sealed the surrender
of the former province. His treatment of Aurelian altogether ignores
the latter's Danubian policy.

Festus, on the other hand, is an undaunted optimist, even with
respect to Dacia which was lost, as he confirms, under Gallienus.
But to this patriot, who always looked on the bright side, there
was no such thing as a definite loss. He always saw a silver lining
somewhere. Thus even the blow of Crassus' defeat is softened by
thought that his death did not go unavenged since the son of the
Parthian king perished as well.[80]

GALLIENUS AND DACIA

In considering the historical truth about the 'loss' of Dacia, one
inevitably wonders whether the epitomists were right in unanimously
maintaining that this catastrophe occurred under Gallienus. The
question should not be avoided, but to my mind, whether they were
right or wrong, their approach is far more important, for it is there
that they reveal the differences which distinguish their personalities.
However, in view of the fact that the above question is generally
treated somewhat superficially, to the disadvantage of the epitomists,
it surely merits our attention. Their accounts are quite unambiguous.
Victor (33,3): 'et amissa trans Istrum quae Traianus quaesiverat.'
He cites the loss of Dacia as the last of a long list of calamities. He is
severe on Gallienus and says that he nearly shipwrecked the
Empire;[81] Eutropius (IX 8,2): 'Dacia, quae a Traiano ultra
Danubium fuerat adiecta, tum amissa'; Festus (8): 'sub Gallieno
imperatore amissa est.'

Wickert,[82] like many others, makes a distinction between the
loss of Dacia under Gallienus and official recognition of the fact
under Aurelian. The latter, the official surrender under Aurelian,
is amply confirmed in the contemporary sources[83] and has not, to
my knowledge, been contested. As regards Gallienus, however, the
picture is different, though with the single exception of one in-

---

[80] Chapter 18: 'ne aliquando Romani ducis mors inulta relinqueretur.'
[81] 33,3: 'rem Romanam quasi naufragio dedit'.
[82] *RE* XXV, col. 355, *s.v.* 'Licinius (84)': 'Dakien, das in den ersten
Jahren seiner Regierung dem römischen Reiche effektiv verloren ging, wenn
es auch erst von Aurelian offiziell aufgegeben wurde (*CIL* III, p. 161).'
[83] *Vita Aurel.* 39,7; Eutr. IX 15,1; Festus 8; Jord. *Rom.* 217; Malal.
XII 301; Synkell. I 721 f. Dind.; Zonar. XII 24.

controvertible piece of numismatic evidence, namely, the fact that no provincial coins were struck after 256. In other words, they ceased under Gallienus.[84]

The modern view is best expressed in the words of one modern historian who stated, with no hesitation and on reasonable grounds, that 'no one now believes that the whole of Dacia was overrun under Gallienus'.[85] Nevertheless, the rate at which Dacia was lost remains a matter of opinion. The chapter was closed by Aurelian's official recognition of the surrender of the province, but much may have happened between the years 253 (the accession of Gallienus) and 270 (the accession of Aurelian). Be this as it may, the epitomists place the burden of guilt upon Gallienus, once again incurring censure for doing so. Alföldi even goes so far as to regard the mentality underlying their version as a sort of conspiracy of the senate and its supporters against an emperor who was in fact abler than their narrow-minded tradition would have us believe.[86]

Even an argument of a literary historical nature has been adduced. Late Roman historical compendia are said to have levelled their allegations against Gallienus 'auf Grund einer literarischen Topik, die den Typus der Tyrannen in einer Stufenweise erfolgten Entartung darzustellen pflegte'.[87] We may be brief on this line of reasoning. It is a law of human nature that power corrupts, and that absolute power corrupts absolutely; one should hence exercise due caution before dismissing a genuine personality development as a literary process. Moreover, there is absolutely no evidence for the use of such a literary artifice.

Alföldi's purely historical arguments are similarly unconvincing. He has to admit that the last coins were minted (as far as we know) in 256. Most commentators make full use of this circumstance, but Alföldi somewhat arbitrarily robs the fact of its significance by saying 'noch Sommer 256 hat man ... die Bronzeprägung hergestellt'. This is not, however, of much use to modern historians, for the point is how long this issue of coin continued to dominate the economy. Alföldi sidesteps the question by pointing out that

---

[84] Cf. *RE* IV, col. 1975, 42 ff.

[85] T. D. Barnes in *JRS* 58 (1968), 264. See also D. Tudor, 'La fortificazione della città romane della Dacia nel sec. III dell'e.n.', *Historia* 14 (1965), 368-380.

[86] A. Alföldi, *Studien zur Geschichte der Weltkrise des 3. Jahrh. n. Chr.* (Darmstadt 1967), 326 (formerly in *CAH* XII [1939], 138 ff.).

[87] Alföldi, *op. cit.*, 326.

the military in these areas were well cared for until Aurelian's time. Neither argument strikes me as being very strong.[88]

The thought of shielding the fourth-century historians, with all their prejudices, is not to be entertained. Their comments on the loss of Dacia are instinct with nostalgia and resentment. For a hundred years every civil servant knew that the final stages of the Dacian tragedy (for any loss of territory was considered a tragedy) had started under Gallienus. Small wonder, then, that the affair was magnified. Modern modifications of their views are justifiable and even necessary. Wickert's balanced view sums up the present state of our knowledge. Alföldi's efforts notwithstanding, there are no real grounds upon which modern historians can defend Gallienus, far less exonerate him.

CONQUESTS

The history of the Imperium Romanum tells not only a tale of conquest, but of administration. Festus was well aware of this, and would certainly have agreed with Florus that *plus est provinciam retinere quam facere*.[89] The term 'retinere' necessitates an explanation of provincial policy and the changes it underwent over the years. Festus preferred the emperor who enlarged the empire by means of conquests, and was convinced, like Eutropius, that Hadrian gave up his campaign of conquest out of jealousy. This view is understandable. In the fourth century Rome was faced with situations in which Hadrian's policy would have meant suicide. Festus devotes ten chapters to conquests and the retention of the newly-acquired territories. Subjection to Rome is, for this 'imperialist', a law of nature. He shows no trace of Florus' love of peace.[90] Not only Corinth,[91] but Rhodes and the Greek islands serve to increase the glory of Rome.[92] An attack on Italy is considered presumptuous, even if it took place in the distant past, such as that of Pyrrhus of Epirus.[93]

---

[88] For problems of a general nature connected with dates between 250 and 260, see Th. Pekáry, 'Bemerkungen zur Chronologie des Jahrzehnts 250-260 n. Chr.', *Historia* 11 (1962), 123-128.

[89] Florus I 33,7. Cf. *Mnem.* 18 (1965), 372; P. Jal, *REL* 43 (1965), 358-383.

[90] Eutr. VIII 6,2; Festus 20. Cf. Jal, *art. cit.*, 374-5.

[91] See above, pp. 7, 142; Florus I 30-34; Livy *Perioch.* 52; Eutr. IV 14,1.

[92] Festus 10: 'Ita Rhodus et insulae primum libere agebant, postea in consuetudinem parendi Romanis clementer provocantibus pervenerunt'. The painful humiliation suffered by Rhodes is in striking contrast to this version of events.

[93] Festus 7: 'Epirotae, qui aliquando cum rege Pyrrho, etiam ad Italiam

More profoundly critical than Eutropius,[94] he does not allow
himself to be misled by Aurelian's gesture of giving the name of
Dacia to the region to the south of the Danube. The author of the
vita Aureliani [95] does not commit himself: his phrasing may have
been derived from the official version, possibly quoted by Eutropius.
No wonder, then, that Festus' words *in solo barbarico* [96] reflect such
pride in the expansion of the Empire under Trajan.[97] 'Traianus qui
post Augustum Romanae reipublicae movit lacertos.' [98] And now,
Valens was to resume Trajan's work.

ROME AND THE EAST

The task of the historian writing in the second half of the fourth
century did not differ much from that of his colleague of the first
half of the second century. In the intervening two hundred and
fifty years of Roman history the dangers threatening her had increased, dangers which Festus and other optimists believed could
be allayed by the emperor in person. It is surely no coincidence
that this passage is so strongly reminiscent of the terms in which
Florus describes the miracle of Rome's rebirth [99] under Trajan:

Festus 20,2:   Florus *praef.* 8:

Traianus, quo post Augustum   (Populus Romanus) sub Traiano
Romanae rei publicae movit   principe movit lacertos.
lacertos, Armeniam recepit a
Parthis ...

transire praesumpserant'. For 'praesumere' meaning 'sich erkühnen', see
Wölfflin, *ALL* 13 (1904), 178.

[94] As L. Homo, *Essai sur le règne de l'empereur Aurélien* (1904), 318,
rightly says: 'Il fallait ménager l'orgueil national et masquer le recul de
l'Empire'. Festus 8 says: 'Traianus Dacos sub rege Decibalo vicit et Daciam
trans Danubium *in solo barbarico* provinciam fecit.'

[95] 39,7.

[96] Wölfflin misses the point here (*art. cit.*, 178) when he contends that
the expression *in solo barbarico* derives from the *H.A.*, whence it was taken
over by Eutropius, Ammianus and in *Epit.* 29,3. Apart from the fact that
the *H.A.* is thus incorrectly dated, he fails to take the fact into account
that these words acquired a special place in the tradition of the *breviaria*,
being intended to arouse the combative spirit in the readers.

[97] Cf. Festus 20.

[98] Perhaps it is this very passage, the imagery of which is derived from
Florus, that earned Festus the name 'der kleine Florus'.

[99] For Roman ideology, see the extensive bibliography given by M. Fuhrmann, 'Die Romidee der Spätantike', *HZ* 207 (1968), 536, n. 22, and elsewhere in the same article.

However, there are certain differences. In Florus, these words form part of the analogy between the Roman Empire and the life of man, the following passage in which is of particular relevance in the present context. 'From the time of Caesar Augustus down to our own age there has been a period of not much less than two hundred years, during which, owing to the inactivity of the emperors, the Roman people, as it were, grew old and lost its potency, save that under the rule of Trajan it again stirred its arms and, contrary to general expectation, again renewed its vigour with youth as it were restored.'[100]

The main focus of Festus' account lies elsewhere. Abandoning the East had proved no act of statesmanship. For this not the people but the emperors were responsible. In this text addressed to the current emperor, Festus paraphrases Florus to suit the needs of the moment. Here, if ever, was an opportunity to appeal to Valens himself, who was about to follow in Trajan's footsteps;[101] the reference to Augustus, the great emperor, adds greater urgency to his appeal.[102]

If one is to isolate those aspects of the subject which Festus considered of greatest importance, it is advisable to analyse the chapters he devotes to the East. A poetic term, *Eoas partes*, introduces this major section of his work.[103] Those regions exposed to the greatest dangers are given fitting emphasis.[104] The passage describing the situation in Armenia and the fighting against the

---

[100] Translation by E. S. Forster in the Loeb edition (1940).

[101] The limitations inherent in nineteeth century *Quellenforschung* emerge with great clarity from Wölfflin's work. 'Unwiderleglich aber beweist (dies) die Abhängigkeit des Festus von Florus. Denn der Topos ist so ungewöhnlich, dass unmöglich zwei Autoren unabhängig von einander auf die nämliche Worte verfallen und dieselben auf den gleichen Kaiser beziehen konnten ... Dass Florus das römische Volk zum Subjekte nehmen musste, ergab sich aus der Anlage seines Werkes, dessen Thema eben der Populus Romanus ist.' (*ALL* 1904, 79.) But this precisely misses the point. The point is the manner in which Festus changes the image. He focuses on the emperor of the past, because he expects future action from the present emperor.

[102] For references for these passages in Florus and Festus, see above, p. 3, 40 and 186

[103] See above, p. 177, n. 12.

[104] Chapter 11: 'semper inter auxilia nostra fuere Cappadoces et ita maiestatem coluere Romanam, ut in honorem Augusti Caesaris Mazaca, civitas Cappadociae maxima, Caesarea cognominaretur.' *RE s.v.* 'Caesarea (5)' wrongly states that, according to Festus, Archelaus ordered Mazaca to be renamed.

Parthians (chapter 14) contains the afore-mentioned [105] assessment
of Trajan's expedition, repeated in chapter 20, which contradicts
the traditional view as we know it from Cassius Dio. This repetition
serves to underline Hadrian's jealousy of Trajan.

A repetition in a work as compact as this may be expected to
serve a particular purpose; and so it does. The failure of the expedition undertaken by the great emperor Trajan must have impressed itself upon Valens and his advisers. The entire episode is
accordingly reduced to a personal grudge. This is Festus' contribution to historical evaluation. The problem of interpretation was
recognized as early as the second century. Most probably Arrian
had already chosen to side with Trajan,[106] albeit for other, military,
reasons. All this, however, does not render Festus' interpretation
any more plausible. The construction he places on the event is
curious: the successor ceases his campaigns of conquest out of
jealousy of his predecessor's successes and consequent prestige. One
would expect an envious successor to have gone to great lengths
in order to surpass his predecessor's campaigns of conquest. A more
subtle line of reasoning was that to which Valens and his advisers
presumably subscribed: that after Trajan's policy of war, *which
had already reached an impasse in* 117, a policy of peace could bring
greater fame to his successor. Hadrian's complete change of course
was designed to show that Trajan's policy, *which had caused the
impasse,* was an utter failure. Now this was an interpretation which
emperor Valens would consider reasonable, but which would be
disastrous for a policy of aggression. Festus therefore had to replace
one interpretation of the past, which might lead to a policy of
peace, with another glossing over Trajan's failure. The words
italicized above express considerations lacking in Festus' account.
The reasoning underlying his case *pro Traiano* is as follows: The
view he defends was known to the military and civil servants alike.
The problem of the historical evaluation of Trajan and Hadrian
had already been recognized long before.[107] Was it likely that peace

---

[105] The following passage is of particular importance: 'sed Hadrianus
qui successit Traiano, invidens Traiano gloriae, sponte sua Armeniam,
Mesopotamiam, Assyriam reddidit'.

[106] Suda, *s.v.* ἀπείρατον and γνωσιμαχῆσαι (A. G. Roos, *Studia Arrianea,*
30); cf. Cassius Dio 68,17,1. The contradictions cannot be explained away
as Lepper tries to do in *Trajan's Parthian War* (Oxford 1948), 6, n. 2.

[107] This particular view cannot be traced any further back than Eutr.
VIII 6,2: 'Traiani gloriae invidens'. The two passages in Festus say: 'invidens

and prosperity would follow the projected expedition in the East ? History taught Festus to aswer this question in the affirmative: in a former age, Diocletian had brought about a period of peace lasting for many years.[108] His example is adduced in order to encourage and inspire Valens. Festus was most concerned lest the latter compare unfavourably with Diocletian.

Pompey, being an empire builder, merits frequent reference, despite the author's avowed aim of brevity.[109] His military exploits in the East (chapter 169) form a brilliant introduction to the sad story, which had to be told since it was common knowledge, of Crassus' defeat at Carrhae. The blow of this defeat would be somewhat softened for the reader if preceded by a description of the subjection of Syria, the land of Seleucus, which had once included Persia. Moreover, as a pagan, Festus had yet another object, to remind his Christian emperor of the fact that Pompey worshipped pagan gods: 'rediens apud Antiochiam Daphnensem lucum, delectatus loci amoenitate et aquarum abundantia, addito nemore consecravit'.[110]

Crassus' war is represented as having been waged against an enemy who had already been subjected: 'Crassus consul adversus Parthos *rebellantes* missus est'.[111] This distortion of the facts is also to be found in Florus.[112] It arises from the idea that the *consuetudo parendi Romanis* admitted of no exceptions, a concept that was even then an imperialistic anachronism. The reader is not spared any of the horrors of Crassus' defeat—he must be convinced of the formidability of the enemy Rome is once again preparing to confront. But the Romans found some comfort in certain details of the dreadful tale, such as, for instance, the success of Lucius Cassius, Crassus' quaestor;[113] there was the fact that the treachery of

---

Traiani gloriae' (chapter 14), and 'Hadrianum gloriae Traiani certum est invidisse' (chapter 20). Cf. also above, p. 42

[108] Chapter 14: 'ac Diocletiani temporibus, . . . Mesopotamia est restituta et supra ripas Tigridis limes est reformatus, ita ut quique gentium trans Tigridem constitutarum dicionem adsequeremur. Quae conditio foederis in tempus divalis Constantii reservata duravit'.

[109] Chapters 5, 11, 14, 16, 19.

[110] End of chapter 16. Cf. Eutr. VI 14,2. Festus' additions, 'rediens' and 'addito nemore', cannot be ascribed to any particular source, see Eadie, *op. cit.*, 75. See also below, p. 215.

[111] Chapter 17.

[112] The relevant passages are discussed in *Mnem.* 18 (1965), 375.

[113] 'Lucius Cassius, quaestor Crassi, vir strenuus, reliquias fusi collegit exercitus. Contra Persas in Syriam irrumpentes ter cum summa admiratione conflixit eosque trans Euphratem redactos vastavit' (ch. 17).

Labienus, a follower of Pompey[114] who helped the Parthians, did not go unpunished. The death of Pacorus on the anniversary of Crassus' defeat was also significant, 'ne aliquando Romani ducis mors inulta relinqueretur'.[115]

Augustus' policy towards the Parthians is hardly discussed. Festus does, however, stress Gaius Caesar's activities in the East (1-3 A.D.), and tells the story of treachery which so nearly claimed him as a victim.[116] The point was that the prince was wounded during this attack and subsequently, according to Festus, died of his wounds. This again is a warning to emperor Valens.[117]

It is not surprising that a 'bad' ruler like Nero should fare ill against the Parthians: both Armenian provinces were lost, and what was worse, 'tum Romanae legionis duae sub iugum a Parthis missae extremo dedecore Romani exercitus sacramenta foedarunt'.[118] This tale of disaster serves to enhance Trajan's welcome intervention. His policy, described above, was regarded by Festus as uniformly wise, whereas he censures Hadrian's policy.[119]

There are two items of information in the chapter on the successes of Lucius Verus, Septimius Severus and Caracalla, that merit special emphasis. In the first place, there is the reference to the joint monarchy of Marcus and Verus, each of whom held a triumph to celebrate their success. The historian is undoubtedly in favour of the principle of joint monarchy.[120] Secondly, Septimius Severus is described as 'natione Afer'. Presumably it was in the interests of emperors of other than Italian origin to point to this African as an example. The abbreviators, who were generally erudite men of senatorial rank, were only too often scornful of the origins of the emperors.[121] In this case, however, the reference to Severus' background is intended as a recommendation. This is a trait peculiar to Festus; Eutropius, who also refers to Severus' origins, gives the fact a totally different emphasis.[122] To Festus, Severus' 'barbarian' back-

---

[114] In spite of the fact that Pompey was a man *expertae felicitatis* (ch. 16), Festus' portrait of him is not too favourable.

[115] Chapter 18.

[116] Cf. Cassius Dio 55, 10; Florus II 32.

[117] Chapter 19.

[118] Chapter 20.

[119] See above, p. 40. ff.

[120] This does not, however, entitle one to assume that Festus dedicated his work to the emperors Valens and Valentinian jointly.

[121] Eutr. VIII 18,1; Victor *de Caes.* 20,22. Cf. p. 46 f., above.

[122] Eutropius was able to overlook Severus' shortcomings because he

ground is a positive circumstance; Valens would do well to model
himself upon him. It is tempting to suppose that Festus was
relatively untrammelled by social scruples about this emperor's
provincial origin simply because he himself was born in Italy and
an aristocrat. The *homo novus* is always more sensitive to considerations of social status than the man who has always been able to take
his own status for granted. Such considerations, however, will never
proceed beyond the realm of speculation because of the unsatisfactory nature of our information on Festus' background. Leaving
them aside, then, so much is clear, that Festus regarded Severus'
conduct towards the Parthians as 'exemplary': 'Septimius Severus,
natione Afer, acerrimus imperator, Parthos strenue vicit, Aziabenos
delevit, Arabas interiores obtinuit et in Arabia provinciam fecit.
Huic cognomina ex victoriis quaesita sunt; nam Aziabenicus,
Parthicus, Arabicus est cognominatus.' [123]

One might almost think that the author is already preparing his
readers for a still greater catastrophe, the defeat, imprisonment and
death of Valerian: 'Valeriani infausti principis, fortunam taedet
referre'.[124] He must first find an impressive close for his description
of Septimius Severus' conquests, though, before introducing his
imperial patron to the chapter of woe which is once again inevitable.
The necessary link is forthcoming in the form of the deeds of
Aurelius (i.e. Severus Alexander), and Gordian III. The latter of
these had had to face at least one problem which Valens cannot
afford to disregard. In the case of Alexander, there is a somewhat
curious addition: *quasi fato quodam in exitium Persicae gentis renatus.*
No doubt he had that other conqueror, Alexander the Great, in
mind. The words 'fato quodam' came easily to Florus, his example.[125]
Festus, however, favours no other ruler with its use in relation to
Persia. This is why I feel it is of particular significance here: will
Valens, too, prove an instrument of Providence? The name Xerxes
(used in all *breviaria*) for the king defeated by (Severus) Alexander
evokes vague memories of the Persian king Xerxes defeated at
Salamis. Perhaps Festus identified them with each other: 'Persarum
regem nobilissimum gloriose vicit' (chapter 22). Gordian III was

---

was also a man of culture (VII 19,1). Cf. T. D. Barnes, *Historia* 16 (1967),
87 ff.
[123] Chapter 21.
[124] Chapter 23.
[125] *Mnem.* 18 (1965), 286. Cf. A. Nordh, *Eranos* 50 (1952), 111-128.

less fortunate: after defeating *ex iuventutis fiducia* the rebellious
Parthians he was killed by his praetorian prefect Philippus.
Eutropius describes him as *admodum puer*.[126] His story is rounded
off with an account, taken verbatim from Eutropius, of the funeral
accorded him.[127]

Festus is now ready to discuss Valerian, whose defeat was the
most serious since Crassus'. He once again demonstrates the
originality of his composition by the way in which *both* failures are
offset by triumphs. Alexander Severus and Aurelian (chapter 24)
frame the picture, so to speak, of the disastrous events of 259-60.

The word *infaustus*, used to characterize Valerian, throws an
ominous light on his fate. The fact that Gallienus and Valerian
commanded but divided sympathies is barely touched upon, no
more, 'sed hunc exercitus, Gallienum senatus imperatorem fecerat':
it does not befit Festus to criticize the decisions of the powers that
be. But he is, after all, a *vir clarissimus* himself, and he is aware
of the right of the senate to acclaim and consecrate the sovereign
(official gestures, perhaps of no real political significance, but
nevertheless senatorial privileges). Although his account of the
resulting conflicts between military leaders, army and senate is less
detailed than that of Eutropius, he is by no means ignorant of
them. Possibly as a precautionary measure, he opposes senate and
army at a moment when the battle over their prerogatives was
less violent than at other times, since Gallienus and Valerian got on
well together. At all events, the bare reference shows Festus'
contempt, even hatred, for the army; the fact that Valerian was
proclaimed by the army and not by the senate makes him (Festus)
feel that it was no wonder that he was defeated. There is thus a link
between (a) '*infausti* principis', (b) 'hunc exercitus imperatorem
fecit', and (c) 'superatus est, et captus in dedecori servitute
consenuit'.

The most galling of all to Roman pride, however, was the fact
that it was ultimately left to Odenathus and his gang of Syrian
peasants to uphold the honour of Rome. Even Syria would have
been in danger of falling into Persian hands, 'nisi, *quod turpe dictu
est*, Odenathus decurio Palmyrenus, *collecta Syrorum agrestium
manu*, acriter restitisset'. When Festus finally does, quod *mirum
dictu*', give the devil his due, he calls him *Romani ultor imperii*, a

---

[126] Eutr. IX 2,2.
[127] Cf. Wölfflin, *ALL* 13 (1904), 173: *exequiae* = body.

studied understatement. Even the word 'turpe', which he used before, was not strong enough to express his bitterness.[128]

In accordance with his usual technique, Festus follows his account of Rome's humiliating rescue by Odenathus with a reference to the fierce struggle against Zenobia.[129] This bore only the slightest connection with his subject, but he had to wipe out the stigma of that mortifying assistance, which he could only do by reminding his readers of Zenobia's humiliation: 'Aurelianus ... Romae triumphans ante currum duxit'.

Carus' career was both glorious and mysterious: there were no rebellious Persians, he had great success and acquired much land, but he was struck down, perhaps deliberately, through the jealousy of the gods. Perhaps the gods let him win on purpose, only to kill him afterwards, out of *invidia*. Such is Festus' theory of history as shown by his comments. 'Cari imperatoris victoria de Persis nimium potens superno numini visa est. Nam ad invidiam caelestis indignationis pertinuisse credenda est. Is enim ingressus Persidem, *quasi nullo obsistente*[130] vastavit ... Cum victor totius gentis castra supra Tigridem haberet, vi fulminis ictus interiit.'[131]

The immediate past

From chapter 25 onwards, it looks as if the historian has extended his ambitions. His style is more literary, and charged with drama. Of course, this change has also been ascribed to a fresh source, but this is extremely unlikely: Festus did not have much time at his disposal. Chapters 1 and 30, and the beginning of chapters 10 and 15, show that the author gave free rein to his literary aspirations whenever he wished or thought necessary. This may well have been the case here, since with the introduction of Diocletian, he arrived in the more immediate past.[132]

---

[128] Chapter 23. The mood in which this is written is comparable to that of Florus' reference to the slaves who helped save Rome after Cannae. I 22,30; '*o pudor—manu servili pugnaret*'; cf. *Mnem.* 18 (1965), 380. For other attitudes to Gallienus' accession, see above, p. 75.

[129] Chapter 24.

[130] The textual alteration suggested by Eadie on the basis of ms. B, 'nullo *eam* obsistente', is, perhaps, superfluous.

[131] For the death of Carus, see below, p. 217. Festus' comments on Carus' death is a typical Roman religious attitude, see R. M. Ogilvie, *The Romans and their Gods* (London 1969), 34.

[132] See Eadie, *op. cit.*, 97, for the suggestion that Festus suddenly started using different sources.

Festus starts [133] with the well-known episode of Diocletian's insulting treatment of Galerius after the latter's defeat near Carrhae.[134] Who knows, perhaps this is a covert reference to the fact that any general's chances of gaining supreme command were rated as almost non-existent. Valens himself wished the war to take place, and he was determined to conduct it himself. It is possible that Festus is intent upon hammering home to the emperor the well-tried maxim that no commander-in-chief should ever evade his responsibilities by delegating them to his subordinates. After Galerius' rehabilitation, Diocletian's success was complete. In spite of minor conflicts, a lasting peace had been achieved. The chapter ends on an optimistic note: 'pax facta, usque ad nostram memoriam rei publicae utilis perduravit'.[135]

This glorious final stage is obviously incomplete without due reference to the statutory chivalry shown the womenfolk of the defeated. 'Uxor eius et filiae captae sunt et cum maxima pudicitiae custodia reservatae. Pro qua admiratione [136] Persae non modo armis, sed etiam moribus superiores esse Romanos confessi sunt.' The surrender of the Persians was partly due to the restraint displayed by the Romans on this occasion—which made it a story for every Roman to rejoice in.[137] The humanization of war had already found a militant champion in Florus. Granted the unity of the empire and of power, no subject, provided he remained a subject, need worry. This was the idea that still dominated Roman ethics. If the conviction of the necessity of absolute supreme authority were to be

---

[133] Chapter 25. See also W. Ensslin, *Zur Ostpolitik des Kaisers Diocletian*, Sitz.-Ber. der Bayer. Akad. der Wiss., Philos.-hist. Abt. Heft 1, 1943; cf. W. H. C. Frend, *Martyrdom and Persecution in the Early Church* (Oxford 1965), 488.

[134] This episode is discussed above in the chapter on Eutropius, p. 117.

[135] The writer is less reserved here than he was in chapter 14: 'quae condicio foederis in tempus divalis Constantii reservata duravit.'

[136] Although Eadie, *op. cit.*, 148, considers this an 'amusing remark', it was intended seriously.

[137] There are two versions of the emperor's behaviour towards his royal prisoners. According to one, Narses' wives were returned to him after the peace of Nisibis, Petr. Patr. *FHG* IV 14 (Müller); Malalas, p. 308 (Ed. Bonn). According to the other, they were compelled to take part in the triumphal procession (Eutr. IX 27; Cassiod. *Mon. Germ. Chron. min.* II, p. 150; Zonaras XII 32 ff.). Festus has the former version, though he does not mention the return of the women as a fact. However, he also considers it likely in view of the Persians' *admiratio*. Cf. W. Seston, *Dioclétien et la tétrarchie* (Paris, 1946), 23; for Diocletian and the East, id., *op. cit.*, 137-189.

lost, the Empire (and hence also the ethics of Rome victorious) would lose its *raison d'être*.

Constantine's actions,[138] which threatened to start a fresh war, eventually culminated in a bloodless confirmation of Roman supremacy. He marched against the Persians with many armies,[139] but the show of power alone proved sufficient. Yet Festus is not satisfied. His criticism of Constantine is curious: he censures him for being too weak, since this attitude had inevitable repercussions in that, under Constantius Caesar, Constantine's son, border raids were frequent.[140] Festus feels that the father had been too lenient in disregarding such maraudings: 'nec tamen pro adsiduis eruptionibus, quae sub Constantio Caesare per Orientem temptaverant, veniam mererentur'. Festus therefore wished Valens to profit by this example and take a firmer line with the Parthians than that favoured by Constantine the Great.

Constantius II was indeed more severe than his father had been.[141] There were not only skirmishes, but 'praeter leves excubantium in limite congressiones[142] acriori Marte noviens decertatum est'. It goes without saying that the emperor did not often take part in these expeditions himself, but twice he took personal charge. Festus decides to describe one of these occasions in some detail, the war in which Narses perished.[143] In this war, at least, the Romans were the undisputed victors. The emphasis laid on the emperor's presence is noticeable—Festus refers to this fact no less than three times.[144]

As he nears the end of his work, the writer appears to become more deeply involved in the problem of Rome and the East. Chapters 28 and 30 are very lively, and one gains the impression that the historian is building up towards a climax. He has a ready answer for the problem why Rome had been unable to solve the

---

[138] Chapter 26.

[139] *agmen = copiae*; see Wölfflin, *ALL* 13 (1904), 174.

[140] Festus refers to sallies (*eruptio*) from out of Persia, even though the emphasis in his account lies on the violation (*irruptio*) of Roman territory.

[141] Chapter 27.

[142] *Congressiones* = (Classical) *congressus*, Wölfflin, *op. cit.*, 174.

[143] The years 348-350 are well covered by E. Albertini, *L'empire romain*, in: Peuples et Civilisations IV (1929), 370: 'on se battit longtemps avec des succès divers, autour de Nisibis: Sapor lassé finit par accepter une paix qui ne lui concédait aucun avantage'. A summing-up by a modern abbreviator which would not have been out of place in the work of his Roman predecessor.

[144] In chapter 27: 'ipse praesens bis adfuit . . .' 'praesente Constantio . . .' 'ubi praesens Constantius adfuit'.

Eastern question: the soldiers were to blame. Under Constantius II, the war would have been brought to a successful conclusion at last, had not the soldiers panicked and, at a critical moment, thought only of how to quench their thirst. In this manner, the satisfying of a personal need interfered, to the detriment of the common good, with the execution of their military duties: 'omnium expeditionum conpensatus fuisset eventus, si locis et nocte adversantibus, percitos ferocia milites ab intempestivo pugnandi tempore imperator ipse adloquendo revocare potuisset.'[145]

A comparatively long chapter is devoted to the tragedy of Julian. His luck deserted him, 'Iuliano in externos hostes expertae felicitatis ... modus defuit',[146] and luck is something everyone needs. Julian had to do without it, and is thus a prime example of the inconstancy of the fortunes of war. The emperor himself was in no way to blame for his defeat, as Festus is at pains to stress by his suggestion that Julian and his army were misled by a Persian guide.[147] The second reason for his failure is again the selfishness of the soldiers: 'apertas Ctesiphontis portas victor miles intrasset, nisi maior praedarum occasio fuisset quam cura victoriae'. In the final analysis, however, it was also the emperor's own fault for refusing to listen to his cautious advisers: 'cum de reditu a comitibus admoneretur, intentioni suae[148] magis credidit.' The three reasons given for Julian's defeat, viz., the inconstancy of Fortune, the egoism of the soldiers and the emperor's own obstinacy, suggest that this comparatively recent episode was the subject of lively debate in the circles Festus frequented. It was impossible for him to avoid the subject, and he dealt with it with great tact.[149]

Of all the stories of his death, Festus' version at any rate avoids any trace of heroics: 'cum incautius per agmen erraret, excito pulvere erepto suorum conspectu ab obvio hostium equite conto per ilia ictus inguinum tenus vulneratus est.'[150]

---

[145] Chapter 27.

[146] Chapter 28.

[147] For a short survey of the relevant sources and a bibliography of modern research, see Eadie, op. cit., 151 ff.

[148] Intentioni suae = consilio suo, Wölfflin, ALL 13 (1904), 175; cf. Festus 15: quo tua pergat intentio.

[149] Festus' extensive discussion of Julian has to my mind no connection with his pagan sympathies (Momigliano, op. cit., 95).

[150] The classical accounts of Julian's expedition and his death are discussed by M. F. A. Brok in De Perzische expeditie van Keizer Julianus volgens Ammianus Marcellinus (thesis, Leiden 1959), 185 f. Cf. the discussion

Jovian, whose was the thankless task of bringing the army back to safety as best as he could, could scarcely expect Festus to be lenient: 'cupidior regni quam gloriae'. [151] Certainly, the difficulties facing the new emperor were beyond the ordinary, the way home was long,[152] and the conditions set by the enemy harsh, [153] but no circumstances could ever extenuate the surrender of Roman territory. The pill is sweetened for the reader by the statement that the Persians were the first to negotiate, but the words have a hollow ring: 'tanta reverentia Romani nominis fuit, ut a Persis prius sermo de pace haberetur'; in fact, the Persians' sole concession was to provide food for the exhausted soldiers. The mere fact, however, that these conditions were accepted was an indignity that cried out for vengeance. It was now up to Valens to draw the only conclusion possible from the facts of history as presented by Festus, that a policy of appeasement could never resolve the Eastern question.

The unpredictable factor

Even a civil servant as conscientious as Festus had difficulty, being a poor historian, in reporting the bare facts of history as far as he knew them. We saw earlier that Festus' personality emerges particularly from the beginning and the end of his work. There are passages elsewhere, however, which go to show that Festus did not regard history merely as the history of man, but as the revelation of the will of the gods. Even in relating certain purely historical details he displays religious feeling, as, for instance, when he refers to the sanctuary at Daphne. A comparison of his account with that of Eutropius is instructive.

Festus 16,4:	*Eutropius* VI 14,2:
(Pompeius) rediens apud Antiochiam Daphnensem lucum, delectatus loci amoenitate et aquarum abundantia, *addito nemore* consecravit.	Aliquantum agrorum Daphnensibus dedit, quo lucus ibi spatiosior fieret, delectatus loci amoenitate et aquarum abundantia.

of the fruitless disputes about the various versions of this Persian expedition given in the sources by L. Dillemann, 'Ammien Marcellin et les pays de l'Euphrate et du Tigre', *Syria* 38 (1961), 87-158, esp. 115 ff.

[151] Chapter 29.

[152] 'via in reditu prolixior (= *longior*) immineret'.

[153] 'condicionibus (quod numquam antea accidit) dispendiosis' (= *iniquis*, used as early as Columella, but no more until Late Latin), see Wölfflin, *ALL* 13 (1904), 175.

The fact that he stressed Antioch and interpolated the words
italicized above requires some explanation. The reasoning underlying these additions may have been as follows. Every expedition
to Parthia, Mesopotamia and Armenia had always started out from
Antioch. It goes without saying that no-one had ever questioned the
beginnings of Roman intervention in Antioch, particularly since
Rome had always been careful to respect local deities and their cults.
One of the most important cult sites was the sacred grove at Daphne
near Antioch,[154] which is referred to by all *breviaria* of pagan
authorship. Festus feared that Valens would allow himself to be
influenced by Christian fanatics, who resented his tolerant attitude
towards pagan shrines and sanctuaries. He thus appropriated
Eutropius' apt phrase, 'delectatus loci amoenitate et aquarum
abundantia', which sounded innocent enough, in the hope of
encouraging the emperor in his tolerance. The most zealous of
Christians could not object to the emperor's predilection for the
scenic beauties, even of a sacred grove, or to their enhancement
by Pompey. The reference to the latter in Eutropius was amplified
by Festus, who presumably hoped that Valens would follow his
example.[155]

In contemplating the actions of men, Festus feels, one should

---

[154] See, for instance, G. Downey, *Ancient Antioch* (Princeton 1963), 73
(Pompey).

[155] A discussion of the possible sources of this passage is an unprofitable
undertaking. Eadie says (*op. cit.*, 75), that some scholars 'emphasized the
differences between Festus and Eutropius: i.e. Eutropius reports that
Pompey made a donation of land on his first journey into Syria, while
Festus states that he made a donation of land and consecrated a nemus
on his return from Syria—and concluded that both the donation and the
consecration were found in a common source, the Chronicon.' Nevertheless,
Festus' changes seem a curious departure from the original if Eutropius
were his (only) source. It has therefore been suggested that Festus' additions
were intended as mere rhetoric, and inadvertently confused the issue of
Eutropius' account. 'Addito nemore', it is alleged, must be rejected as an
historically incorrect interpolation by Festus, since this grove was a 'lucus
famosusque vetustissimusque'. This reasoning is unsatisfactory. It was
by no means impossible for a great general to add to a sanctuary or to an
ancient grove. The date at which this donation was made, is immaterial to
Festus. The main point is that he has a particular interest in the emperor's
attitude to ancient pagan sanctuaries. Festus is a more religious man, or
perhaps one ought to say that he writes from a more deeply religious point
of view, than Eutropius. The latter, who is strictly formal, almost ritualistic,
is interested chiefly in the proper conduct of the consecration of the emperors.
Which of the two is right from the historical point of view will never be
known.

never disregard divine intervention in human affairs. His quasi-mystical belief in the 'return' of Alexander the Great, reborn, so to speak, as Alexander Severus, is to be sought in vain in Eutropius.

Festus 22:

Aurelius Alexander *quasi fato quodam in exitium Persicae gentis renatus*, iuvenis admodum Romani gubernacula suscepit imperii.

Eutr. VIII 23:

successit ... Aurelius Alexander ... iuvenis admodum, susceptoque adversus Persas bello Xerxen, eorum regem, gloriosissime vicit.

This passage of Festus', with its concept of the personification of Roman glory in a Macedonian name, helped to lay the foundations of the Life of the last of the Severi in the *Historia Augusta*.

The death of an emperor allows one to gauge the depth of a historian's emotional involvement with his subject, particularly if this event is attended by extraordinary circumstances. The author even of a *breviarium* is then given a chance to reveal his personality. The death of emperor Carus is a case in point, which may be illustrated by comparing the following texts:

a. Festus 24,2:

Cari imperatoris victoria de Persis nimium potens superno numini visa est. Nam ad invidiam caelestis indignationes pertinuisse credenda est. Is enim ingressus Persidam quasi nullo (eam) obsistente vastavit, Colchen et Ctesiphontem, urbes Persarum nobilissimas, cepit. Cum victor totius gentis castra supra Tigridem haberet, vi fulminis ictus interiit.

b. Victor, *Caesares* 38,3-5:

Ubi fusis hostibus, dum gloriae inconsulte avidior Thesiphonta urbem Parthiae inclitam transgreditur, fulminis tactu conflagravit. Id quidam iure ei accidisse referunt; nam cum oracula docuissent adusque oppidum memoratum perveniri victoria licere, longius delatus poenas luit. Proinde arduum fatalia devertere, eoque futuri notio superflua.

c. *Vita Cari* 8,2:

Verum cum avidus gloriae, praefecto suo maxime urgente, qui et ipsi et filiis eius quaerebat exitium cupiens imperare, longius progressus esset, ut alii dicunt morbo, ut plures fulmine, inter-

emptus est. 9.1: plerique dicunt vim fati quandam esse, ut
Romanus princeps Ctesifontem transire non possit, ideoque
Carum fulmine absumptum quod eos fines transgredi cuperet
quo fataliter constituti sunt.

d. Eutr. IX 18.1:

Et cum castra supra Tigridem haberet, vi divini fulminis periit.

It was generally believed that Carus was killed by lightning.
Victor's moralism leads him to dramatize the event: in his arrogance,
the emperor wished to overstep the limits the gods had set to his
victory. The true cause of his death was hubris. The story as told by
Festus is somewhat different: he says not a word about the oracles
referred to by Victor, he merely tells of the pride that came before
a fall. The *vita Cari* in the *Historia Augusta* enlarges upon this
theme, but also reports another version according to which the
emperor died 'naturally', in his bed. Eutropius needs no more than
the bald statement, 'cause of death, a stroke of lightning'.[156]

The manner of the emperor's death became the subject of heated
dispute, as not only Festus but the *Historia Augusta* tells us: 'fama
emersit fulmine interemptum eum quem, quantum scire possumus,
aegritudine constat absumptum.' This passage, purporting to be a
quotation from a letter, inspired the author to make some curious
comments [157] which show that we are now in the thick of a fourth-
century debate on the influence of the gods on the course of history.

The encouragement of humility could easily, of course, quite
apart from the cause of Carus' death, be taken to advocate a
defeatist attitude towards Persia. The writer of the *vita* does not
believe in divine intervention in this particular case. He reminds
his readers of the firmness shown by Galerius towards the Persian
Narses in 296-297. Presumably this reasoning would hardly have
impressed Festus, whose approach is that of the group to which he
belonged by virtue of his office. It is interesting to note that Victor
tells us wherein lay the emperor's presumption: he disregarded an
oracle warning him to go no further than Ctesiphon. Festus, who
also refers to Ctesiphon, is obviously cognisant of this detail. He
merely sees no need to impart it since he assumes that his readers
are equally familiar with the facts. The modern theory that Carus

---

[156] *Mnem.* 21 (1968), 281.
[157] *Vita Cari* 8,2; 8,7 (letter) and 9 (commentary).

was murdered [158] is unsupported by the classical sources, but then, no modern discussion has dealt adequately with the curious religious cause of his death given by the epitomists.

An emperor's fortunes are a precarious matter, as Julian's fate had shown. Both he and Carus before him proved the fact that even the most powerful of rulers must bow before Providence; even a brief historical summary could not but agree. One might only hope that Valens would share the good fortune of Alexander Severus.

STRUCTURE AND TERMINOLOGY

If Festus was aware that his work belonged to a particular literary genre that set certain requirements, the fact need not concern us here. In my view, this severely practical man writing to very definite purpose was not much concerned about the requirements of a literary genre. He had a better use for his time. This is not to say that he had not his own special brand of originality, which also extended to his rendering of material first presented by others, for instance, Eutropius. I have no intention of illustrating this originality by means of examples from his work, since this has already been done so excellently by Wölfflin, long ago.[159] There is one conclusion of his, however, with which I cannot agree, namely, that Festus must have known the work of several other authors. My aim throughout has been to demonstrate that we should seek the background of his information, not in the extant written sources, but rather in items of out-dated information passed on by successive generations of imperial officials.

To this oral source we may trace certain expressions which give the writings of many authors their *couleur locale*. The word *clibanarius*,[160] for instance, which occurs in Eutropius.[161]

Formerly thought to be a Persian word used as an alternative to *catafracti*, the cuirassiers,[162] it is nowadays assumed to be a soldiers' term of Greek origin. It was also used by Ammianus Marcellinus. It is always possible, of course, that Festus borrowed

---

[158] *CAH* XII 322 (H. Mattingly) and *RE*, *s.v.* 'Aurelius (77)' (Henze).

[159] *ALL* 13 (1904), 69 ff., 173 ff.

[160] Chapters 15 and 24.

[161] Eutr. IX 6,1 (also in connection with military action in the East). Also in Ammianus 16,10,8. and 16,12,21.

[162] Wölfflin *op. cit.* For the Greek origin, see H. Frisk, *Griechisches etymol. Wörterbuch* (Heidelberg 1954), *s.v.* κλίβανος.

the word from Eutropius, but it is equally possible that it was in common use in civil service jargon.

In chapter 25, Festus refers to the limitanei.[163] This passage merits our attention, particularly as it has escaped the notice of specialists on the composition of the army in late imperial times. The reason for this omission is not hard to find. These writers all based their studies on Mommsen's excellent article, 'Das römische Militärwesen seit Diocletian'.[164] Mommsen cites numerous references to the *limitanei*, but apparently overlooked Festus. The most recent study of the significance of the *limitanei*[165] also fails to mention this passage. The text runs as follows: 'Et cum vix impetrasset, ut reparato de limitaneis Daciae exercitu eventum Martis repeteret, in Armenia maiore ipse imperator (Galerius) ... cecidit'.

The context in which it occurs is the well-known story of Galerius' humiliation by Diocletian as a punishment for his defeat in the East.[166] Then come the lines quoted above, in which Galerius goes to great lengths to persuade his superior to allow him to continue his military undertaking, subsequently crowned with success. Once again, Festus gives such a drastic summary of an historical event as to impair one's perspective of the episode as a whole.

It sounds most unlikely that Galerius recalled the *limitanei*, older and often physically weaker troops,[167] from Dacia to serve on the eastern front. It is possible that Festus placed this unusual measure in the wrong context, and that it properly belongs in the history of Galerius' struggle in his own provinces, in the year 293 and later. The situation being extremely critical at that time, I imagine that the *limitanei* and also naval military units may have been temporarily withdrawn from their normal duties. There is sufficient evidence to show that the navy commanded considerable military resources,[168] which could be mobilized to meet situations calling for their specialized experience. Had these troops, however, accustomed as they were to special treatment and secure prospects, suddenly been sent to face the profoundly different circumstances obtaining in the

---

[163] See the penetrating comments by T. D. Barnes, *JRS* 58 (1968), 264.

[164] *Hermes* 24 (1889), 195 ff. (= *Ges. Schr.*, VI 200 ff.).

[165] *RE*, Suppl. XI (1968), col. 876-888 (A. R. Neumann).

[166] See above, p. 116 (Eutropius), and p. 212 (Festus).

[167] *Cod. Th.* VII 22,8 (dating from the year 372). Cf. Neumann, *RE*, *art. cit.*, col. 880, line 58.

[168] See Neumann. *art. cit.*, 886-7.

East, they would have been more than a hindrance to Galerius than a help.

A further possibility is suggested by certain parallel passages in Victor and Eutropius.[169] These tell us that Galerius' Persian expedition necessitated the mustering of fresh troops. So much is known. It is not unlikely that Festus employed a technical term in use for certain troops from the Danubian frontier in order to designate the units sent to reinforce the emperor's troops. The fact that he chose precisely the name of those troops which were not transferred, is an error characteristic of a man who liked to use military jargon but did not stop to think that his use of a particular term may have been entirely inappropriate.[170]

The present, more accurate, dating of the *Historia Augusta*[171] demands a renewed investigation into the first occurrence of the *limitanei*.[172] Wölfflin still regarded its use in the *Historia Augusta* as primary. Nowadays we know that it was first used as a noun in Festus, and as an adjective in Cod. Theod. XII, 1, 56.[173] In itself this does not significantly add to our knowledge of the units themselves, the more important question being when *limitanei* were first used in the Roman army. The most recent research has shown that frontier troops of that name may even antedate Alexander Severus. If this is so, the use of the term in the *vita Sev. Al.* 58,4 is not necessarily an anachronism,[174] nor may this accusation justifiably be levelled against Festus.

In chapter 27, Wölfflin noted a linguistic error to which he gave wider relevance, namely, confusion of cause and effect. The context of the passage in question is that at night the soldiers search for wells, armed with torches, which make them an excellent target for the enemy. Festus says: 'nimbo sagittarum obruti sunt, cum

---

[169] Victor 39, 34; Eutr. IX 25.

[170] This suggestion has been made with some necessary reservations. Even after the most recent extensive discussion of the *limitanei*, many questions remain unanswered. For some of these, see Syme, *Ammianus*, 46 ff., and the references listed in n. 6, *ibid.*

[171] See Chastagnol, *Historia* 4 (1955), 173-188 and the same author's contributions in the *Historia-Augusta-Colloquia* of 1963 and 1964/5; Syme, *Ammianus*, p. 107.

[172] *ALL* 13 (1904), 175: 'limitaneis, ein Wort des Spätlateins, doch schon von den Scriptores hist. Aug. gebraucht'. *Sev.* 58,4; *Prob.* 14,7.

[173] Barnes, *JRS* 58 (1968), 264.

[174] Syme is quite right in saying that the use of this word in the *vita Alexandri* may be imaginative rather than anachronistic, *op. cit.*, 47, n. 2. Neumann, *art. cit.*, col. 879.

stolide *ad dirigendos certius in se ictus* lumina ipsi per noctem accensa praeberent.' As Wölfflin rightly remarks, 'Da die Angriffe der Perser von den Römern nicht beabsichtigt waren, so hätte der Autor schreiben müssen: unde factum est ut ... certius dirigeren- tur.'[175] He goes on to comment, 'Seine Schulbildung genügte nicht, um ihm gegen die Verwechslung von Finalkonstruktion und Konsekutivkonstruktion zu schützen', thus exposing, I feel, the chief weakness in the work of this, perhaps the least gifted of the epitomists. His mind did not work with the lucidity which is such a salient characteristic particularly of Eutropius' work.

One of the chief difficulties confronting one in attempting to explain Festus' errors is that he makes so many that one is occasion- ally tempted not to recognize extenuating circumstances, let alone grounds for exoneration. However, far be it from the historian to degenerate into a hanging judge. In fairness to Festus, moreover, we must hasten to add that modern historians often write with a set purpose corresponding to Festus'. His approach to history, divested as it is of the biographical backgrounds of emperors and military leaders is, in a sense, surprisingly modern. The personality of an emperor only rarely plays a part in the work of Festus. It is usually subsidiary to some great military aim. The moderns are often, therefore, far more appreciative of Festus than of Eutropius and Aurelius Victor.[176] Perhaps this modern appreciation is in turn merely a product of the times.

CONCLUSION [177]

Each of the three *breviaria* discussed above was written for a different purpose. One cannot expect a writer to write like his contemporaries if their aims and approach are quite different. Aurelius Victor is the writer of fear, Eutropius is resigned, and Festus has great hopes for the future. We do not know whether Victor composed his work in accordance with well-defined in- structions; as far as we know, he followed his inclinations. If so, he was not bound to take any particular line and is thus a valuable witness. Eutropius was certainly commissioned to write his *breviarium*: 'ex voluntate mansuetudinis tuae', 'in accordance with

---

[175] Wölfflin, *art. cit.*, 175.

[176] For instance, in F. A. Lepper, *Trajan's Parthian War* (Oxford 1948), 15.

[177] Cf. *Mnem.* 21 (1968), 282.

the wishes of your Majesty'. The fact that he nevertheless managed to retain a certain degree of independence and preserve his integrity as a senator, is an extraordinary achievement. In this respect Festus is inferior to him, though he is no less sincere. He was perfectly willing to accommodate himself to the limited terms of the commission he received when the emperor decided to reconquer the East, since he was himself an obvious champion of a traditional expansionist policy. It is in this attitude that he differs most from his example, the more humane Florus, but also from his contemporaries, who were full of forebodings for the future.

Pessimism, impartiality, and optimism—these three words suffice to express the salient characteristic of each of our three writers, Victor, Eutropius, and Festus.

SELECT BIBLIOGRAPHY

Work was completed on this book in 1969. It has therefore been impossible to take more recent publications into consideration. This is especially to be regretted in the case of the following books:

Chastagnol, A. *Recherches sur l'Histoire Auguste* (Bonn 1970).
Syme, R. *Emperors and Biography* (Oxford 1971).
Bonner Historia-Augusta-Colloquium 1968/1969 (Bonn 1970).

Texts

Eadie, J. W., *The Breviarium of Festus, a Critical Edition with Historical Commentary* (London 1967).
Jal, P., *Florus. Oeuvres. Texte établi et traduit*, 2 vols. (Paris 1967).
Pichlmayr, Fr.,—R. Gruendel *Sexti Aurelii Victoris Liber de Caesaribus* (Teubner 1966).
Ruehl, Fr., *Eutropi Ab Urbe Condita* (Teubner 1909).

Lexica

Daremberg, Ch. et E. Saglio, *Dictionnaire des antiquités grecques et romaines d'après les textes et les monuments* (Paris 1877-1919).
Paulys Realencyclopädie der classischen Altertumswissenschaft.
Reallexikon für Antike und Christentum.

Books and articles

Alföldi, A., 'Das Problem des "verweiblichten" Kaisers Gallienus', *ZNum* 38 (1928), 56-203.
——, *A Conflict of Ideas in the Late Roman Empire* (Oxford 1952).
——, *Studien zur Geschichte der Weltkrise des 3. Jahrhunderts nach Christus* (Darmstadt 1967).
——, 'Die Vorherrschaft der Pannonier im Römerreiche und die Reaktion des Hellenismus unter Gallienus', in: 25 *Jahre Röm.-Germ. Kommission* (Frankfurt am M. 1930), 11 ff (= *Studien zur Geschichte de Weltkrise des 3. Jahrhunderts nach Christus*, [Darmstadt 1967], 228-284).
Alföldy, G., *Die Legionslegaten der römischen Rheinarmeen*, Epigr. Studien 3 (Köln-Graz 1967).
Astin, A. E., *Scipio Aemilianus* (Oxford 1967).

Badian, E., *Foreign Clientelae* (Oxford 1958).
——, *Roman Imperialism in the Late Republic* (Oxford 1968[2]).
Balsdon, J. P. V. D., *The Emperor Gaius* (Oxford 1934).
Barb, A. A., 'The survival of Magic Arts', in: Momigliano, *Conflict* (1963), 100-125.
Barnes, T. D., 'The Family and Career of Septimius Severus', *Historia* 16 (1967), 87-107.
——, review of Eadie, *Breviarium of Festus, JRS* 58 (1968), 263-265.
——, 'Three notes on the *vita Probi*', *CQ* 20 (1970), 198.
Bickermann, E. J., 'Die römische Kaiserapotheose', *ARW* 27 (1929), 1-31.
Bicknell, P., 'The Emperor Gaius' Military activities in A.D. 40', *Historia* 17 (1968), 496-505).
Birley, A., 'The oath not to put senators to death', *CR* 12 (1962), 197-199.

den Boer, W., 'Religion and Literature in Hadrian's Policy', *Mnem.* 8 (1955), 123-144.
——, 'Florus und die römische Geschichte', *Mnem.* 18 (1965), 366-387.
——, 'Rome à travers trois auteurs du quatrième siècle', *Mnem.* 21 (1968), 254-282.
Brok, M. F. A., *De Perzische expeditie van Keizer Julianus volgens Ammianus Marcellinus* (thesis, Leiden 1959).
Broughton, T. R. S., *The Magistrates of the Roman Republic*, 2 vols. (New York 1951-52).
——, *Supplement to the Magistrates of the Roman Republic* (New York 1960).
Bruhl, A., *Le souvenir d'Alexandre le Grand et les Romains* (Paris 1930).
Burckhardt, J., *Die Zeit Constantins des Grossen* (Wien, Phaidon-Ausgabe, 1935).

Calderini, A., *I Severi. La crisi dell'Impero nella III secolo* (Bologna 1949).
Cameron, A. D. E., 'Litterary Allusions in the Historia Augusta', *Hermes* 92 (1964), 363-377.
——, 'The Roman Friends of Ammianus', *JRS* 54 (1964), 15-28.
——, 'Two glosses in Aurelius Victor', *CR*, n.s. 15 (1965), 20-21.
——, review of Straub, *Heidnische Geschichtsapologetik*, *JRS* 55 (1965), 240-248.
——, 'Macrobius, Avienus, and Avianus', *CQ*, n.s. 17 (1967), 385-399.
——, review of Eadie, *Breviarium of Festus*, *CR*, n.s. 19 (1969), 305-307.
Camus, P. M., *Ammien Marcellin* (Paris 1967).
Carney, T. F., *A Biography of C. Marius*, Proceedings of the African Classical Associations, Supplement Number 1 (1961).
Charlesworth, M. P., 'Gaius and Claudius', *CAH* X (1934), 653-701.
——, 'Flaviana', *JRS* 27 (1937), 54-62.
——, 'Imperial Deportment. Two texts and some Questions', *JRS* 37 (1947) 34-38.
Chastagnol, A., 'Notes chronologiques sur l'Histoire Auguste et le Laterculus de Polemius Silvius', *Historia* 4 (1955), 173-188.
——, *La préfecture urbaine à Rome sous le Bas-Empire* (Paris 1960).
——, 'Le problème de l'histoire Auguste: Etat de la question', *Historia-Augusta-Colloquium, Bonn* 1963 (Bonn 1964), 43-71.
——, 'Zosime II, 38 et l'Histoire Auguste', *Bonner Historia-Augusta-Colloquium* 1964/1965 (Bonn 1966), 43-78.
——, 'Emprunts de l'*Histoire Auguste* aux "*Caesares*" d'Aurelius Victor', *Rev. Phil.* 41 (1967), 85-97.
Cichorius, C., *Römische Studien* (reprint Darmstadt 1961).
Clarke, G. W., 'The Date of the Consecratio of Vespasian', *Historia* 15 (1966), 318-327.
Collins, J. H., *Propaganda, Ethics, and Psychological Assumptions in Caesar's Writings* (thesis, Frankfurt am M. 1956).
Corbett, P. B., 'The "De Caesaribus" attributed to Aurelius Victor: points arising from an examination of the MSS and of the Teubner edition of F. Pichlmayr', *Scriptorium* 3 (1949), 254-257.
Crees, J. H. E., *The Reign of the Emperor Probus* (repr. Rome 1965; 1st. ed. 1911).

Damerau, P., *Kaiser Claudius II. Gothicus* (268-270 *A.D.*), Klio Beih. 33 (N.F. 20), (1934).
Damsholt, T., 'Zur Benutzung von dem *Breviarium* des Eutrop in der *Historia Augusta*', *Class. et Med.* 25 (1964), 138-150.

Davies, R. W., 'The 'Abortive Invasion' of Britain by Gaius', *Historia* 15 (1966), 124-128.

Demandt, A., *Zeitkritik und Geschichtsbild im Werk Ammians*, thesis Marburg (Bonn 1965).

Dillemann, L., 'Ammien Marcellin et les pays de l'Euphrate et le Tigre', *Syria* 38 (1961), 87-158.

von Domaszewski, A., *Die Personennamen bei den Scriptores Historiae Augustae*, Sitzungsberichte der Heidelberger Akademie der Wissenschaften, Philos.-hist. Kl. 1918, Abh. 13.

Downey, G., *Ancient Antioch* (Princeton 1963).

Durry, M., 'Sur Trajan père', in: *Les empereurs romains d'Espagne* (Paris 1965), 45-61.

Duff, J. Wight, *A Literary History of Rome in the Silver Age* (London 1927).

Duncker, K., *De Paianio Eutropii interprete*, Progr. Greiffenberg 1880.

Eadie, J. W., 'The Breviarium of Festus: a Fragment in Copenhagen', *Bull. Inst. Cl. Stud.* (London) 14 (1967), 93-95.

Echols, E. C., *Sextus Aurelius Victor's Brief Imperial Lives* (Exeter, New Hampshire, 1962).

Enmann, H., 'Eine verlorene Geschichte der röm. Kaiser und das Buch *De Viris illustribus urbis Romae*'. *Philologus*, Suppl.-Bd. IV (1884), 357-501.

Ensslin, W., *Zur Ostpolitik des Kaisers Diocletian*, Sitz.-Ber. der Bayr. Akad. der Wiss., Phil.-hist. Abt., Jhrg. 1942, Heft 1 (München 1942).

Fitz, J., *Ingenuus et Régalien*, Collection Latomus 81 (1966).

Frend, W. H. C., *Martyrdom and Persecution in the Early Church* (Oxford 1965).

Fuchs, H., *Der geistige Widerstand gegen Rom in der antiken Welt* (Berlin 1938).

Fuhrmann, M., 'Die Romidee der Spätantike', *HZ* 207 (1968), 529-561.

Garroni, A., 'L'iscrizione di Rufio Festo Avieno e l'autore del "Breviarium Historiae Romanae" ', *Bull. Com.* 43 (1915), 123-135.

Garzetti, A., *Nerva* (Rome 1950).

Graindor, P., *Athènes sous Hadrien* (Cairo 1934).

Gross, K., 'Aurelianus', *RAC* I (1950), Col. 1004-1010.

Häussler, R., 'Vom Ursprung und Wandel des Lebensaltervergleichs', *Hermes* 92 (1964), 313-341.

Hahn, I., 'Prooemium und Disposition der Epitome des Florus', *Eirene* 4 4 (1965), 21-38.

Hartke, W., *De saeculi quarti exeuntis historiarum scriptoribus quaestiones* (thesis, Berlin 1932).

——, *Geschichte und Politik im Spätantiken Rom. Untersuchungen über die Scriptores Historiae Augustae*, Klio Beiheft 1940 (reprint 1962).

——, *Römische Kinderkaiser* (Berlin 1951).

Hasebroek, J., *Untersuchungen zur Geschichte des Kaisers Septimius Severus* (Heidelberg 1921).

Helm, R., 'Hieronymus und Eutrop', *RhM*, N.F. 76 (1927), 138-170, 254-306.

Henderson, B. W., *The Life and Principate of the Emperor Hadrian* (London 1923).

Herter, H., 'effeminatus', in: *RAC* IV (1959), Col. 620-650.

Hohl, E., 'Vopiscus und die Biographie des Kaisers Tacitus', *Klio* 11 (1911), 178-229, 284-324.

Hohl, E., 'Zur Historia-Augusta-Forschung', *Klio* 27 (1934), 148-164.
——, 'Die H.A. und die Caesares des Aur. Vikt.', *Historia* 4 (1955), 220-228.
Homo, L., *Essai sur le règne de l'empereur Aurélien* (Paris 1904).
——, 'L'empereur Gallien et la crise de l'Empire romain au IIIe siècle',
  Rev. Hist. 38e Année, Tome 113 (1913), 1-22, 225-267.
——, *Les empereurs romains et le Christianisme* (Paris 1931).
Hopkins, M. K., 'Eunuchs in Politics in the Later Roman Empire', *Proc.
of the Cambr. Philol. Soc.* 189 (N.S. 9), (1963), 62-80.
Hopkins, R. V. Nind, *The Life of Alexander Severus* (Cambridge 1907).

Jal, P., *La guerre civile à Rome* (Paris 1963).
——, 'Nature et signification politique de l'ouvrage de Florus, *REL* 43
  (1965), 358-383.
Jankowski, N., 'Das gallische Gegenreich (259-274 n.C.) und seine soziale
  Basis im Spiegel der *Historia Augusta*', *Helikon* 7 (1967), 125-194.
Jones, A. H. M., 'Inflation under the Roman Empire', *Ec. Hist. Rev.*, Second
  Series, Vol. 5 (1952-1953), 293-318.
——, 'Collegiate Prefectures', *JRS* 54 (1964), 78-89.
——, *The Later Roman Empire* (Oxford 1964).

Kaniuth, A., *Die Beisetzung Konstantins des Grossen. Untersuchungen zur
  religiösen Haltung des Kaisers* (Breslau 1941).
Keller, E., *Eusèbe, historien des persécutions* (Genève 1912).
Kienast, D., 'Nerva und das Kaisertum Trajans', *Historia* 17 (1968), 51-71.
Koep, L., 'Divus, in: *RAC* III (1957), Col. 1251-1257.
——, 'Die Konsekrationsmünzen Kaiser Konstantins und ihre religions-
  politische Bedeutung, *Jahrb. f.A.u.Chr.* 1 (1958), 94-104.
Koep, L. and A. Herrmann, 'Consecratio', in: *RAC* III (1957), Col. 269-294.
Kotula, T., 'Rzymskie millennium', *Meander* 16 (1961), 69-84.

Lambrechts, P., 'Caligula dictateur littéraire', *Bull. de l'Institut historique
  belge de Rome* 28 (1953), 220-232.
Lana, J., *Velleio Patercolo o della propaganda*, Università di Torino, Pubbl. d.
  Fac. di Lettere e Filosofia, vol. IV, fasc. 2 (Turin 1952).
Landsberg, F., *Das Bild der alten Geschichte in den mittelalterlichen Welt-
  chroniken* (thesis, Basel 1934).
Laqueur, R., *Eusebius als Historiker seiner Zeit*, Arbeiten zur Kirchege-
  schichte 11 (Berlin und Leipzig 1929).
——, 'Das Kaisertum und die Gesellschaft des Reiches', in: *Probleme der
  Spätantike* (Stuttgart 1930), 1-38.
Latte, K., *Römische Religionsgeschichte* (Munich 1960).
Lepper, F. A., *Trajan's Parthian War* (Oxford 1948).
——, 'Some Reflexions on the "Quinquennium Neronis" ', *JRS* 47 (1957),
  95-103.

MacMullen, R., *Enemies of the Roman Order* (Cambridge, Mass., 1966).
——, 'The Celtic Renaissance', *Historia* 14 (1965), 93-104.
Mariotti, Sc. review of Eadie, *Breviarium of Festus*, et ali., *RFIC* 95 (1967),
  503.
Marrou, H.-I., *Histoire de l'éducation dans l'Antiquité* (Paris 1948; 1955³).
Matthews, J., 'Continuity in a Roman Family; The Rufii Festi of Volsinii',
  Historia 16 (1967), 484-509.
Mattingly, H., 'The Imperial Recovery', in: *CAH* XII (1939), 297-351.
Mazzarino, S., *Aspetti sociali del quarto secolo* (Rome 1951).

Mazzarino, S., *La fine del mondo antico* (Milan 1959).
——, *Il pensiero storico classico II*, 2 (Bari 1966).
Millar, F., *A Study of Cassius Dio* (Oxford 1964).
——, 'Emperors at Work', *JRS* 57 (1967), 9-19.
Momigliano, A. D., *Claudius: The Emperor and his Achievement* (Oxford 1934; repr. Cambridge 1961).
——, (ed.) *The Conflict between Paganism and Christianity in the Fourth Century* (Oxford 1963).
Mommsen, Th., 'Ammians Geographica', *Hermes* 16 (1881), 602-636 (= *Ges. Schr.* VII [1909], 393-425).
——, 'Das römische Militärwesen seit Diocletian', *Hermes* 24 (1889), 195 f. (= *Ges. Schr.* VI, 200 ff.).
Moreau, J., *Lactance, De la mort des persécuteurs* II (n.d.).
——, 'Krise und Verfall. Das dritte Jahrhundert n. Chr. als Historisches Problem'. Heidelberger Antrittsvorlesung, 11. Januar 1961, *Heidelb. Jahrb.* 5 (1961), 128-142; also in: *Scripta minora*, herausgegeben von W. Schmitthenner (Heidelberg 1964), 26-41.
——, *Excerpta Valesiana* (Teubner 1968²).

Nordh, A., 'Virtus and Fortuna in Florus', *Eranos* 50 (1952), 111-128.
Norman, A. F., *Libanius' Autobiography (Oration I)* (Oxford 1965).

Oliva, P., *Pannonia and the Onset of Crisis in the Roman Empire* (Prague 1962).
Oost, S. I., 'The Death of the Emperor Gordian III', *CPh* 53 (1958), 106-107.
——, 'Cyrene 96-74 B.C.', *CPh* 58 (1963), 11-25.
Opitz, Th., 'Sallustius und Aurelius Victor', *Fleckeis. Jahrb.* 29 (= *Jahnsche Jahrbücher für Philologie und Paedagogik* 127), (1883), 217-222.

Paribeni, R., *Nerva* (Rome 1947).
Paschoud, F., *Roma Aeterna, études sur le patriotisme romain dans l'occident à l'époque des grandes invasions* (Neuchâtel, Inst. suisse de Rome, 1967).
Pekáry, Th., 'Bemerkungen zur Chronologie des Jahrzehnts 250-260 n. Chr.', *Historia* 11 (1962), 123-128.
Petschenig, M., 'Bericht über die Litteratur zur späteren römischen Geschichtschreibern bis einschliesslich 1890', *Bursians Jahresberichte* 72 (1892), 1-74.
Pflaum, H.-G., *Essai sur les Procurateurs équestres sous le Haut-Empire romain* (Paris 1950).
——, 'La séparation des pouvoirs civil et militair avant et sous Dioclétian (et *De Caes.* 33, 34)', *BSAF* 1958 (1960), 78-79.
Phillips, E. J., 'The Emperor Gaius' abortive invasion of Britain', *Historia* 19 (1970), 369-373.
Picard, G.-C., 'Néron et le blé d'Afrique', *Les Cahiers de Tunésie* (Tunis, Faculté des Lettres) IV (1956), 163-173.
——, *Les trophées romains. Contribution à l'histoire de la religion et de l'art triomphal à Rome* (thesis, Paris 1957).
Pighi, J. B., *De ludis saecularibus populi Romani Quiritium*, ed. altera (Amsterdam 1965).
Platnauer, M., *The Life and Reign of the Emperor Septimius Severus* (Oxford 1918; reprint Rome 1965).

Reusch, W., *Der historische Wert der Caracallavita*, Klio Beiheft 24 (N.F. 11), (1931).
Roos, A. G., *Studia Arrianea* (Leipzig 1912).

Rostovtzeff, M., *Social and Economic History of the Roman Empire* (Oxford 1967²).
Rougé, J., 'L'histoire auguste et l'Isaurie au IVe siècle', *REA* 88 (1966), 282-315.
Rühl, S. F., *Die Verbreitung des Justinus im Mittelalter* (Leipzig 1871).

Salmon, E. T., *Samnium and the Samnites* (Cambridge 1967).
Schmid, W., 'Eutropspuren in der Historia Augusta', *Historia-Augusta-Colloquium, Bonn 1963* (Bonn 1964), 123-133.
Seeck, O., *Die Briefe des Libanius zeitlich geordnet* (Leipzig 1906).
——, *Geschichte des Untergangs der antiken Welt* (Berlin 1907-1913, Stuttgart 1920-1921).
Seel, O., *Die Praefatio des Pompeius Trogus*, Erlanger Forschungen, Reihe A: Geisteswissenschaften, Bd. 3 (1955).
Seston, W., *Dioclétien et la tétrarchie* (Paris 1946).
Sirinelli, J., *Les vues historiques d'Eusèbe de Césarée durant la période pré-nicéenne* (Dakar 1961).
Sperber, D., 'Calculo - logistes - ḥashban', *CQ*, n.s. 19 (1969), 374-378.
Starr, C. G., 'Aurelius Victor, Historian of Empire', *AHR* 61 (1955-1956), 574-586.
——, *The Awakening of the Greek Historical Spirit* (New York 1968).
Steidle, W., *Sueton und die antike Biographie* (Munich 1951).
Straub, J. A., *Vom Herrscherideal in der Spätantike* (1939).
——, 'Caligula', in: *RAC* II (1954), Col. 827-837.
——, 'Caracalla', in: *RAC* II (1954), Col. 893-901.
——, 'Commodus', in: *RAC* III (1957), Col. 252-266.
——, *Heidnische Geschichtsapologetik in der christlichen Spätantike. Untersuchungen über Zeit und Tendenz der Historia Augusta* (Bonn 1963).
Stroheker, K. F., *Der senatorische Adel im spätantiken Gallien* (Tübingen 1948).
Suolahti, J., *The Roman Censors. A study on Social Structure* (Helsinki 1963).
Sutherland, C. H. V., 'Denarius and Sestertius in Diocletian's Coinage Reform', *JRS* 51 (1961), 94-97.
Syme, R., *Tacitus* (Oxford 1958).
——, *Sallust* (Berkeley and Los Angeles 1964).
——, *Ammianus and the Historia Augusta* (Oxford 1968).

Taeger, F., *Charisma* (Stuttgart 1957-1960), esp. vol. II.
Thiel, J. H., 'Trajanus', *Kon. Ned. Akad. van Wetenschappen, Akademie-dagen VIII* (1955), 15-43.
Tibiletti, C., 'Il proemio di Floro, Seneca il Retore e Tertulliano', *Convivium* N.S. 3 (1959), 276 ff.
Tudor, D., 'La fortificazione della citta' romane della Dacia nel sec. III dell' e.n.', *Historia* 14 (1965), 368-380.
Tuncan, R., 'Le délit des monétaires rebellés contre Aurélien', *Latomus* 28 (1969), 948-959.

Vittinghoff, F., 'Der Staatsfeind in der romischen Kaiserzeit', *Neue Deutsche Forschungen*, Bd. 84 (Berlin 1936), 87-89.
Vitucci, G., *L'Impereratore Probo* (Rome 1952).

Walker, B., *The Annals of Tacitus* (Manchester 1952).
Walser, G. and Th. Pekáry, *Die Krise des römischen Reiches* (Berlin 1962).
Werner, H., *Der Untergang Roms*, Forsch. zur Kirchen- und Geistesgeschichte 17 (Stuttgart 1939).

Wild, J. P., 'The Caracallus', *Latomus* 23 (1964), 532-536.

Willger, H. J., *Studien zur Chronologie des Gallienus und Postumus* (thesis, Saarbrücken 1966).

Wölfflin, E., 'Aurelius Victor', *RhM* 29 (1874), 282-308.

——, 'Epitome', *ALL* 12 (1902), 333-344.

——, 'Zur Latinität der Epitome Caesarum', *ALL* 12 (1902), 445-453.

——, 'Das Breviarium des Festus', *ALL* 13 (1904), 69-97, 173-180.

Yavetz, Z., *Plebs* and *Princeps* (Oxford 1969).

Zancan, P., *Floro e Livio* (Padua 1942).

INDEXES

A) GEOGRAPHICAL NAMES

B) PERSONAL NAMES

D) MODERN AUTHORS

ERRATA

P. 67, l. 29 *Read* Diadumenus *instead of* Diodumenus

P. 161, l. 6 *Read* Aemilianus *instead of* Aemilius